ANTISOCIAL DRIVERS

ANTISOCIAL DRIVERS

Prosocial Driver Training for Prevention and Rehabilitation

By

ROBERT R. ROSS, Ph.D.

Professor, Department of Criminology
University of Ottawa
Ottawa, Ontario, Canada
Director, Cognitive Centre of Canada

and

DANIEL H. ANTONOWICZ, Ph.D.

Adjunct Professor, Department of Psychology
Carleton University
Ottawa, Ontario, Canada

CHARLES C THOMAS • PUBLISHER, LTD.
Springfield • Illinois • U.S.A.

Published and Distributed Throughout the World by

CHARLES C THOMAS • PUBLISHER, LTD.
2600 South First Street
Springfield, Illinois 62704

ISBN 0-398-07496-8 (hard)
ISBN 0-398-07497-6 (paper)

Library of Congress Catalog Card Number: 2004043978

With THOMAS BOOKS *careful attention is given to all details of manufacturing
and design. It is the Publisher's desire to present books that are satisfactory as to their
physical qualities and artistic possibilities and appropriate for their particular use.*
THOMAS BOOKS *will be true to those laws of quality that assure a good name
and good will.*

Printed in the United States of America
UBC-R-3

Library of Congress Cataloging-in-Publication Data

Ross, Robert R., 1933-
    Antisocial drivers : prosocial driver training for prevention and rehabilitation / Robert R.
Ross, Daniel H. Antonowicz.
        p. cm.
    Includes bibliographical references.
    ISBN 0-398-07496-8 – ISBN 0-398-07497-6 (pbk.)
    1. Automobile driver education. 2. Automobile driving. 3. Automobile drivers–Psychology.
4. Road rage. I. Antonowicz, Daniel H. II. Title.

TL152.6.R67 2004
629.28'3–dc22   2004043978

ACKNOWLEDGMENTS

The *Cognitive Model* for the prevention of antisocial behavior and the rehabilitation of antisocial youth and adults is a product of a thirty-five-year research project that was initially funded by the Ontario Mental Health Foundation's research grant to Dr. Ross at the Department of Psychology, University of Waterloo. Dr. Don Meichenbaum served as a consultant during the early stages of the project and Bryan McKay served as Senior Research Associate. Later stages of the project were conducted while Dr. Ross was Professor of Criminology at the University of Ottawa and Honorary Research Associate, Faculty of Law, University of Edinburgh. Dr. Ross' research was encouraged, supported, and guided by Dr. Andy Birkenmayer.

Dr. Ross' development of the cognitive model and his training of hundreds of Trainers and Instructors in the delivery of the *Reasoning and Rehabilitation* programs based on the *Cognitive Model* has been supported and encouraged by colleagues and friends in many countries and, in particular, by James Hilborn in Estonia and the directors and staff of Cognitive Centers in Beirut (Alex Abdennur); Spain (Vicente Garrido); Scotland (Bruce Kidd); Texas (Frances Cox, Ray Gingerich, Dianne Magliola, and Barbara White); Wales (Peter Davies, Robin Morris-Jones and the late David Sutton); and by Brad Bogue and Richard Greene in Colorado.

The creativity and counsel of Roslynn D. Ross, co-author of the original *R&R* program, and the advice of Principal Bambi D. Ross on educational theory and practice are acknowledged and appreciated. Jim Ross played devil's advocate throughout the writing of this book and unwittingly made many contributions. Thankfully, his driving on the highway is better than his driving on the golf course.

This book is dedicated to the late Alan Morrice whose fascination with cars and concern about offensive driving behavior stimulated the production of this book.

CONTENTS

ANTISOCIAL DRIVERS

Chapter 1

THINKING AND DRIVING

Why are so many drivers inconsiderate, selfish, and rude? Why do so many drivers act as though they have never learned basic social skills? Why are there so many antisocial drivers – individuals who frequently drive in a manner that disregards the rights of others to be treated courteously, fairly, and safely?

Auto-Metamorphosis?

Driving seems to bring out the worst in people. Prosocial behavior ends and antisocial behavior begins for many individuals as soon as they get in their car. Polite behavior is replaced by rudeness; friendliness by hostility; kindness by callousness; empathy by egocentricity. Many individuals drive as if too much carbon monoxide has seeped into their cars and killed the cells in their brains that normally regulate their behavior.

If Looks Could Kill

Anyone who spends time on the road is exposed to antisocial driving. Some individuals are content to respond to the offensive behavior of antisocial drivers with a shrug of their shoulders. Some react by shaking their heads or *tut-tutting*. However, many drivers have become intolerant. Some have exhausted their lexicon of profanity in cursing at drivers whom they judge to have the intelligence or moral values of a reptile. Some react by pointing their middle finger in a perpendicular direction. Such reactions may enable them to ventilate their anger; however, they seldom have any long-term deterrent or educational benefit in terms of motivating antisocial drivers to abandon their egocentric, ill-mannered, or care-less driving behavior.

Contagion

After being subjected to the ill-mannered, irritating, aggravating, and dangerous behavior of other drivers on our roads and highways day after day, many drivers have responded by adopting the attitude, "if you can't beat them; join them." Many otherwise upright, law-abiding citizens have reacted to their daily exposure to antisocial driving by behaving as though the rules that usually guide their social behavior are neither necessary nor appropriate on the road. Many drivers have been trained in *defensive* driving. Many more appear to have been trained in *offensive* driving.

Traffic researchers used to refer to antisocial drivers as "deviant drivers." We reject that label because there are now so many of them that they are no longer deviant, at least in the statistical sense. Antisocial driving is contagious. It is becoming the norm in most countries. It already is the norm in many countries.

Retaliation

Many individuals react to the antisocial behavior of other drivers by engaging in retaliatory behavior that is just as antisocial as the behavior of those whose driving upset them. The most extreme form of antisocial driving occurs when incivility and retaliation spiral into violence in the form of "Road Rage." However, the majority of retaliatory acts do not involve direct violence. Many take the form of aggressive, risky driving maneuvers that increase the antagonism between the drivers and can spell disaster on the highway without a blow being struck.

Careful Drivers Beware

Many antisocial drivers are intolerant of *careful* drivers. Resenting cautious drivers who inconvenience them or delay them, they respond by engaging in high-risk maneuvers without regard to civility, legality, or safety. Individuals who choose to drive carefully and cautiously now do so at their peril.

Beware of Careful Drivers

The reaction of many individuals to the perceived risks to their safety posed by antisocial drivers is anxiety or panic. Their fear may cause them to become so hesitant and indecisive that their driving becomes hazardous both to themselves and other drivers.[1]

End of the Road

Some individuals have been so traumatized by their encounters with antisocial drivers that they have given up driving altogether. Fear of driving may develop at any age. However, in an aging population, a growing number of drivers are becoming increasingly hesitant to drive as they come to realize that they no longer are able to cope with antisocial drivers whose impulsive, rapid, risky, or aggressive maneuvers tax the aging driver's declining vision, hearing, and reaction time. Ironically, governmental concern about the inordinate number of collisions among aging drivers tends to focus on the deterioration in the driving *skills* of the greying population rather than on the driving *style* of those with whom they must interact on the road.

THE ANTISOCIAL DRIVING CULTURE

Driving is a learned behavior. Like all learned behaviors, it is strongly influenced by one's culture. The decline in courtesy, cooperation, good manners, and concern for others; and the increase in aggressive, risky, reckless, and selfish behavior on the roadways may well be a function of similar changes in society at large.

Antisocial driving should not be viewed as a new phenomenon spawned by the complexities of modern life or the stresses of traffic congestion or the development of powerful engines. Antisocial driving used to be called "Jehu," a phenomenon that has been around for centuries: "*The chariots shall rage in the streets; they shall jostle one against another in the broad ways*" (Book of Nahum, Ch. 2, Verse 4, Holy Bible).

However, it can be argued that the current population of drivers has been raised in a norm of aggressive driving; a "hurry up and wait" and a "me first" mentality. They have been subjected to countless advertisements that extol the horsepower of cars, but fail to note that they can be demolished even when they are driven at rates of speed that require only a fraction of such power. Many automobile manufacturers label their products with the names of wild animals, and proudly proclaim

---

1. Research on driving-related fear has been reported by Taylor, Deane & Podd (2002).

their ability to go from zero to sixty in less than seven seconds while failing to inform us that doubling the speed of the car quadruples the force of drivers, passengers, and family pets exiting through its windshield. Having been exposed to media and video game presentations of entertainment such as high-speed car chases and "wreck 'em" car derbies, many drivers have come to view the highway as a sportsfield, or a battlefield. Aggressive driving has become a hallmark of machismo.

PROSOCIAL DRIVERS

If antisocial driving is simply a symptom of deterioration in social values, we must wonder why there are still many individuals who drive courteously and safely. There still are many "prosocial drivers" – individuals who drive carefully with due consideration for the well-being of others. They may be an endangered species.

This book addresses the question of why some drivers are so well behaved whereas other drivers appear to be so depraved. However, our major focus will be on indicating what can be done to turn the latter into the former. How we can reduce the *car*nage on our roads by persuading antisocial drivers to become prosocial drivers? How can we prevent beginning drivers from acquiring antisocial driving habits? Those questions are addressed in this book by examining the findings from three large bodies of research that have not previously been integrated:

- **Traffic research** that has identified personal factors that are associated with driving violations and risky or careless driving;
- **Psychological research** that has identified personal factors that are associated with antisocial behavior;
- **Criminological research** that has identified personal factors that are key to the success of programs that reduce antisocial behavior.

As we shall see, each body of research points to the same factors.

THE SEARCH FOR 'BAD DRIVERS'

Research designed to identify what it is about individual drivers that can account for their poor driving behavior has a long but controversial history. Several hundred studies have been conducted on psychopathology and on a variety of personality factors such as emotional stability, depression, introversion/extraversion, achievement motivation, anxiety, biorythm, and even astrological signs.[2] The results of such studies have not been encouraging.

Most studies have found no relationship, or very weak correlations between personality factors and collision involvement (Arthur & Graziano, 1996; Elander, West & French, 1993; Matthews, Dorn & Glendon, 1991; Wilde, 1994c). A review of research led to the conclusion that "the relative contributions of . . . stable, enduring aspects of personality or lifestyle to risk for motor vehicle accidents remain obscure" (Simpson & Beirness, 1993).

Antipersonality

Research on a possible link between personality and collisions became unpopular as increasing emphasis came to be placed on other factors that could be more reliably measured and remedied. Traffic researchers as well as the automobile industry, government agencies and safety organizations came to focus on car design and highway engineering as a way to reduce collision risk. There have been thousands of studies of automobile design, traffic, weather, visibility, speed, and road conditions and a host of other factors that influence the likelihood that 'accidents will happen.'

The focus of research moved from studying the personality of drivers who were involved in collisions to studying how to minimize the damage to the drivers and their passengers resulting from such collisions. The emphasis came to be placed on improving occupant protection by maximizing the integrity of the passenger compartment with, for example, padded dashboards, collapsible steering wheels, and ergonomically efficient instrument panels. Substantial progress was made in developing occupant restraint systems such as seat belts and air bags that undoubtedly reduce the severity of injuries but do little to reduce the frequency of the collisions that yield such injuries.

Other researchers concentrated on car engineering and automated controls and warnings that might help drivers avoid a collision in the first place. Major progress has been achieved in the design of such components

---

2. One insurance company even ranks "car accident" claimants by their star signs. The company asserts that the most "accident prone drivers" are Geminis whom they say are typically described as "restless, easily bored, and frustrated by things moving slowly" (National Manager of an insurance company quoted in the *Toronto Globe & Mail*, Feb 22, 2002).

as brakes, steering, lighting, and tires and in the development of electronic devices such as alcohol ignition interlocks that prevent drink/drivers from starting their cars.

Automobile manufacturers are now designing so-called "safe cars" with equipment that can detect and react evasively to impending collisions. Such engineering developments may provide a welcome addition to the protective armamentarium of drivers and a significant contribution to traffic safety but they do little to teach drivers to drive safely or motivate them to do so. They may, in fact, reduce the driver's concern for safety. They may lead drivers to take more risks by promising them that the car will take care of them.[3] Some might argue that "Safe Car" is an oxymoron.

There should be little argument but that shortcomings in cars and roads have been and continue to be a major factor in collisions and that impressive gains have been made in designing cars that can be driven safely and roads that can be navigated safely. Unfortunately, although some modern automobiles are smarter than the supercomputers developed in the 1950s, they still rely on a safe driver. "Smart Cars" may be a welcome addition to efforts to combat collisions. "Smart Drivers" would also be welcome.

In spite of major improvements in highway and automobile design, collision avoidance technology and police surveillance techniques, drivers continue to drive their well-engineered cars into other well-engineered cars and into abutments, trees, and pedestrians who are not so well protected. They do so not only when they are driving poorly designed or poorly maintained cars, or when they are drunk or fatigued, or when they have consumed over-the-counter cold and allergy remedies, or when they are engrossed in cell-phone conversations, but literally at any time.

Designing safe roads and safe cars is necessary but not sufficient. Can we design safe drivers?

Cars or Drivers of Cars?

Some cars and some roads have far more than their "fair" share of collisions. However, research indicates that in most instances it is what individuals do with those cars on those roads that cause collisions. Bad

---

3. The *Risk Homeostasis* theory of Professor Emeritus, Gerald Wilde suggests that the safer a car makes people feel, the greater are the chances that their drivers will take (Wilde, 1994, b).

cars, bad roads, bad weather and bad luck undoubtedly make it much more likely that collisions will occur; but many, if not most collisions may also be the result of bad attitudes, bad manners, bad judgment, or bad behavior.

Driver behavior is a major determinant of the likelihood of collisions. That conclusion is supported by research dating from the early 1940s when Ross (1940) reported that poor road conditions and defects in cars accounted for no more than ten percent of collisions and that the remaining 90 percent could only be ascribed to driver characteristics. Similar findings were reported in the 1980s (McKenna, 1983; Rumar, 1985; Sabey & Taylor, 1980). Such research indicated that human actions are a sole or a contributory factor in ninety to ninety-five percent of collisions. More recent research has also indicated that most collisions can be attributed to "human error" (Elander et al., 1993). It has become increasingly obvious that there must be something about drivers, or some interaction between drivers, cars, and the driving environment that needs to be understood. Individual factors cannot be ignored.

One might wish that cars would behave like other physical objects that are subject only to Newton's laws of motion. However, cars are driven by people. Many of those people respect neither the laws of physics, nor the rule of law, nor the rules for decent human interaction.

COGNITION AND DRIVING

Although research has yielded little reliable evidence of a strong link between personality and collisions, that does not mean that individual factors are insignificant. Research that we will review in subsequent chapters indicates that *some* individual factors are associated with both driving violations and collision risk. The research examined not the drivers' personality or their psychopathology or their temperament; but their *cognitive* skills; their emotional skills; their *social* skills; and their *attitudes, beliefs and values.*

A growing number of studies have demonstrated that safe driving requires competence in a number of basic cognitive skills: the ability to *attend* to salient aspects of one's driving environment; to *recognize* potential hazards; to accurately assess risks; to *calculate* the consequences of one's driving actions; and to realistically *judge* one's own driving skills. Factors such as inattentiveness, faulty information-processing, inadequate risk assessment, and impulsive or careless decision-making have all been implicated in collision involvement and driving violations.

EMOTIONAL COMPETENCE

Safe driving also requires emotional competence – the ability to control one's emotions rather than let one's driving be controlled by them. It requires the cognitive/emotional skills that enable one to cope with conflict and stress that are ever present on the road. Prosocial driving requires the ability to recognize and identify one's feelings and emotions and to effectively manage their expression. Safety on the roads requires more than 'traffic calming,' it also requires 'driver calming.'

DRIVING SKILL IS A SOCIAL SKILL

Most of the research on the personal factors associated with risky driving and collisions viewed driving as an *individual* activity. However, driving does not occur in a social vacuum. Safe driving requires the ability to quickly and accurately predict the behavior of other individuals and to behave in ways that minimize the possibility of interpersonal *clashes* that can result in *crashes*. Driving is a highly complex, highly unusual, and highly demanding social activity that requires many of the social skills that are required for competence in any social activity (Grayson, 1992). Safe and courteous driving requires adequately developed *social* cognitive skills and values that enable interpersonal understanding and that engender concern for other people's rights, safety and well-being.

Behind Closed Doors

Many drivers do not view driving as a social activity and, therefore, do not think that social skills are required on the road. Comfortably ensconced in their mobile metal boxes, drivers may feel they are the only people on the road.

The modern driver may be more involved in interaction with people other than the drivers who surround them on the highway. Many drivers spend their time on the road preoccupied in cell phone conversations with others and lamenting the fact they must put people 'on hold' while they shift gears.

Some traffic researchers point out that the car offers the driver a "cocoon of privacy" and, thereby, actually *prevents* individuals from interacting with others (Lofland, 1973). The privacy of cars can foster feelings of social isolation that, in turn, can spawn a feeling of normlessness in which we think 'anything goes.' You do not need social values if you no longer are a social being.

Social isolation can also engender depersonalization and dehumanization. Drivers may come to view other drivers with whom they share the road only as inanimate objects — cars, not people. When other people are viewed as non-persons there is little reason to treat them with the same courtesy and consideration as 'real people.' Civility is designed for people, not machines.

Highway Anomie

Most interpersonal activities are shaped and controlled by rules and social conventions. Rules for social interaction stem from community. On the highway, the community is amorphous. On the highway, we are "a nation of transient strangers without a real system of social bonds" (Caldwell, 1999). On the highway, there is no community; there is only traffic. Accordingly, individuals may feel there is no need for their behavior on the road to be constrained by the definitions of acceptable behavior that normally guide social interaction. The absence of social bonds in the driving environment makes civility fragile.

Anonymity Breeds Contempt

Many antisocial drivers believe that, on the road, there is seldom any social consequence for bad manners. It is usually not possible for us to identify the antisocial drivers who offend us. All we are likely to see is their rear license plate as they speed away knowing full well that they may never meet us again and no one will know who they are. Individuals who believe that they cannot be identified may temporarily suspend the personal controls that normally restrain them from committing acts that might harm other individuals (Novaco, 1991). Anonymity can disinhibit antisocial behavior.[4]

---

4. Tinted windows increase anonymity. They are also associated with a high frequency of acts of antisocial driving such as failing to signal, and speeding when traffic lights change (Wiesenthal and Janovjak, 1992).

When The Cat Is Gone

Many drivers engage in antisocial behavior on the road believing that traffic regulations can be ignored without consequence because there are so many cars and so few police that on the vast majority of occasions on which they choose to transgress, detection is unlikely. They may feel that the car provides a sanctuary from the consequences of rule-breaking.

SOCIAL VALUES

Reliance on *external* controls to curb antisocial behavior on the road is unlikely, by itself, to be successful. The social/legal safety of our roads may tempt drivers to disregard both the official and the informal rules and conventions that guide and govern other types of social interactions. Prosocial driving requires more than traffic lights, traffic cops, and traffic courts. Prosocial driving also requires *internal* controls.

Some drivers display excellent social skills except when they are behind the wheel. However, the socially skilled behavior of some antisocial drivers may represent only superficial charm used as an instrument for personal gain in social situations. They may believe that there are few personal gains for them in displaying courtesy and consideration for others in traffic. They may believe that performing such behavior in traffic only slows their progress. Drivers who usually *appear* to be socially skilled and caring may drop their veneer in the interpersonal safety of their cars.

Safe driving requires prosocial values that are sufficiently strong that the driver's internal controls are not compromised by the freedom provided by the absence of social and legal consequences for transgression. Prosocial driving requires both the ability and the inclination to consider, appreciate, and respond to the needs and safety of other drivers and not only to one's own needs and safety. However, research that we will review indicates that antisocial driving is often associated with the pursuit of exclusively personal goals.

COGNITION AND ANTISOCIAL BEHAVIOR

The research we describe in this book demonstrates that the personal factors that traffic researchers have found to be associated with antisocial driving are the same factors that criminological researchers have found to be associated with other forms of antisocial behavior, including aggression in children; bullying in school; risk taking and conduct problems in adolescents; vandalism; child abuse; alcohol and drug abuse; juvenile delinquency; delinquency in college students; interpersonal violence; and criminal behavior.

Criminological research has found that the following personal characteristics are associated with a variety of types of antisocial behavior:

Impulsivity: Many antisocial individuals are impulsive and impatient. They fail to think before they act and frequently respond without considering the possible consequences of their actions. Their focus on their immediate needs limits their ability to tolerate delay. Many are so focused on satisfying their immediate needs that they persist in risk-taking behaviors even when such behaviors frequently lead them into difficulty.

Sensation-seeking: Many antisocial individuals evidence a penchant for activities that involve thrill and excitement and involve risk.

Unrealistic thinking: Many antisocial individuals evidence a lack of objectivity in their thinking. They underestimate risk, fail to recognize problems, and overrate their ability to avoid such problems.

Problem-solving: Many antisocial individuals have difficulty in the thinking skills that are required for solving the problems that we all encounter in our interactions with other people. They have difficulty in calculating the possible consequences of their behavior. They fail to understand the cause and effect relationship between their behavior and people's reaction to them. As a result, they frequently experience interpersonal conflict and lack the skills to adequately cope with both the conflict and the stress it engenders.

Egocentricity: Many antisocial individuals tend to see the world only from their own perspective and fail to consider how other people think or feel. Their lack of sensitivity to other people's thoughts or feelings severely impairs their ability to anticipate how their behavior might affect other people and contributes to their lack of concern for the possible consequences of their behavior on others.

Values: Many antisocial individuals think only about how their behavior affects themselves, not how it affects other people. The principle that governs their actions is: "*If it is good for me, it's good.*"

Each of those characteristics has also been found to be associated with antisocial driving.

Questionable Assumptions

Virtually all society's efforts in the field of traffic safety from training and testing novice drivers to deterring careless, risky, dangerous, and drunk drivers by surveillance, enforcement and punishment strategies have been based on the assumption that drivers are rational individuals who modify their behavior in accord with consequences – who are able to accurately assess risk, who are able to control their emotions, who have values that make safe and courteous driving important, and who understand and are concerned about the feelings of other drivers. In the case of many antisocial drivers, those are erroneous assumptions.

A Formula For Failure?

The prevalence of antisocial driving might be ascribed to social and cultural factors such as the pace and stress of modern life and the individualism and self-centeredness of modern society. However, such explanations have provided few practical strategies for changing the behavior of antisocial drivers.

Conceptualizing ill-mannered, careless, or risky driving as antisocial may not appear to offer much more help in terms of ideas as to how such driving might be reduced. There is a widespread belief that changing antisocial behavior is a formidable, if not impossible task. However, there is a solid body of criminological research that has clearly and convincingly demonstrated that antisocial behavior *can* be changed. The research includes statistically sophisticated meta-analytic analyses of several hundred independent, controlled studies that have demonstrated that antisocial individuals *can* be rehabilitated.

CHANGING ANTISOCIAL BEHAVIOR

Unfortunately, successful programs are outnumbered by interventions that have failed to reduce antisocial behavior. Analyses of more than forty years of controlled evaluations of programs designed to rehabilitate antisocial individuals have revealed that effective programs differ from ineffective programs in at least one major way. Almost all programs that have been effective in rehabilitating antisocial individuals have achieved their success by applying techniques which foster the development of the same cognitive skills, thinking and reasoning skills, social skills, coping skills, problem-solving skills, and values that research has identified as being associated with antisocial driving.

Effective programs include techniques that can improve antisocial individuals' impulse control; increase their reasoning skills, and how they process information; enhance their sensitivity to the consequences of their behavior; improve their ability to comprehend the thoughts and feelings of other people; increase their problem-solving skills; acquire emotional control; broaden their view of the world; and help them to develop alternative interpretations of social rules, and social obligations. Many programs that include such training "'work." Most programs that do not, fail.

We shall identify the specific social cognitive skills and values that when improved by training are key to the success of programs that seek to change the behavior of antisocial individuals. We shall also review research that indicates that inadequate development of those skills or a failure to apply them in driving situations is associated with frequent traffic violations and collisions.

We shall also describe a program that has successfully taught those skills and values around the world to groups of individuals who comprise some of the most antisocial drivers. The program is a product of a thirty-five-year research project involving a sequential series of empirical studies on the efficacy of programs for reducing antisocial behavior. The project led to the development of a cognitive-behavioral program that teaches cognitive/emotional skills and values that are required for prosocial competence and are antagonistic to antisocial behavior.

The program is based on more than a hundred rigorously evaluated programs that a variety of researchers in North America and Europe have found to be effective in preventing or reducing antisocial behavior. It has been successfully implemented in fourteen countries around the world with more than forty thousand antisocial individuals. They include alcohol and drug abusers, adolescent and adult felons, chronically recidivistic offenders, and violent offenders. Many of those successfully treated had extensive histories of convictions for traffic violations, license suspensions, and driving without a license. Many had been repeatedly convicted for drink/driving offenses and some had a history of convictions for dangerous driving or criminal vehicular manslaughter.

THE PROSOCIAL DRIVER TRAINING PROGRAM

We shall also describe a version of the program that focuses on teaching prosocial cognitive skills, emotional skills, and values that are associated with courteous and safe driving. The program is a multifaceted, cognitive-behavioral, education program for teaching these prosocial skills and values to adolescent and adult drivers with poor driving records and/or antisocial driving habits. It is also designed to be delivered to potential drivers before, or while they are being trained to drive to ensure that they have acquired such skills and values before they are granted a license.

While We Are Waiting

We make no apology to those who might argue that the education or reeducation of individual drivers is an inadequate response to the problems of antisocial driving. We have no argument with the view that the reduction of antisocial driving requires an ecological perspective. Cultural and situational factors are a major determinant of how one chooses to drive. They also influence how individuals believe they are supposed to drive. We recognize that the reduction of antisocial driving requires not only changing the behavior of drivers but also changing the host of technological, political, economic, social, and cultural factors that play a major role in engendering antisocial driving.

We certainly would not quarrel with the view that we need increases in police surveillance and enforcement of traffic laws. A significant decrease in the rate of violations and "accidents" is unlikely to be achieved without them.

We also believe that if we wish to reduce the carnage on our roads and make our highways safe, we must modify social and judicial attitudes concerning acceptable and safe driving (particularly drinking and driving). We must develop a culture of driving wherein cautious driving is no longer viewed as 'wimpy' and where offensive and risky driving is viewed not as exciting, entertaining, or 'macho'; but as antisocial.

While we are waiting (very patiently) for such large scale social change we believe that a major contribution to society can be made by equipping antisocial drivers with skills, attitudes, and values that are antagonistic to offensive driving and that can prevent young persons who are about to become drivers from becoming antisocial drivers.

Chapter 2

ANTISOCIAL DRIVING: A THORN BY ANY OTHER NAME

Referring to the behavior of drivers who flout the rules of the road, or who are discourteous, uncooperative, selfish, impulsive, aggressive, thoughtless, or rude as "antisocial" is not simply pejorative name-calling. They have been called much worse things. It also is not original. It is based on more than thirty years of research. We review that research in Chapter 4. We identify in Chapter 3 the variety of types of individuals who engage in such driving. First, we need to clarify what we mean by "antisocial driving."

Antisocial driving includes such acts as driving under the influence of alcohol or drugs; violating traffic laws by failing to stop at red lights; speeding up at yellow lights; failing to signal before turning; tailgating; failing to yield the passing lane to faster drivers; chronic slalom-like lane-changing on an expressway; and a host of other illegal driving behaviors. The antisocial quality of such acts is probably obvious to anyone who witnesses them or is a victim of them. The antisocial quality of the failure to wear seat belts is also readily apparent given the well-known protection against injury and death that they provide. There should be little doubt that compromising the safety of the driver, other drivers, and pedestrians by knowingly failing to exercise adequate care and caution when behind the wheel, or knowingly failing to adequately maintain one's car's brakes or steering or tires is also antisocial. However, there are other driving behaviors that we believe should be viewed as antisocial. They include not only deliberate violation of traffic laws but also deliberate violations of informal rules for cooperative and safe driving.

17

VIOLATIONS OR ERRORS?

Research has established that as many as ninety percent of collisions are caused by "driver error." However, the term, "Driver Error" can be very misleading. It is essential to differentiate between "driving errors" and "driving violations" (Aberg & Rimmo, 1998; Blockey & Hartley, 1995; Reason, Manstead, Stradling, Baxter & Cambell, 1990). A large proportion of collisions arise not from drivers making unintended errors or mistakes but from their "deliberate violations of safe driving and co-operative driving practices and/or from flagrant and deliberate law-breaking involving violations of highway codes" (Parker, West, Stradling & Manstead, 1995 b).

It is violations, not unintended errors or lapses that are most strongly linked to collision-involvement in the case of both private car drivers (DETR, 2001; Kontogiannis, Kossiavelou & Marmaras, 2002), and professional drivers (Sullman, Meadows & Pajo, 2002). A tendency to speed and disregard traffic rules is among the best predictors of future collisions (Norris, Mathews & Riad, 2000). Violators are also more likely to be involved in collisions. They have been referred to as "Crash Magnets" (Stradling, 1997).

Many collisions are a consequence of the driver's lack of experience, or their lack of driving skill. However, "the problem of traffic crashes is much more one of drivers doing things that they know they ought not to do, than of drivers not knowing what to do" (Evans, 1991).

Although collisions can be a result of driving violations or unintended driving errors, they are more likely to be the result of both. The cause of most collisions is the driver making an error when they are violating (Stradling & Parker, 1996).

Deliberate Errors

It is also necessary to distinguish between *unintended* violations and *deliberate* violations. Some violations are unintended. They may 'only' be slips or lapses. For example, failing to observe a road sign or failing to notice that one's driving behavior inconveniences or jeopardizes the safety of others. Such violations may reflect unintended errors of judgment. However, most violations are committed by drivers who are fully aware that they are breaking the established rules of the road. They are aware that they are acting in ways in which they should not act, and they do so deliberately.

No Harm Meant

Although some violations are intentional in that the driver fully intends to break a traffic rule, it may not be the driver's intention to negatively impact anyone. Nonetheless, whether or not they are intended to hurt anyone, such acts are antisocial since they *deliberately* contravene rules designed to ensure good order and/or safety. The behavior is antisocial although the motive may not be. Their intention may not have been to harm other individuals or damage their property. Their intent may have been to put their own needs ahead of those of other drivers. Most have no design upon others except to beat them.

A consideration of deliberate violations is crucial to our understanding of the personal factors that are involved in collision risk. However, since making even a minor error can result in a fatal collision, one must also ask if there are personal characteristics that lead some drivers to be particularly prone to making unintended "driving errors." Some drivers seem to believe that they can get Mulligans when they drive poorly on the highway.

> *To err is human, but when the eraser wears out before the pencil, you're overdoing it.*
>
> J. Jenkins

Violations Are Rewarding

It is the rare violation that incurs an immediate legal penalty for the driver. In fact, most breaches of traffic laws are immediately rewarding since they give the driver an apparent advantage in terms of proceeding more quickly to their goal without the inconvenience that may result from obeying the rules. Violating can also be rewarded by the thrill of speed, the opportunity to express aggression, the experience of exerting power and control over one's world, and the feeling of 'having got away with it.' Thus, for many drivers, violating is immediately and positively reinforced. The immediate gratification is a much stronger motivating force than the delayed negative consequences drivers may experience *if* they are caught. Violating can quickly become a habit.

It is not surprising that in the year 2000 in England and Wales the number of "motoring offences" increased by five percent to a record high of 10.5 million (Ayres, Hayward & Perry, 2003).

There are many drivers who repeatedly violate traffic regulations. Twenty percent of female drivers and forty percent of male drivers have been found to be High Violators. Violations among young drivers are even more prevalent. More than fifty percent of male drivers aged seventeen to twenty-five and almost forty percent of female drivers aged seventeen to twenty-five are frequent violators (Stradling & Parker, 1996). Those are the drivers about whom this book is most concerned.

Non-Crimes

> *Crimes sometimes shock us too much;*
> *vices almost always too little.*
>   August Hare

Many antisocial driving behaviors involve breaking laws but they are not called "crimes." They 'only' break the Rules of The Road. The distinction between legal and illegal behavior on the road is often only a matter of degree (Corbett & Simon, 1992). Drivers can break the rules simply by extending their lawful driving actions (for example, by just a little more pressure on the accelerator).

Acts that occur while driving tend to be viewed as different from acts that occur elsewhere. Many acts of antisocial driving constitute what criminologists refer to as "folk crimes" – illegal acts that are not stigmatized by the public as criminal. Many driving offenses, such as speeding, are regarded in this way by a large proportion of the public.

Criminalizing "law-abiding traffic violators" would cripple an already overburdened justice system and would make criminals out of a large proportion of the population for behaviors in which they engage every day. However, the fact that driving violations are more common than the common cold does not make them less antisocial.

No Offense

Antisocial driving also includes driving behavior that does not breach any traffic law. Many acts of antisocial driving do not violate traffic laws, but are flagrant violations of cooperative driving practices. We are also concerned with those drivers who may not violate traffic rules, but repeatedly violate the formal and informal codes for courteous driving.

Antisocial driving includes failing to exhibit common courtesy to other drivers. It includes acts that annoy other drivers, inconvenience them, irritate them, ignore their needs and rights, and jeopardize their safety and well-being. Many driving behaviors which violate the rules for cooperative driving behavior are not an offense, but they are offensive.[5]

Antisocial driving includes such behaviors as braking in an effort to force the driver behind not to drive so closely; driving closely to the car in front in order to force its driver to go faster or get out of the way; refusing to allow another driver to legitimately enter your lane; excessive horn-sounding; and swearing or yelling at other drivers, or making obscene gestures to protest against their driving. It includes such acts as knowingly failing to adjust one's driving to road conditions, or weather conditions, or traffic conditions, or the mechanical limitations of one's car. It also includes acts of highway littering in which drivers throw garbage such as bottles, coffee cups, and even unwanted pets out of their windows as they drive along unconcerned about the impact of their behavior on the environment or on the pets.

Antisocial driving is by no means limited to drinking/driving. It also includes driving while impaired by fatigue or by emotional states that detract from the driver's ability to focus attention on the driving task and make him/her a threat to the lives of other drivers and their passengers. Such behavior is seldom penalized in law if they are not associated with a collision. There are no 'breathalyzers' for such conditions.

"But, your Honor, my client was driving,"

Reading some automobile advertisements leads us to wonder whether advertisers create or only reflect social values. For example, one advertisement describes the merits of its car in the following manner:

> *Distant thunder, cold as stone, one by one each car succumbs. Something wicked this way comes. Naught-to-sixty in 5.8 seconds: Once a figment of the imagination, now a fixture of intimidation . . .*

It remains to be seen whether the increasing prevalence of antisocial driving is fostering the perception that incivility is acceptable when driving. Should the car excuse antisocial behavior?

---

5. The Court of Appeals in Texas has dismissed a lower court's conviction of a man for disorderly conduct for giving other drivers the "finger" (*Texas vs. Coggin,* October, 2003). However, in Germany, civility on the roads is still regulated – it is verbotten to make various rude gestures. Fines have even been levied for calling other drivers 'fools.' Establishing and enforcing such regulations in other countries and punishing them by means of fines might at least reduce government deficits.

No Problem

> *On the whole, human beings want to be good,*
> *but not too good and not all the time.*
>
> George Orwell

Many drivers who frequently violate traffic laws and drive without considering the needs of other drivers do not view their behavior as antisocial. Some firmly believe that driving is not subject to the rules and conventions that define civilized interpersonal behavior. Many drivers appear to believe that incivility while driving is socially acceptable. However, antisocial driving is not only offensive. It is also dangerous.

Very few antisocial acts have personal and social consequences that are as severe as the potential consequences of antisocial driving. Antisocial driving can cause injury to people, cars and property that have staggering effects in terms of the costs of insurance, the costs of policing and the costs for the judicial and public health systems. Compared to most forms of illegal behavior, antisocial driving is much more likely to result in property damage and personal injury and is much more likely to be lethal in its consequences.

Since on September 13, 1899 when Henry Bliss became the first person to be killed by a car, more than 30 million people have become 'road kill.' Such 'road-kill' significantly decreased in the 1990s (Robertson, 1998). However, approximately, 885,000 people died in automobile collisions in 1993 alone – 2,400 deaths each day; one a minute. An injury occurred every second. More people are killed by cars than by guns – even in the U.S.A. Such everyday events are seldom newsworthy (Hertsgaard, 1998).

Accidents Are Not Accidental

One reflection of the informal social acceptance of antisocial driving is the fact that we label the consequences of antisocial driving differently than we label the consequences of other antisocial behaviors. Antisocial driving often causes what are typically referred to as "accidents." "Accident" implies unintentional, unpredictable, and unavoidable. The label enables us to euphemize as random or chance events the consequences of driving behaviors that involve negligence, impulsivity, carelessness, callousness, inattentiveness, or indifference. Most do not deserve to be dismissed as chance occurrences. A more accurate label would be "collision." Accidents are rare. Collisions are not.

Mixed Messages

Some types of antisocial driving would qualify as "aggressive driving" – the driving behaviors that are the target of "aggressive driving" laws that many jurisdictions have enacted. The definitions of "aggressive driving" in such laws – and in much of the research literature – vary considerably but most correspond to that of the National Highway Traffic Safety Association that defines "aggressive driving" as "when individuals commit a combination of moving traffic offenses so as to endanger other persons or property," or "the operation of a motor vehicle involving three or more moving violations as part of a single continuous sequence of driving acts, which is likely to endanger any person or property" (NHTSA, 2000).

Accordingly, driving acts that are "only" careless; discourteous; inconsiderate; rude; or thoughtless would not merit the "aggressive driving" label in law unless they violated traffic offenses or breached traffic regulations. Antisocial driving is a much more common phenomenon.

Although some acts of antisocial driving constitute violations of traffic laws and, thereby, may qualify as aggressive driving, many others do not breach any traffic law, and are not illegal. Victims might believe that the most important law that antisocial drivers violate is the law of natural selection.

Antisocial driving does not necessarily reflect aggression. More frequently it is characterized by a more fundamental human shortcoming – selfishness. Antisocial driving includes a wide variety of driving acts that reflect a lack of concern for the feelings, needs, and rights of other people. Antisocial driving is 'care-less' driving in which individuals operate their vehicle with only themselves in mind.

We believe that labeling life-threatening, risky, rude, or discourteous driving as "aggressive" fails to do justice to the essential antisocial quality of such acts. Drivers who use their cars as a way of exhibiting their power or expressing their "masculinity" may view the "aggressive driver" label not as a condemnation, but as a badge of honor.

BAD DRIVERS ARE NOT BAD DRIVERS

It is also misleading to refer to antisocial drivers as "bad drivers." Unfortunately, the label "bad driver" has two different meanings. It may refer to someone who lacks the driving skills to competently maneuver a vehicle. However, in that sense, many antisocial drivers are not "bad drivers." Many are highly competent drivers. Antisocial drivers include some taxi drivers, some truck drivers, some bus drivers, some professional racing drivers and many others who are able to maneuver their vehicles with impressive skill and dexterity. Their "bad driving" does not indicate that there is something lacking in their *driving* skills. It may indicate that there is something lacking in their *social* skills.

BAD DRIVERS OR BAD PEOPLE?

The term "bad driver" can also be misleading because it suggests that the person whose driving offends us is a bad person. Some "bad drivers" are discourteous, foul mouthed, rude, hostile, inconsiderate, intemperate, arrogant, or callous in every aspect of their lives. They drive as they live — they not only drive badly, they live badly. However, many "bad drivers" behave badly only when they drive. Something about driving a car can transform nice people into rascals. Many drivers who act like rogues when behind the wheel of a car are otherwise well-mannered, considerate, and kindly ladies and gentlemen whose behavior is usually law-abiding and socially acceptable.

Chapter 3

WHO ARE THE ANTISOCIAL DRIVERS?

Antisocial drivers are not a homogeneous group. Research has not yet yielded classification schemes that can reliably differentiate antisocial drivers into discrete types that can be shown to benefit from different intervention approaches. However, our review of the available research indicates that drivers can be grouped into the following general types depending on the manner in which they customarily drive and the manner in which they usually live.

DRIVING HOOLIGANS

Many of the boors who behave badly in the driver's seat behave just as badly elsewhere. Driving is just another situation in which they demonstrate their lack of manners and their poor social judgment.

There is no reason to expect that people who behave badly at home or at work or at play would behave well when they are driving. It is much more likely that they would exhibit the same offensive behaviors when driving as they do elsewhere.

> It would appear that the driving habits, and the high accident record, are simply one manifestation of a method of driving that has been demonstrated in their personal lives. . . . If his personal life is marked by caution, tolerance, foresight, and consideration for others then he will drive in the same manner. If his personal life is devoid of these desirable characteristics then his driving will be characterized by aggressiveness and over a long period of time he will have a much higher accident rate than his more stable companion.
>
> Tillman and Hobbs (1949)

The research we review in the next chapter indicates that, as Tillman & Hobbs observed many years ago, drivers whose personal life history is characterized by antisocial behavior and attitudes are unlikely to change their lifestyle when they sit behind the wheel of a car. They frequently violate traffic rules and they are more likely than other drivers to be involved in collisions. They are not specialists who are deviant, aggressive, malicious, or discourteous and flout the law only when they are driving. They are antisocial wherever they are.

Such drivers are also not specialists in the manner in which their antisocial behavior is expressed on the road – they do not limit their violations to one prohibited driving act such as running red lights, but tend to be indiscriminate in their offending. They are likely to violate most types of traffic laws and to do so on frequent occasions. Wherever they are, Road Hooligans ignore or flout social conventions. They are ill-mannered, inconsiderate of others, and concerned only with their own immediate needs. They often evidence callous disregard for the needs and rights and even the safety of others. Their behavior is clearly antisocial.

Some of these antisocial drivers have a remarkable history of collisions. Many also have a lengthy record of convictions for traffic violations – convictions that in many cases appear to have had little impact on their subsequent driving behavior. Many of them view Traffic Court as a revolving door which enables them to enter, receive a tongue lashing and a "final" warning, then depart with a sneer ready to drive again in ways that later bring them back to court for another "final" warning.

Many Road Hooligans are adolescents who test the limits of social tolerance wherever they are. Many of them view the highway as a video-arcade game. However, it must not be thought that Road Hooligans are only young drivers. Antisocial driving is also exhibited by many older drivers. Aging does not guarantee maturing. Many individuals fail to learn social skills no matter how much life experience they acquire. Many Road Hooligans are middle-aged Yuppies or Senior Citizens who, like the adolescent Road Hooligans, are social boors wherever they are. They grow old without growing up. They are the kind of drivers who make you want to emigrate. Unfortunately, they are to be found in every otherwise civilized nation.

Not all adolescent drivers are Road Hooligans. Many adolescents drive with the utmost caution and respect for their car and for other cars as well as for the people in them. Other young and old adults should follow their example.

Males are not the only Road Hooligans. Some are females. When it comes to driving, whether it is prosocial or antisocial, females are gaining equal rights (Quigley & Tedeschi, 1989). Teen-age girls are driving more, and the youngest ones are involved in an alarming number of collisions (NHTSA, 2000). Our interviews with many female drivers indicates that they feel that the car is the one place where they have equal power to males – power that they are able to use or abuse just as much as many males do.

It should also not be thought that all Road Hooligans are drunk drivers. Many are. However, most Road Hooligans live and drive antisocially whether they have been drinking or not. Even without alcohol they are high-risk drivers.

The antisocial drivers we have dubbed "Road Hooligans" are the most easily recognized, but they are by no means the only individuals who drive antisocially. They are distinguishable from other antisocial drivers by the fact that they do not confine their antisocial behavior to the car. They drive as they live – indifferent to the dictates of fair and decent behavior and in many cases impervious to society's sanctions against antisocial behavior.

> *We take the same mind with us wherever we go.*
> Road Sage

ROAD CHAMELEONS

There are exceptions to Tillman & Hobbs' conclusion that people drive as they live. Many antisocial drivers are nice people who are boors only when they drive. Many of the drivers who jeopardize our safety on the highways are otherwise upstanding citizens who are somehow transformed into scoundrels when in cars. Antisocial inclinations that are usually inhibited elsewhere, can quickly become disinhibited in the car. The car is a convenient place to unleash obnoxiousness.

Unlike Road Hooligans, the Road Chameleons seldom behave in their 'off-road life' in ways that are ill-mannered. However, like chameleons, they appear different in different environments. In driving situations their normally civilized behavior is temporarily suspended and they act as though they think that, on the road, offending people is perfectly justifiable. They frequently drive as though they believe that other drivers are not entitled to be treated courteously, civilly, or even fairly.

The driving behavior of Road Chameleons may appear to be "out of character" not only because it is ill-mannered but also because it is frequently illegal. Many individuals who are otherwise law-abiding citizens become lawbreakers when they are behind the wheel of a car.

Survey research indicates that almost all drivers admit to occasionally breaking at least one traffic law. Eighty-eight percent of drivers admit that they break speed limits at least 'sometimes' and twenty-two percent admit driving over the alcohol limit on some occasions. Moreover, some drivers confess that they break 'minor' traffic laws on frequent occasions (Corbett & Simon, 1992). However, the findings of the British Crime Survey indicate that less than one-fifth of the general adult population admit to even one of a list of eight *non-driving* violations such as tax evasion. These data suggest that many people 'stick to the road' in terms of their antisocial behavior and although they commit driving offenses, they do not break the law in other ways. At least they *say* that they do not. At least in Britain they say they do not. Many antisocial drivers say that they do not live as they drive. That is easy for them to say. Maybe they are being honest.

Road Chameleons are individuals who frequently behave antisocially when they are driving but do not appear to be antisocial at other times. However, appearances can be deceiving. Our research suggests that although many drivers appear to have well-developed prosocial values that guide their behavior in most circumstances, they may not have such qualities in sufficient strength to withstand the conflicts, stresses, and temptations that are frequently encountered in driving situations. Civility for them may only be a veneer. The car is a shield that protects them while they are being nasty. How such individuals behave behind the wheel of a car is most likely to be a pretty good reflection of how they would behave in non-driving situations if they were afforded the same protections from detection, social censure or prosecution that they 'enjoy' in their car.

Road Chameleons do not drive as they live. Many *would* live as they drive – if they thought they could get away with it.

HIGHWAY VIGILANTES

A third type of antisocial driver is the driver who drives antisocially for apparently prosocial reasons. They frequently react or overreact to the antisocial driving of others by engaging in very risky driving themselves. They do so in order to "teach them a lesson."

Lamenting the lack of police surveillance, or inadequate enforcement of traffic laws, they proceed to take the law into their own hands. Their negative assessment of the efficiency of the justice system may be accurate, but their attempts to correct the behavior of other drivers that they find offensive is often just as antisocial and dangerous as the driving that they think they are correcting.

Some Highway Vigilantes doggedly block the passing lane in an ill-advised attempt to control drivers behind them whom they believe are driving too fast Some refuse to respond or even acknowledge the horn blowing, light-flashing driver who wishes to pass. Some just tap on their brake pedal to activate their brake lights in order to communicate to the following driver that he/she should slow down because they themselves have no intention of speeding up or pulling over to allow the driver behind – who is driving over the speed limit – to pass them. Some slam on their brakes to deter the driver behind them from getting too close and, as a result become firmly attached to a total stranger. Some swerve into the other lane when the following driver finally gives up and tries to pass on the wrong side. Some do all of the above. The consequences of such conflicts can be fatal, particularly when the driver behind decides to use an alternative way to pass when none is available.

Road Vigilantes comprise a mixed group of drivers. Some are only extending to the highway a behavioral style that they evidence in non-driving situations. Many are egocentric individuals who, whether they are in a car or not, think everyone must behave in accordance with their own selfish needs. Some are "holier than thou" characters who appear to believe that everyone must conform to their personal standards of behavior. They assume the role of our moral guardians. They experience moral outrage at the rule violators and engage in vengeful aggression against those whom they feel have wronged them. Wherever they are, they condemn dissenters. It is no problem if they confine their *angst* to writing letters to the editor. Unfortunately, the chastisement they apply to those whose behavior they find unacceptable can have very serious consequences when exercised at high speed on the highway. They act as the policeman, judge, and jury. Their ill-advised attempts at correcting other drivers can turn them into the executioner.

Other types of Road Vigilantes would never think of reacting to the offensive behavior of other individuals in non-driving situations in the same dramatic and extreme way they do without hesitation while in the relative safety of their cars. Like the Road Chameleons, they are otherwise peace-loving citizens who ordinarily tolerate or ignore discourteous behavior and simply avoid the perpetrators. However, for some reason, when they are driving, they are transformed into motorized bounty hunters who use their cars as urban assault vehicles in their fight against those whose driving offends their principles.

Many Road Vigilantes act as though the motivation for their risky driving is prosocial when in reality they are motivated by hostility, or anger, or revenge. Some thrive on harassing, humiliating, and tormenting other drivers.

Many Road Vigilantes are lacking in the skill to respond to driving stress and conflict without losing control of their emotions. Their vigilantism is neither principled nor reasoned. It is reactive.

Most drivers view the antisocial driving of other drivers as a breach of norms of acceptable driving behavior. Road Vigilantes also view it as a personal affront. Many experience anger and a desire for personal revenge or retaliation (Oldenquist, 1988).

The efforts of such "do-gooders" to influence other drivers are seldom effective in improving the driving behavior of the targets of their "vigilantism." One must question the adequacy of their problem-solving skills and their values.

Ironically, drivers who frequently violate traffic rules are the ones who are most likely to express irritability and annoyance towards other drivers (Parker, Lawton, Stradling & Manstead, 2000).

ROAD RULERS

Many drivers think they should have the same control on the road as they have with their remote controls in their living rooms. They act as though their car is a castle and they are the King or Queen of the Road. They think they can make their own Rules Of The Road – rules that serve only themselves.

MOBILE BULLIES

Some antisocial drivers are bullies whose cowardice is temporarily suspended by the ability of their car's engine to make them feel powerful.

Some drive antisocially because their vehicle enables them to easily control, harass, frighten, intimidate, and even traumatize other people. Some bully us by high speed and risky driving maneuvers that make us respond like chickens avoiding roosters. A powerful engine not only gives power to the car's drive-shaft; it also enables the driver to minimize the risk of retaliation. Cars can turn milquetoasts into monsters.

TRAVELLING HEDONISTS

Many antisocial drivers are stimulus-seekers for whom high-risk driving is primarily a form of recreation. Driving is a sport for them. It is a sport which they force us to play even though we are unwilling players. Their games can readily become a blood sport.

Many Road Hedonists are risk-takers in many aspects of their lives. Risky driving is simply another opportunity for them to indulge themselves in the emotional and physiological arousal they gain by testing fate. Some are normally not risk-takers but find that risky, high-speed driving gives them a non-chemical high similar to what Freud labeled "kinesthetic eroticism."

Many Road Hedonists find risky driving more stimulating than most other social activities in which they engage. Some Road Hedonists use the road as a stage on which they indulge their narcissism in displays of high speed and high-risk maneuvers by means of which they can impress audiences whom they might not be able to impress in any other way.

Some Hedonists do not realize that the risky driving they enjoy is distasteful or distressful for other drivers. Many do, but don't care. Their personal enjoyment is all that matters to them.

STREET SABOTEURS

The car can be used as a weapon. It is, in fact, the most powerful weapon that most people will ever have at their disposal. It can be used to inconvenience other people, frighten other people, and even physically harm other people. It is an instrument that is used by many drivers as a means of expressing anger, hostility, and aggression.

Anger is a frequent passenger in the cars of many drivers. Long before the invention of the rush hour, the anger-generated adrenalin

rush that prepares us to defend or attack was an essential mechanism
for survival against predators who might come out of the bush. The
dangers we now face are more likely to come out of the adjoining lane.
Now we are less concerned with the risk of running into a wild animal
than with running into a radar trap. Other cars encroaching on our
space on the road or in the parking lot are the modern enemy.

As society becomes more orderly, individuals are expected and even
required to put a lid on their anger. The direct expression of aggression
has become severely curtailed in modern, complex, urbanized environments. Zero tolerance for aggression is now in vogue, particularly
in the workplace. Many organizations have removed the necessity of
individuals resolving conflicts between themselves. That is what com-
mittees, tribunals, and courts are for.

Interpersonal conflicts are now less likely to be resolved by the individuals openly and directly confronting one another. That has become
the responsibility of negotiators or lawyers. Briefs and motions have
become the vehicle for the expression of aggression. Warring parties
seldom are allowed to confront each other even when their squabbles
reach open court; their angst is suppressed by procedures, precedents,
and maneuvers that convert the expression of antagonism into legal
argument.

Antagonists are now controlled by negotiators, mediators, and other
"disinterested parties" who strive to reduce emotion in order to reduce
conflict. We seem to be trying to make anger an anachronistic emotion.

The suppression of aggression may help resolve conflicts but it may
also lead to the perpetuation of hostility, grudge, and vindictiveness.
Gaylin (2001) has argued that we now live in a state of contained anger.
Keeping the lid on anger has become a requirement for individuals
living together in our highly organized society. Individuals may become
"warehouses of unexpressed aggression" (Abdennur, 2000). Confrontation may have come to be controlled or suppressed; but aggression has not.

Anger can be contained but it is not easily eliminated. Where does
the anger go? Some people displace their anger from their office to their
home where they berate their mother-in-law or bark at their dog. Some
displace it from their office to their intestines and develop ulcers. Some
live in chronic stress and develop pervasive irritability. Some attempt
to swallow their anger by gulping Prozac®. Aggression is often displaced
from the office to the highway where it is taken out on other drivers. It

can take as much as six hours to reduce stress-response levels to normal following five minutes of anger – long enough to drive twelve miles at 60 miles per hour. Angry drivers take more than their cars out on the road.

There may be zero tolerance for the expression of aggression in the workplace or the courtroom, but not on the road. Driving provides an ideal opportunity for the expression of displaced aggression. All it takes is a little turn of the steering wheel, or a slam of the brake pedal, or a little tap on the accelerator.

Drivers can express aggressive feelings and make other individuals suffer without even being aware that they are doing so. Aggression may be expressed in a more passive form such as by driving at the speed limit in the passing lane on an expressway, or by taking an inordinate length of time in intersections and thereby delaying the progress of other drivers while appearing to be driving cautiously.

> *Keeping another person waiting is a basic tactic for defining him as inferior and oneself as superior.*
>
> Thomas Szasz

The car provides an ideal vehicle for "interpersonal sabotage." The car provides both the power and the opportunity to make other people suffer without having to confront those individuals on a personal level. The car also enables drivers to express their anger in a way in which their personal identity is not revealed.

Many drivers believe that expressing aggression is an essential driving skill. They truly believe they are just following the norm for driving behavior. Many even argue that their fast, aggressive driving is in the best interest of efficient traffic flow. Many claim that this is the reason one seldom sees a police car watching for speeders during rush hour.

Cars provide a fertile environment for the expression of anger. High speed or risky driving can increase emotional arousal so much that even relatively minor transgressions by neighboring drivers and minor encroachments on our "territory" may be perceived as an indignity and trigger our anger. Such irritations are an unavoidable aspect of the modern driving situation that drivers must learn to tolerate. Many have not learned to do so. Many have no intention of doing so.

Many antisocial drivers who use their cars in a hostile manner are simply extending to the road an interpersonal lifestyle that is characterized by belligerence and aggression. They elbow their way through life whether they are driving or not. They qualify, in this respect, as "Driving Hooligans." However, many other individuals who behave aggressively when in their car are seldom aggressive in other aspects of their lives. Their aggressive driving enables them to achieve the expression of anger or hostility – a cathartic release that they may not find possible in other aspects of their lives. They feel secure enough in their moving metal and glass house to 'throw stones' at those who frustrate or offend them and they feel free to attack individuals in ways that they would never dream of doing in other circumstances. On the road they think no one will kick sand in their faces.

ROAD RAGERS

The most extreme of the many forms of antisocial driving is Road Rage – felonious criminal acts in which the driver is fully intent on causing discomfort, harm, or injury to others. However, it is by no means the only form or even the most common form. Road Ragers constitute only a small percentage of the population of antisocial drivers. A recent study of 526 motorists found that sixty percent reported having lost their tempers when driving (AAA, 1997). However, losing one's temper does not necessarily translate into an attempt to injure someone. Without downplaying the seriousness of Road Rage, we must note that drunk drivers cause 85 times as many deaths as are caused by Road Rage (Glassner, 2000). In our view, the attention that the media has devoted to sensational acts of Road Rage has *lessened*, not *heightened* our concern for other less dramatic forms of antisocial driving that lead to far more fatalities than do acts of Road Rage.

SUBSTANCE ABUSING DRIVERS

Many antisocial drivers are individuals who mix their drinks with their driving in a potentially lethal cocktail. There is a variety of subtypes of substance-abusing drivers. Some drive under the influence infrequently, but once is too often. Some are anesthetized by alcohol and/or drugs very frequently and engage in risky driving on many of the occasions when they are under their influence. Some substance abusers become impervious to the risks of driving when they temporarily dilute their senses and their judgment with alcohol or other substances.

We will discuss drink/driving more thoroughly in Chapter 5 when we review research that indicates that many drink/drivers drive antisocially not only when they have been drinking but also when they are sober.

PROSOCIAL DRIVERS

There is another group of individuals who drive as they live. These are individuals who are just as courteous, considerate, controlled, concerned, careful, and cautious when they drive as they are in any other social situation.

Some drivers do not break the law whether they are on the road or not. They act as though established rules for decent social interaction apply everywhere. They do not believe that such rules should be disregarded just because they are driving and are surrounded by others who appear to believe that the road is a special place where social rules do not apply and antisocial behavior is acceptable. They do not identify with or endorse social norms that condone or promote antisocial driving.

Stress factors associated with driving, particularly those occasioned by congested traffic and conditions of cut and thrust driving, may test their emotional control and test the strength of their beliefs and convictions. However, some drivers have acquired prosocial skills and values in sufficient strength to protect them from the urge or the temptation to relax their prosocial attitudes when driving. They may feel the same revulsion and anger that others do about the antisocial driving that they encounter, but they have skills and values that enable them, and motivate them to refrain from engaging in antisocial behavior on the road.

Everybody Does It

Many would argue that no matter how they are driven, all cars and, therefore, all those who drive them can be considered to be antisocial because they pollute the environment and threaten the world economy by their unquenchable thirst for oil. Margaret Wente has dubbed "fuel-guzzling SUV" drivers as "*mobile eco-criminals.*"[6] Admittedly, the focus of this book is much narrower. Our focus is the *socially* toxic environment

---

6. Globe & Mail, March 7, 2002

that is caused by how too many of those SUV's — and other "fuel-guzzling" vehicles — are driven.

Most individuals probably drive antisocially on some occasions at some point in their driving career. Some simply grow out of it. Some change as a result of law enforcement. Some change their ways because of an accumulation of frightening experiences resulting from their antisocial or risky driving.

Some may learn only through experiencing a collision. The deterrent effects of collisions are often short-lived, but collisions can be effective teachers for *some* drivers. However, such 'crash courses' cannot be recommended as "best practice" in efforts to teach safe driving.

Many others fail to learn. They continue to drive antisocially on frequent occasions. Those are the drivers with whom this book is most concerned. Some learn very slowly. Many die before they learn.

ANTISOCIAL VS. PROSOCIAL DRIVERS

Antisocial drivers represent a heterogeneity of social and demographic characteristics and personal attributes. However, there may be some commonality in the underlying factors that can help us to understand the similarity in their driving behavior.

Criminological research that we review in this book indicates that individuals who behave antisocially can be differentiated from those who behave prosocially on the basis of their level of development in a number of cognitive and emotional skills and values. We shall present evidence that demonstrates that inadequate development of such skills is related to antisocial driving and other forms of antisocial behavior. They are skills and values that can and should be taught both to potential drivers who are seeking their licenses and to experienced drivers who drive as though they should never have been licensed.

Chapter 4

ANTISOCIAL DRIVING AND ANTISOCIAL BEHAVIOR

Research demonstrating a link between "poor driving" and antisocial behavior began in England in the 1940s when a study by Tillman & Hobbs (1949) found that taxi drivers with "high accident histories" had a history of aggression against authority dating from their early childhood. They also found that, in the general population of drivers, sixty-six percent of a "high accident group" (four or more collisions) were known to law enforcement agencies compared with only nine percent of collision-free drivers.

Tillman & Hobbs (1949) reported that the "high-accident" taxi drivers displayed antisocial behavior throughout their life. They had school records of truancy and disciplinary infractions. They had frequently been brought before the Juvenile Court. They were likely to have police records for offenses other than traffic violations. Their social problems were frequently known to various agencies such as Children's Aid Societies, Family Service Bureaus, and Public Health Departments. Their work history was that of frequent short-time employment, and their relationship to their employers was poor. A history of promiscuity was common. They were unfaithful to their spouses and assumed little responsibility for their families. They showed very little concern over mechanical problems in their cars. They were discourteous to their passengers and quickly became annoyed at other motorists. Their driving was marked by the same aggressiveness, impulsiveness, and lack of concern for others that characterized their social and personal lives.

The "low accident" group, in contrast, were non-aggressive; had little history of school problems; had good employment records; and had harmonious family backgrounds. They were considered to be well-adjusted personalities who had stable friendships. They drank only moderately, if at all. They evidenced neither marital infidelity nor promiscuity. They were quiet, reserved individuals who were conscientious about their work. They were serious while driving even to the point of refusing to talk when driving. They were sensitive to the possibility of mistakes being made by other drivers. They appreciated the mechanical limitations of their vehicles. They were concerned about the welfare of others and were courteous to their passengers and to other drivers.

Tillman and Hobbs concluded that "a man drives as he lives." That conclusion has been quoted again and again by many traffic researchers since it first appeared fifty years ago. It has just as frequently been rejected by others.

A large number of early studies yielded support for Tillman and Hobbs' findings by demonstrating that adaptive behavior in traffic is related to general social adaptation and conformity to institutionalized patterns of social behavior. The studies found that "poor driving," as indicated by the frequency of both fatal and non-fatal collisions, was associated with the driver's lack of conformity (e.g., Conger, Gaskill, Glad, Rainey, Sawrey, & Turrell, 1957). It was also associated with social maladjustment (McGuire, 1976; Williams & Malfetti, 1970).

Early studies found that a history of collisions and traffic violations was associated with social adjustment problems including conflict in family relationships; disturbances in parental family life; and problems with authorities (Mayer & Treat, 1977; McFarland, 1966; McGuire 1973; Williams & Malfetti, 1970). Such early research supported Tillman & Hobbs' conclusion that drivers whose personal life is characterized by a lack of caution, tolerance, and consideration for others tend to drive in the same careless, thoughtless, discourteous, and aggressive manner over a long period of time and are likely to have a much higher collision rate.

Rediscovering The Past

Although many early studies indicated that collisions are a correlate of being antisocial, the research methodology employed in most of the studies was flawed. Consequently, the investigation of the relationship between antisocial behavior and driving received little continuing support from a traffic research community that became more interested in studies in highway engineering and automotive technology that could be much better controlled than was possible in studies in sociology, psychology, or criminology.

Some researchers have continued to pursue research on the relationship between driving and antisocial behavior. Their work indicates that whereas the early studies may not have been high quality research, some of their conclusions may well have been valid. More recent and better quality research that we will review has indicated that both collision risk and driving violations are, indeed, related to social deviance (Hartos, Eitel & Simons-Morton, 2002; Lawton, Parker, Stradling & Manstead, 1997; Meadows, Stradling & Lawson, 1998; Underwood, Chapman, Wright & Crundall,1999; West & Hall, 1997).

West & Hall (1995) concluded on the basis of their own research, and their review of the research of many others, that "the relationship between collisions, driving violations, driving speed, attitude to driving violations and social deviance are among the best-established in the field of accident liability."

CRIMINALS AS DRIVERS

It is not only general social maladjustment, antagonism towards authority, interpersonal conflict, and social deviance that have been found to be common among drivers with high collision histories. It also is criminal behavior.

Evidence of a relationship between traffic violations and other types of involvement with the police was reported as early as the 1960s when it was found that among drivers with a record of criminal offenses, most had a history of traffic offenses. Willett (1964) and Kroj & Helleman (1971) found that a considerable percentage of drivers convicted of various motoring offenses had a police record for non-motoring offenses. Moser (1974) also reported that the greater the driver's history of criminal offenses, the stronger was the relationship between criminality and traffic violations.

The relationship between traffic violations and involvement with the police for non-driving offenses has been confirmed by recent research that concluded that a history of "aggressive criminal offenses" is related to a history of repeated traffic violations (Noordizi, 1990). In programs run by probation officers in the U.K. for individuals convicted of offenses such as car theft, joyriding, or driving while their license was suspended, seventy-five percent of participants had previous convictions for theft; sixty percent had convictions for burglary; and fifteen percent had convictions for violence against persons.

It has been established that a history of convictions for *non*-driving offenses is one of the most reliable predictors of the driver's likelihood of committing traffic violations (Blockley & Hartley, 1995). Both collisions and violations are correlated with attitudes that support breaking the law (Furnham & Saipe, 1993). A strong relationship between various types of crime and collisions has also been found among youths ranging in age from 12 to 24 (Junger, Terlouw, & Van Der Heidjen, 1995).

A record of criminal behavior has even been found among many drivers who park illegally. Thirty-three percent of owners of illegally parked cars have a criminal record (Chenery, Henshaw & Pease, 1999).

Drinking/Driving, Disqualified Driving, Dangerous Driving, and Crime

A study of serious traffic offenders in the U.K. (drivers convicted of drink driving, disqualified driving, or dangerous driving) indicated that many have committed "mainstream offenses" such as violence against the person; burglary; robbery; theft; handling stolen goods; criminal damage; and drug offenses (Rose, 2000). It was also found that disqualified drivers had criminal histories similar to that of criminal offenders – seventy-nine percent had a criminal record. Moreover, drink/drivers were twice as likely as the general population to have a criminal conviction – forty percent of drink/drivers had a criminal record. Approximately fifty percent of dangerous drivers had a previous conviction for criminal offenses and twenty-five percent were reconvicted within a year.

Persistent traffic offenders should not be thought of as otherwise law-abiding citizens. Drivers who repeatedly commit *traffic* offenses are likely to commit *criminal* offenses as well. This fact is not well recognized by the general public. Nor is it easily accepted by those among us who have been ticketed sometime for breaking traffic rules – and more often have done so without being caught.

Criminals On The Road

The police recognize the link between traffic offenses and other criminal acts. They have found that many criminal offenders are apprehended as a result of being stopped for traffic violations. The Association of Chief Police Officers in the U.K. has adopted the principle that "policing the roads means policing crime" (DETR, 2000). Similarly, Joslin (1994) has declared that, "My own traffic officers arrest more persons for crime than do my CID." The West Midlands Police (1997) reported that "36 percent of all arrests made by traffic officers were for crime."

Most drivers are not criminal, but most criminals are drivers.

Cars For Crime

The contribution of cars in the commission of crimes – including bombings and drive-by shootings – as well as in the 'get away' from the scene of the crime has been 'celebrated' in film and media presentations throughout the history of the automobile. These fictional presentations too often reflect real life. Too often they become reflected in real life.

Collisions And Crime

It is not only violation of traffic laws that is associated with other forms of illegal behavior. It is also collisions. A record of collision is frequently found in the history of jailed criminals. Compared to the general population, criminals are more than five times more likely to be involved in collisions. They are also approximately twenty times more likely to be involved in collisions that are fatal (Junger & Tremblay,1999).

Criminal Professional Drivers

The relationship between collisions and crime has been found not only among the general driving population, but also among some professional drivers. For example, among bus drivers, collision rates are correlated with a history of criminal convictions (Parker et al., 1995).

DRIVING AND VIOLENCE

A positive relationship between driving and violent crime has been found even at the population or aggregate level. For example, collision rates in twenty-seven countries have been shown to be associated with indices of violent crime, homicide rates, and indices of fatalities caused by murder, suicide, and other forms of violence. Traffic fatality rates in a state are strongly correlated with that state's homicide rate. The best predictor of rates of traffic collision fatalities in the United States in 1977 was the rate of homicide (Sivak, 1983). Moreover, Mizel (1997) has found that the majority of "aggressive drivers" are relatively young males who have histories of violence.

Licensed To Kill

The automobile can, and often has been used by both male and female drivers of all ages as a weapon in assaults and homicides (MacDonald, 1964; McGuire, 1960; Sivak, 1983). Many police officers have been victims of "assault by auto."

Mizell has documented 2,300 cases of vehicular homicide in the six-year period from 1990 to 1996. They include instances where drivers have intentionally driven their cars into crowds of people. Cars have also been used as battering rams by drivers who have deliberately crashed into offices, private homes, restaurants, hotels, government buildings, and even schools and hospitals (Mizel 1997).

The vehicles used in such assaults have included not only cars, vans, and SUVs, but pickup trucks; bulldozers; tow trucks; forklifts; and tractor-trailers. The vehicle in one incident was a heavily armed tank stolen from the military.

The weapons that have been used in assaults include tire-arms, jack handles; baseball bats; knives; bayonets; ice picks; razor blades; swords; beer and liquor bottles; rocks; soft-drink cans; hamburgers; crowbars; lead pipes; batons, wrenches; hatchets; mace; and pepper spray. One driver was killed by a paint roller thrown through his windshield in response to a dispute over a parking spot (Mizel, 1997). The favorite weapon of older drivers is a walking cane.

Several instances have been reported of aggressive drivers taking their golf clubs from their car's trunk and wielding them as weapons. It has not been reported whether they swung them more competently on the road than on the golf course.

The Family Car As A Hearse

Driving one's car into a solid object such as a wall or another car or steering it off the edge of a cliff or a bridge has been one of the popular techniques for committing suicide (Sivak, 1983). More common is suicide in the car with the aid of a garden hose and carbon monoxide.

Vehicular Murder-Suicide

It is well known that victims of fatal car crashes are often victims of drivers whose suicidal mission ended not only their own life but, either intentionally or inadvertently, also ended the lives of other individuals. However, reliable statistics are difficult to obtain because post-mortem psychological assessments are difficult to conduct, leaving us to wonder how many such crashes there are.

PSYCHOPATHS AT THE WHEEL

Not deeply vicious, he carries disaster lightly in each hand.
Cleckley, 1955

Reckless driving is considered to be a symptom of "Antisocial Personality Disorder" in the Diagnostic and Statistical Manual of the American Psychiatric Association, the major classification system for mental disorders. A number of studies have reported that mild psychopathy is common among drivers with high collision histories (e.g., Tsuang, Boor & Fleming, 1985).

Court-referred aggressive drivers have been found to be more likely than controls to meet the criteria not only for Personality Disorder but also for such conditions as Alcohol Dependence and Intermittent Explosive Disorder (Galovski, Blanchard & Veazey, 2002).

ANTISOCIAL ATTITUDES AND VALUES

Murderers and psychopaths represent the extremes of antisocial behavior. They certainly do not represent the vast majority of drivers who are involved in collisions or the vast majority of antisocial drivers. Violations and collisions are common not only among psychopaths and criminals but also among drivers who may never have been convicted of a criminal offense. However, research indicates that many drivers who have a history of a high frequency of collisions, but have not been arrested, evidence antisocial attitudes and values.

Violations and collisions are common among drivers who may never have been convicted of criminal offenses but describe themselves as "less law-abiding" (Moser, 1974). Many early studies found that differences between "good and bad drivers" were related to the extent to which the driver identified with general social values and that the self-image of drivers without "accidents" and violations was that of a safe and responsible driver and of a person who had respect for the law (Williams & Malfetti, 1970).

Drivers with frequent collision histories have poorer attitudes to the laws that govern driving behavior (McGuire, 1976). Moreover, "high accident adolescents" are more likely than low accident youth to evidence a disregard for social morals and a defiance of authority (McFarland, 1968). Drivers with disrespect for the law are more prone to collisions than drivers with the opposite characteristics (Clark, 1976). High collision risk drivers of various ages were found to evidence pronounced antisocial attitudes and to express antagonism to authority (McGuire, 1976).

More recent research indicates the salience of a lack of regard for authority and the law in terms of "problem driving" (e.g., Arthur, Barrett, & Alexander, 1992; Donovan, Queisser, Salzberg, & Umlauf, 1985). Analysis of the research literature indicates that "undersocialization" distinguishes "problem" from "non-problem drivers" (Arthur et al., 1992). "Tolerance of deviance" has also been significantly correlated with risky driving (Jessor, Turbin, & Costa, 1997). Normlessness may be the norm among risky drivers (Iversen & Rundmo, 2002).

Collision risk is associated with social deviance not only in the general driving population but also among professional drivers such as bus drivers (Lancaster & Ward, 2002; West, Elander, & French, 1993).

Violations and Collisions

Several recent studies have confirmed the view that collision risk is associated with the individual driver's tendency to violate traffic laws (Meadows, 1994; Parker et al., 1995; Reason et al., 1990; Sabey & Taylor 1980; Stradling & Parker,1996). Such studies have found that drivers who score high on measures of violation of traffic laws are significantly more likely to have been involved in collisions in the past. They are also more likely to be involved again in the future (Parker et al., 1995). Particularly alarming is the evidence that a history of frequent violations is also found in the case of fatal collisions – involvement in fatal crashes is frequently preceded by convictions for traffic offenses (Rajalin, 1994).

DELINQUENT DRIVERS

The driving research literature is replete with evidence that young drivers are disproportionately represented in statistics on risky driving, traffic violations, drink/driving, and collisions (e.g., Cooper, Pinili, & Chen, 1995; Evans, 1991; Jonah, 1986; Laberge-Nadeau, Maag & Bourbeau, 1992; Mannering, 1993). Motor vehicle crashes in the United States and many other countries are the most common cause of death for people under thirty-four years of age. Motor vehicle injuries account for more than forty percent of all deaths among sixteen to nineteen-year-olds (Williams, 1996).

The greater collision involvement among young drivers may not only be a function of their lack of driving experience (Brown & Groeger, 1988; Jonah, 1986). It is also related to the manner in which they drive. Young drivers (17–25) violate traffic laws more frequently (Evans & Wasielewski, 1982; Jonah, Dawson & Smith, 1982; Stradling & Parker, 1996; Wasielewski, 1984; Yu & Williford, 1993). They also speed more frequently than do adults. They drive through yellow lights more frequently. They wear safety belts less frequently.

It is not only adults and researchers who think that young drivers take more risks than older drivers. Young males themselves view themselves as more reckless (Groeger & Brown, 1989).

The high collision rates of young males is less likely to be associated with a lack of driving skills than with *deliberate* risk-taking (Williams, Lund & Preusser, 1986). They take more risks than older drivers (Deery, 1999). Many young male drivers have knowingly and intentionally engaged in high risk driving. Many of them do so regularly (Jessor et al., 1997). However, it is not only in driving that they evidence risk-taking.

Research by Beirness and Simpson (1988) found that many youths who had been involved in collisions also exhibited a number of high-risk or problem behaviors in non-driving situations. Their frequency of collisions was associated with a lifestyle characterized by a variety of antisocial, high-risk behaviors such as smoking, drug use, heavy drinking, and other behaviors likely to negatively impact their health. In contrast, youths who had not been involved in collisions evidenced more concern with their health and well-being and were less likely to engage in any kind of high-risk activities. The converse is also true; it has been found that youths who are not involved in delinquency or accidents are those who function well in their family, are future oriented, and like school (Junger et al., 1995).

Thus, antisocial driving among youth including deliberate risk taking and violations of traffic laws may represent not just age and inexperience but a more general syndrome of adolescent behavior problems including illicit alcohol and drug use and delinquency.

Jessor suggests that risky driving reflects a tendency to violate rules, social norms or laws and is one of a cluster of problem behaviors that comprise a general antisocial lifestyle (Jessor, 1987a,b). His view is supported by Beirness & Simpson's (1988) studies of collision involvement among youth. They found that risky driving such as intentional risk-taking, impaired driving, and the failure to use seat belts was associated with measures of other problem behaviors such as frequency of drug or alcohol use; riding with a drinking driver; and frequency of drunkenness. Collision involvement was also found to be positively related to non-driving problem behaviors.

"Tolerance of deviance" and involvement in delinquent-type behavior is significantly correlated with risky driving among adolescent drivers (Jessor et al., 1997). Compared with low-risk adolescent drivers, adolescents with a history of high risky driving have been found to be almost five times more likely to report their acceptance of high deviance (Hartos et al., 2002).

Antisocial Motives

The research literature (and probably every driver's experience) makes it clear that some driving acts are fully intended to inconvenience, or frighten, or antagonize other drivers. The perpetrator drives in such a way that he/she hopes will either offend or intimidate other drivers. There can be little doubt that such driving is antisocial.

Vengeance

Antisocial driving often involves deliberate acts of retaliation by drivers against other drivers who have offended them in some (often minor) way. Individuals who feel that other drivers have been aggressive toward them, or have violated their driving territory, or placed their well-being in jeopardy, or are driving too slowly, or too fast may respond by seeking revenge against the transgressors (Wiesenthal, Hennessy & Totten, 2000). Such motivation has been found to frequently underlie "driving aggression" (Gulian, Mathews, Glendon & Davies, 1989; Matthews et al., 1991).

Similar revenge motivation is frequently found in other forms of antisocial behavior such as spousal abuse (Hyden, 1995); delinquency (Palmer & Hollin, 2000); gang violence (Cusson, 1989); arson (Bradford & Dimock, 1986; Koson & Dvoskin, 1982); theft (Castelnuovo-Tedesco, 1977); and suicide (Croake, 1982). In each case, the vengeance is intended to provide relief from physical or emotional discomfort that is perceived by the perpetrator to be caused by the target of their revenge (Cramerus, 1990; Lane, Hull, & Foehrenbach, 1991).

The actions of drivers that may actually be entirely innocent may be perceived by other drivers as potentially harmful and may be interpreted as purposeful and personal. Such attributions of hostile intent may engender a need for revenge and lower the aggrieved drivers' inhibitions against harming their transgressors.

Hostility and Aggression

Numerous early studies found that risky drivers exhibit excessive hostility (Bauer, 1955; Conger et al., 1957; Mayer & Treat, 1977; McGuire, 1976; Pelz & Schuman, 1968; Selzer & Vinokur, 1974). A related factor that was found to account for collision involvement is a reduced capacity to manage or control hostility (Conger et al., 1957).

Collision involvement was also found to be related to a history of aggression (e.g., McGuire, 1976; Selzer & Vinokur; 1974; Zelhart, 1972). For example, Pelz and Schuman (1968) found that young drivers with a history of several collisions and violations displayed more physical aggression such as fighting, than those who had no history of collisions or violations.

More recent studies have yielded support for the early findings. Aggression has been found to be associated with the frequency of traffic violations (Galovski & Blanchard, 2001, 2002; Galovski, Blanchard & Veazey, 2002; Yagil, 2001). A strong association between anger and both the number of traffic violations and the number of near-accidents has also been found (Iversen & Rundmo, 2002; Underwood et al., 1999). Driver aggression and even violence was found to be most common among drivers who had received extremely high levels of demerit points for "willful traffic violations" (Hennessy, 2000).

Drivers with the greatest number of collisions and violations have been shown to have the highest scores on measures of hostility and aggression (Lancaster & Ward, 2002; Donovan & Marlatt, 1982; Wilson &

Jonah, 1988). High hostility is one of the best predictors of future "accidents" (Norris et al., 2000). Moreover, high anger drivers report more frequent and more intense anger and engage in more aggression and risky behavior in daily driving, more frequent close calls and moving violations, and greater use of hostile/aggressive and less adaptive/constructive ways of expressing their anger (Deffenbacher, Lynch & Richards, 2003). Hostility combined with high levels of driving-related aggression, competitive speed, driving to reduce tension, sensation seeking, and assaultiveness characterize a subtype of high-risk driving behavior in young novice drivers identified by Deery & Fildes (1999). High anger and hostility are also associated with drunk driving (Lancaster & Ward, 2002).

Thoroughness in Decision-Making

A review of the literature from 1973 to 1994 indicates that there are several personal characteristics associated with aggressive driving (Lowenstein,1997). They include life stress at home or work; quick irritation; a tendency to dehumanize other drivers; and a tendency to express rather than internalize aggression.

The Car As A Vehicle For Aggression

It must be noted that many individuals are no more likely to experience anger while driving than in non-driving situations. However, those individuals who experience high levels of anger are more likely to be outwardly aggressive while driving than they are in non-driving situations (Lawton & Nutter, 2002).

Clearly, whether or not the individual driver behaves aggressively on the road depends not only on his/her aggressive lifestyle but also on the nature of the situation (Lajunen & Parker, 2001). Many otherwise non-aggressive individuals may feel that it is both appropriate and safe to use their car as a means of expressing anger. One woman in England halted a soccer game by driving her car onto the playing field while the game was in progress, locking the doors and walking angrily away. She did so because she was frustrated that a fan parked his car in front of her house, blocking her driveway.

Violators As Victims

Drivers with a history of frequent traffic violations are not only more likely than drivers without such records to crash into other drivers, they are also more likely to be involved in collisions where other drivers crash into them (Meadows, 1994; Parker et al., 1995b). 'Victims' of passive collisions are at higher risk of being involved in similar collisions in a second reporting period (Parker, West, Stradling & Manstead, 1995b). This relationship also applies to fatal collisions.

At the risk of being accused of victim-blaming, we must point out that passive involvement in accidents cannot always be viewed as the result of bad luck. In many cases it may be a function of bad behavior – the victim's bad behavior.

ANTISOCIAL BEHAVIOR AND DRIVING: IN SEARCH OF THE LINK

The research we have reviewed in this chapter has established that there is a consistent relationship between collisions, violations of traffic regulations, violations of safe and cooperative driving practices, and antisocial attitudes and behavior. West and Hall (1995) have suggested that such relationships indicate that there is some as yet unidentified factor that is operative in the driving situation but is also a much broader personal characteristic.

One such factor that has been implicated is low self-control. The "General Theory of Crime" proposed by Michael Gottfredson and Travis Hirschi holds that all forms of deviant, criminal, reckless, and "sinful behavior" can be explained by a common theory based on the fact that all have one thing in common: a tendency to pursue immediate benefits without concern for long-term costs (Gottfredson & Hirschi, 1990). Evidence in support of their theory has been reported for a wide variety of apparently distinct antisocial acts (Hirschi & Gottfredson, 1994). Further support for their position has been yielded by a meta-analysis of the existing empirical studies (Pratt & Cullen, 2000).

Many would argue that it is doubtful that such disparate behaviors as smoking, traffic violations, burglary, and rape can all be adequately explained by one factor (lack of self-control). Research that we will review in the next chapter indicates that lack of self-control is only one of a number of factors that are common to a wide variety of antisocial acts.

Research we will review has established that inadequate development in the cognitive skills, social skills, and values that are essential both for self-control and for general prosocial competence is associated not only with antisocial attitudes and behavior but also with inadequate driving skills and antisocial driving styles. In particular, impulsivity, risk-taking, inattentiveness, sensation seeking, carelessness, impatience, inadequate emotional control, and egocentricity have been found to be associated with both antisocial behavior and driving violations and collision risk. We will present evidence that indicates that such factors may account for the link between antisocial behavior and antisocial driving. We shall also present evidence that multifaceted program interventions that target the range of such factors are required to reduce antisocial behavior.

Chapter 5

THINKING DRINKING
AND DRIVING

The factor that has been most frequently and most fervently identified as the primary personal factor in collision risk is alcohol consumption (e.g., Rajalin, 1994).

Individuals convicted of Drink/Driving offenses consume not only excessive quantities of alcohol; they also consume excessive amounts of court time. Alcohol-related driving offenses are the most frequent offenses dealt with by the criminal justice system. In the United States, more people are arrested for driving under the influence (DUI) or driving while intoxicated (DWI) than for any other reported criminal infraction.

An estimated one out of every 122 licensed drivers in the U.S. have been arrested for DUI/DWI offenses (Buntan-Riklefs, 1992). However, arrests are only part of the story. For every single DUI arrest, there are approximately 300–1200 drink/drivers who are not arrested. Moreover, more than one in four drivers admit to having engaged in drinking and driving in the previous year (Wanberg & Milkman, 1998).

Bad Drinkers Are Bad Drivers

There is a large body of evidence attesting to the role that alcohol plays in impairing driving ability (e.g., Richman, 1985). Even blood alcohol levels well below legal limits can impair accuracy in the attention processes involved in driving (Rossello, Munar, Justo & Arias, 1998). However, the more you drink the more likely it is that you will be involved in collisions; and the more you drink the more likely it is that you will violate traffic rules (Pelz & Schuman, 1968).

Drink Drivers Are Bad Drivers

The fact that drivers who have been drinking drive badly is well known. At least it should be well known. A fact that is less well known is that many drinking drivers drive poorly not only when they are drunk but also when they are sober (Hedlund, 1994).

There are several bodies of research that cast doubt on the assumption that DWI offenders are simply otherwise nice guys who drive well but happen to have driven after drinking on one or more occasions:

- Drivers who have a history of drink/driving offenses are likely to have a history of collisions committed when they had *not* been drinking (Williams et al., 1986). Drink/driving is associated with a pattern of high-risk driving practices without alcohol involvement (Donovan, 1993; Hedlund, 1994). Compared to drivers with no DWI convictions, the records of DWI offenders include more violations for driving offenses other than drink/driving.
- Individuals who are at the highest risk for DWI convictions are drivers with multiple, non-alcohol-related driving violations (Buntan-Riklefs, 1992). Their offenses include not only minor traffic violations but major driving offenses (Argeriou, McCarthy & Blacker, 1985; Donovan et al., 1990; Maisto, Sobell, Zelhart, Connors & Cooper, 1979; Vingilis, 1983; Wilson & Jonah, 1985).
- The converse is also true – drivers with poor driving records (not drinking related) are more likely than drivers without such records to be convicted for driving while intoxicated (Donovan, Umlauf & Salzberg, 1985; 1990). The likelihood of a driver acquiring a drink/driving conviction increases as the number of his/her non-alcohol-related driving violations increases from zero to three. It substantially increases with four or more traffic offenses. Drivers with multiple (non-drinking) moving violations are ten times more likely than the general driving population to be convicted for a DWI offense (Donovan et al., 1990).
- Drivers with poor driving histories (not involving drink/driving) evidence problem drinking behavior that is very similar to that of drink/driving offenders (Donovan et al., 1985; Scoles, Fine & Steer, 1984).

Drink/Drivers are Bad Drinkers

- Drink/drive offenders are not only more likely to have a history of problem *driving*, they are also likely to have a history of problem *drinking* (McCord, 1984; Selzer & Vinokur, 1974; Seltzer, Vinokur & Wilson, 1977). DWI offenders have been found to display attitudinal and personality characteristics that are less often found among social drinkers than they are in individuals diagnosed as alcoholics (Donovan, Marlatt & Salzberg, 1983).

Linking Drinking and Driving

How can we account for these relationships between bad driving and bad drinking? Might there be an underlying factor that might explain the relationships? Our analysis of the research literature suggests that both represent antisocial behavior and that the antisocial behavior may reflect antisocial values and shortcomings in social/emotional competence.

DRINKING/DRIVING AND OTHER ANTISOCIAL BEHAVIORS

Drink/driving offenders are likely to have a history of problem drinking and a poor driving record. However, they are also likely to evidence a history of a variety of other antisocial behaviors. Research indicates that drinking/driving reflects not simply an alcohol abuse problem but a more general tendency to violate norms and rules. It is one of a cluster of both antisocial driving behaviors (Donovan, 1993) and antisocial non-driving behaviors (Jessor, 1987a,b; Shope & Bingham, 2002; Strand & Carr, 1994).

Drinking, Driving and Crime

The antisocial behavior includes illicit drug use and a variety of other delinquent or criminal behaviors (Barnes & Welte, 1988; Jessor, 1987a,b; Johnson & White, 1989; Kochis, 1997; Wells-Parker, Anderson, Landrum, & Snow, 1988).

A recent study in the U.K. found that drink drivers were twice as likely as the general population to have a conviction for a criminal offense. Forty percent of drink drivers were found to have a criminal record (Rose, 2000).

Many studies have indicated that drivers with poor driving histories and drivers who drive under the influence of alcohol share a number of common attitudes and behaviors that are associated with risky driving and collisions (cf. Donovan et al., 1993; Donovan et al., 1985; Jessor, 1987a,b; Jonah, 1986; Mayer & Treat, 1977; McFarland, 1968; McGuire, 1976; Tsuang, Boor & Fleming, 1985). Drink/driving may be part of a larger constellation of psychosocial and behavioral deviance.

Drinking and driving has been found to be related to individual differences in measures of social conventionality. Thus, young adults who drink/drive evidence higher levels of social unconventionality (Donovan et al., 1993) and greater tolerance of deviance (Jessor, 1987a,b).

Drivers with a poor driving record often evidence a pattern of social deviance that is also common among DWI offenders (Donovan et al., 1985; Scoles et al., 1984). For example, they have been found to have higher levels of both overt and covert hostility, particularly driving-related hostility and aggression (Donovan et al., 1985). Their antisocial driving cannot be blamed only on their antisocial drinking. Some factor that is common to antisocial driving, antisocial drinking, and other antisocial behaviors may need to be addressed in interventions designed to reduce the frequency of each of them and their interactions.

It is simplistic to think that DWI offenders are just ordinary people who are affected by alcohol in the same way that the liquid potion consumed by Dr. Jekyl turned him into the monstrous Mr. Hyde. On the contrary, many DWI offenders may be more like Mr. Hyde than Dr. Jeckyl even when they have consumed no magic potion.

CLASSIFICATION OF DWI DRIVERS

Research indicates that high-risk drivers with convictions for drinking/driving differ on measures of antisocial attitudes and behavior from drivers with no drinking/driving convictions and no record of accidents or violations. However, DWI offenders are not all alike.

There are significant differences among drink/drivers on a variety of personality measures and in terms of the generality of the behaviors and attitudes that are associated with their alcohol-involved driving (Arthur & Graziano, 1996). Studies have identified a number of subtypes among DWI offenders on dimensions such as personality and driving-related attitudes (e.g., Anderson, Snow & Wells-Parker, 2000; Donovan & Marlatt, 1982; and driving and non-driving arrest records (Wells-Parker, Cosby & Landrum, 1986).

IMPLICATIONS FOR INTERVENTION

Limiting intervention to models that emphasize alcohol as the primary contributing factor fails to consider the role of personal factors that contribute prominently to both alcohol abuse and driving risk (Donovan, Marlatt & Salzberg, 1983; Richman, 1985; Stacey, 1985).

Regardless of their differences; regardless of their motivation; and regardless of the underlying personality, and attitudinal factors that lead them to do so, drivers who drink and drive are behaving in an antisocial manner. They may have no intention of harming anyone, but in too many cases they do dreadful or deadly harm to others.

Enacting, enforcing, and publicizing laws against drinking-driving may serve to discourage those drivers from drinking and driving who believe that there is a strong likelihood that they will be caught and punished. However, punishment measures are most effective for those who are never likely to engage in the sanctioned behavior. There are many drivers who are undeterred by what they consider to be the remote possibility that they will be detected, apprehended, and eventually punished. More than severe penalties are required to decrease the incidence of drinking/driving. Increased surveillance, detection, and prosecution are essential, but a much more comprehensive approach is required that also targets individual and social attitudes to drink/driving, and to driving under the influence of other substances.

The results of research on the relation between drinking and driving raise doubts about the potential value of the multitude of educational programs that focus only on the *driving* behavior of DWI drivers. Clearly, it is essential that intervention programs must teach not only responsible *driving* behavior but also responsible *drinking* behavior. For example, some programs attempt to teach moderate, "non-problem" consumption or what are termed, "use don't abuse" behaviors (Brow, 1980; Miller, Nirenberg & McClure, 1983; Ross & Lightfoot, 1985). Thus, programs must teach participants the consequences of drinking and driving and how alcohol and other substances affect driving skills.

Reviews of intervention programs for individuals arrested for driving while intoxicated that include such alcohol education and counseling components have indicated that some may have a positive effect on the subsequent drinking and driving behavior at least of social drinkers (e.g., Mann, Anglin, Rahman, Blessing, Vingilis & Larkin, 1995; Mann, Leigh, Vingilis & De Genova, 1983). Systematic and metaanalytic reviews of alcohol education and treatment programs aimed at the drinking driver indicate that, in general, they have reliable, though small (7–9%) beneficial effects on drinking-driving recidivism and alcohol-related crashes (Mann et al., 1983; Wells-Parker, Anderson, Landrum, & Snow, 1988; Wells-Parker, Bangert-Drowns, McMillen & Williams, 1995). Moreover, some research would suggest that alcohol education is also required for many problem-drivers who have not (yet) been arrested for drink/drive offenses (Scoles et al., 1984).

The research also indicates that more than alcohol education or driver education is required for the many DUI and DWI offenders who evidence both problem-*drinking* and problem-*driving*. Programs must also target the social skills, attitudes and values that are associated with both their antisocial driving and their antisocial drinking. They must be taught to modify their *drinking*. They must be taught to modify their *driving*. We shall present evidence in Chapter 9 that indicates that they first must be taught to modify their *thinking*. Ignition interlocks may be effective in preventing drunk driving (Cohen & Larkin, 1999; Weinrath, 1997), but also required for the prevention of antisocial driving are *cognition interlocks*. We need more than "Drunk Tanks." We also need "Think Tanks."

Chapter 6

COGNITIVE SKILLS FOR DRIVING

There are two general personal factors that can influence the individual's driving behavior: driving skill (how well one *can* drive) and driving style (how one *chooses* to drive). The research we present in this book indicates that *cognitive* factors play a central role in both.

PSYCHOMOTOR SKILLS AND VISION

A broad range of cognitive skills have been implicated as integral to the driving task (Groeger, 2000). Driving requires skills in basic operations such as steering, accelerating, braking, tracking, observing hazards, and traffic situation management. It is clear that unless and until they acquire mastery in operational skills, all drivers are unsafe. A fundamental requirement for the development of competence in such basic skills is adequacy in perceptual and cognitive functions such as vision, eye-hand coordination, speed of response, and the ability to focus and sustain attention. Those functions have been the subject of many of the studies of the individual factors in collision involvement.

Delayed or inadequate development in such perceptual and cognitive factors delay the driver's acquisition of operational skills and maneuvering skills and increase collision risk particularly early in the individual's driving history when the novice driver is beginning to learn basic driving skills. Deterioration in these functions associated with injury, disease, and aging must also be considered a major collision-risk factor. Moreover, all drivers are at risk when their visual functions and psychomotor skills are compromised by fatigue or consumption of alcohol and other drugs (AOD).

Although some minimum level of competence in psychomotor skills is clearly required for most driving tasks, researchers have usually found only low correlations between collision rates and measures of basic psychomotor functions such as reaction time (Ranney, 1994). Skill in most of the psychomotor functions required for driving usually peak around the age of twenty. Ironically, the age at which their psychomotor skills are optimal is the age when drivers are most at risk of collisions. That suggests that additional factors determine the driver/collision relationship.

Visual factors undoubtedly contribute to driving performance. However, several studies indicate that, taken by themselves, such variables are not highly correlated with collision frequency (Owsley et al., 1991). However, driving is a complex visual task and it is unlikely that the routine assessment of visual function by means of the Snellen Chart alone (as has been done in many studies) could reliably predict collision frequency. Much more sophisticated assessment of visual functions is required, but very rarely conducted.[7]

Psychomotor and visual skills are undoubtedly necessary but they are by no means sufficient for safe driving. Such skills are required at the operational level for driving but additional skills are required at the tactical level or the strategic level.

Because operational skills can be acquired very quickly, drivers soon think that they have complete control of the driving task whereas they have learned only one part of it (Summala, 1985). Safe driving also requires more complex perceptual and judgmental skills. In addition to operating skills, drivers must acquire mastery in many more complex and higher-order tasks such as detecting and assessing hazards and risks and determining how best to avoid or react to them.

HAZARD RECOGNITION AND RISK ASSESSMENT

Drivers must learn to anticipate risks; continually scan their surroundings to detect risks; clearly identify potential or actual risky traffic situations; assess their severity; and maneuver their vehicles to avoid, or

---

7. Advances in vehicle and street lights have helped to counteract *some* of the problems associated with drivers' visual difficulties. However, much more attention must be paid to visual factors. For example, the ergonomic clustering of dashboard instruments and gauges helps to make them more readily accessible but the miniaturization by which such engineering advances are accomplished taxes the vision of many aging drivers.

safely respond to such circumstances. The driver who has not acquired such skills or fails to apply them to the driving situation is likely to be at considerable risk of crashing or causing other drivers to crash.

INFORMATION PROCESSING

Eye health and visual function measures indicate only the visual information that is available to drivers. However, drivers must also *attend* to the information, *evaluate* the information and *determine* which aspects of the information are relevant. Accordingly, any attempt to understand driving behavior must also consider cognitive functions such as information processing.

Individuals differ considerably in the manner in which they access and process information; in the way they attend to and select information, and in the way they assess the importance of such information. Research has indicated that drivers who evidence ineffective information processing are more likely to experience collisions (Fergenson, 1971; Reason et al., 1990).

Selective Attention

Most driving situations are complex and present the driver with information that is essential to the driving task. However, they are also presented with a great deal of information that is irrelevant and/or disruptive. In order to perceive, interpret, and understand a potential hazard, drivers must be able to focus their attention on the hazard while filtering out other stimuli. They must *select* the information they should attend to based on their understanding of its relevance to the driving task. Selective attention and the ability to rapidly switch attention so that it is directed to the appropriate stimuli in the driving environment is required for driving, particularly in congested traffic; at high speed; and in 'rush-hour combat'. The driving environment can change in the blink of an eye.

Failure to visually scan the traffic environment can lead to a complete failure to notice hazards. Failure to exercise selective attention can lead to making an erroneous judgment of the potential seriousness of the hazards that are noticed.

Selective attention is one of the strongest and most consistent predictors of collision involvement. Numerous studies have found significant correlations between measures of selective attention and collisions (Arthur, Barrett, & Alexander, 1992; Arthur & Doverspike, 1992; Arthur, Strong & Williamson, 1994; Aviolo, Kroek & Panek, 1985; Barrett, 1968; Elander et al., 1993; Hansen, Pallota, Christopher & Conaway, 1989; Kahneman, Ben-Ishar & Lotan, 1973; Parasuraman & Nestor, 1991; Ranney & Pulling, 1989).

The excessive involvement of young drivers and aging drivers in collisions may be partly a function of the fact that selective attention is usually not fully developed until age eighteen. It also deteriorates after age forty four (Parasuraman & Nestor, 1991; Pearson & Lane, 1991; Ranney & Pulling, 1989).

Divided Attention

> *Civilization is a limitless multiplication of unnecessary necessities.*
>
> Mark Twain

Individuals have limited resources in terms of the number of activities and tasks they can attend to at any one time. In driving situations, all we can usually handle at one time is one activity (Brookhuis, deVries & deWaard, 1991; McKnight & McKnight, 1993). However, 'progress' in automotive engineering has added more and more sophisticated devices to the modern car that encroach on the driver's perceptual space.

We are no longer distracted only by activities such as applying makeup; manicuring; shaving with electric razors; eating hamburgers and drinking (hopefully, only soft drinks); calming our children or our dogs in the back seat; arguing with relatives in the passenger seat; or attempting to seduce the person in the adjoining seat. We added radios, then cassette players, then C.D.'s, then phones, then Fax machines, then internet access, then windshield TV. . . Steering wheel or console mounted entertainment devices now can play CDs, CD Roms, MP3s and DVDs. Some provide for our reading distraction, an illuminated display of what's playing and the name of the artist. The drive-*in* movie has been replaced by the 'driv-*ing* movie'. Now we can just go out to our driveway to watch movies, or to enjoy our favorite music in our mobile concert hall.

One might think that by reducing tension and stress, listening to music would be a distraction that would reduce the likelihood of a collision. However, the kind of music may be critical. Thus, fast tempo music may make some people drive faster and violate traffic rules more, according to a study by Warren Brodsky of Ben-Gurion University. University students listened to music as they drove in a simulator. As the music tempo increased, drivers increased their speed. With fast music they also ran more red lights, changed lanes more frequently and had more collisions.

Road hazards may not be noticed as we concentrate on our hands-free (but not attention-free) phones and other creature comforts which enable drivers to attend to stimuli far removed from what should be the driver's visual and auditory environment. Many drivers now spend their time at the wheel preoccupied with events occurring in countries thousand of miles away rather than with the events that are unfolding right in front of their car. We are being driven to distraction.

Drivers who share the road with us also have to compete for our attention with a bewildering myriad of road signs and parking regulations that they may need to consult a lawyer to comprehend.

We can, of course, do many things at once. However, research has demonstrated that when we do many things at the same time we do not do any of them well. We do none of them as well as we do when we do them separately. Even when only two tasks are being performed simultaneously, each task reduces the brain activation that would be involved in the other tasks and each causes interference as we engage in mental juggling among them.

Even at the visual level we do not see as much when we are engaged in multitasking. We do not adequately process the visual information that we see even when we look right at something. The classic "inattentional blindness" experiment was conducted by Daniel Simons of Harvard. People who watched a video of basketball players passing the ball were asked how many passes had been made and then were asked if they saw anything else. Almost fifty percent failed to report that a man dressed as a guerilla walked through the players and beat his chest. Drivers may not "see" a road hazard or a pedestrian or another car even when they are looking right at them.

It is not only electronic devices that may distract us. Conversation can also be distracting, particularly if it involves child passengers. One study found that forty percent of drivers engaged in writing or reading while behind the wheel. It also found that drivers were engaged in some form of distracting activity about sixteen percent of the total time their vehicles were in motion. Thankfully, drivers engaged in most of their distracting activities while the vehicle was stationary (Stutt, 2003).

Internal distractions can also be highly distracting. Most drivers divide their attention between the driving environment around them and the everyday affairs and emotions that they carry with them into the car. Such mental activity can compromise the driver's ability to attend to and process the information to which they must respond for safety (Recarte & Nunes, 2000).

The problem is not only caused by our taking our hands off the steering wheel to activate a cell phone and steering the car with our elbows, our knees, or our noses. It is not that simple. The problem is also that the attention we must direct to matters other than driving reduces the attention we can pay to our driving. The attention we must direct to our driving also limits the attention we can pay to the other matters. The result is that it is not only the driving that suffers. Business decisions, for example, are less likely to be well thought out when they are reached in the 'office on wheels.' Moreover, the memory of what one said in such mobile meetings is often very poor.

It is not possible to stop thinking (as any one who has tried to do so has learned). Accordingly, one cannot completely avoid the intrusion of non-driving related thoughts.

Only if one is aware of the potential hazard of external or internal distractions can one minimize them by pulling over to the side of the road or by continually redirecting one's attention to the driving task – provided one is motivated to do so and has acquired adequate skill in focusing attention.

Sustained Attention

Drivers must not only *select* the features of the driving environment to which they direct their attention, they must also *maintain* their attention at all times.

The development of the ability for sustained attention is an age-related process such that young drivers are more likely to fail to maintain their focus throughout their time at the wheel (Murphy-Berman, Rosell, & Wright, 1986). Young people with high levels of attentional difficulties are at greater risk of involvement in a collision, in drinking and driving, and in traffic violations (Woodward, Fergusson & Horwood, 2000).

Regardless of their age, when driving under conditions which are understimulating such as long, boring highways and very familiar routes, many drivers fall into a zombie-like trance. Their car is then free to act on its own.

There are, of course, many causes of attentional difficulties including visual and neurological problems. However, failure to pay attention may simply reflect careless disregard.

DRIVING SKILL VS. DRIVING STYLE

It is the operational skills that constitute the driving skill that driving schools typically teach (more or less well), that licensing tests assess (more or less accurately), and that drivers continue to exercise (more or less haphazardly). However, there is more consistent evidence of the relation between collision liability and driving *style* than between collision liability and driving *skill* (Quimby, 1986).

Research has clearly indicated that driving style is strongly and consistently associated with collision risk (Reason, Manstead, Stradling, Parker, & Baxter, 1991; West & Hall, 1997). What drivers *choose* to do is at least as important as what they are *able* to do.

Psychomotor skills are required for safe driving, but such skills are not and cannot be applied in a vacuum. Their application to the driving task is controlled and directed by higher-order motives, attitudes and values. Inadequacy in psychomotor skills or failure to effectively apply them to the driving task can compromise safety. However, inadequacy in higher-order cognitive and social skills and values can also interfere with the application of otherwise competent psychomotor and car-handling skills and thereby compromise safety (Hattakka, Keskinen, Gregersen, Glad & Hernekoski, 2002).

The car is not only a means of transportation. Our choice of cars is a reflection of who we are and how we want to be judged by others. We select our cars in much the same way that we choose our clothes. We make our selections on the basis of the image we wish to convey about who we are, or think we are, or wish other people to think we are. Through our choice of car and even through our way presenting it for public view we proclaim not only our social status but our lifestyle.

The car represents an extension of the self – many people have a narcissistic investment in their car – they wash it, they polish it, some pamper it more than they do their spouse.[8] Would that adolescents cleaned and tidied their rooms the way they do their car.

---

8. Shania Twain's "You Don't Impress Me much" puts to music the tendency of many men who treat cars better than they 'treat' women.

We adorn cars with personal accoutrements such as dice, crucifixes, or gold crowns; or with personalized license plates that narcicisstically announce our identity. Many display bumper stickers that proclaim their moral values – or the lack thereof. We wear our cars. Some even marry their cars.[9]

Many individuals gauge their self-esteem by the kind of car they drive. This is in part because that is a factor that others use to assess them. For example, there is a tendency to view men who drive cautiously as lacking in testosterone. Adolf Hitler experienced "dagger-thrusts to my pride" when reminded of his inability to drive (Trevor-Roper, 1976).

We communicate who we are not only by *what* we drive but also by *how* we drive. We proclaim our identity and our personality and our social status through our selection of driving styles. Some want to be viewed as fast and sleek; some as thrill seekers; some as risk-takers; some as successful and sexy; some as sedate, conservative, and safe. Our cars serve as a moving billboard on which we tell the world who we are, how we wish to be treated, and how we will treat others.

Drivers make judgments about what speed they will drive and what risks they will take. They decide what will be their threshold for overtaking and what space they will have between them and the car in front. They decide how they will (or will not) adjust their driving to adverse conditions. They decide whether they will drive when they have had too little sleep or too much alcohol. They decide whether they will obey traffic laws and conform to informal laws of driving. They decide how competitive they will be and how they will respond to what they may view as threats to their convenience and safety or encroachment on their personal space. They also decide what values will guide their driving behavior and what kind of driver they wish to indicate they are. In short, they choose the manner in which they will apply the operational skills they have acquired. They decide how they will drive.

Some drivers choose to drive fast, some too fast, some slow and some too slow. Some choose to conform to all the traffic rules and unwritten codes of conduct for the road, and view them as requirements for safety

---

9. A driver in Tennessee was unsuccessful in obtaining a license to marry the 1996 Mustang that he called his "fiancee" even though his application form listed "her father" as "Henry Ford" and her blood type as "10-W-40" (*Corporate Knights* magazine, November, 2003). Much more successful was the wedding ceremony held in Melanie Wells in 2001 for 250 drivers who wished to marry their Mazda Miatas (*Forbes Magazine* April, 2001).

and good traffic flow. Some choose to drive as though they view such rules only as restrictions on their personal freedom; or as obstacles that interfere with their progress and their driving enjoyment; or as nuisances that must be circumvented, regardless of the potential consequences either for other drivers or themselves. Some are cautious, and considerate of others; others are careless, reckless, impatient, aggressive, and drive as though they are the only ones who have a right to be on the road.

Driving manners are more likely to be related to one's personal characteristics than to one's training in a driving school. Driving style is unlikely to be accurately assessed in a half-hour driving test conducted under the watchful eye of a driving examiner. Driving style is based less on driving skill than on such factors as motivation, responsibility, and values that are difficult to assess. Our failure to accurately assess such personal characteristics may, in part, account for the failure of driving tests to assess driver safety (West & Hall, 1995).

The personal factors that are most reliably associated with an antisocial driving style are cognitive factors that are also known to be associated with antisocial behavior. These factors wil be examined in the next chapter.

Chapter 7

COGNITIVE SKILLS AND ANTISOCIAL DRIVING

There is a growing body of research that demonstrates that antisocial driving is associated with the inadequate development of a number of cognitive skills and values that has also been found to be associated with other forms of antisocial behavior.

IMPULSIVITY

The early worm gets caught.
John Igo

Impulsivity has long been associated by traffic researchers as a risk factor in driving. Many drivers, particularly young drivers, are impatient, impulsive and careless, and give little thought to the potential consequences of their driving actions. Their impatience may lead them to indulge in behaviors that are the antithesis of safe driving. Many drivers get upset when they have to wait for anything or anybody, particularly other drivers who do not drive as fast as they want them to.

Impulsivity has been found to be associated with reckless driving and intoxicated driving and with traffic violations and collisions (Evans, 1991; Lancaster & Ward, 2002; Loo, 1979; Pelz & Schuman, 1968; Wilson & Jonah, 1988). Impulsivity is one of the most common characteristics of drivers with a history of three or more collisions and with drivers involved in fatal collisions (Mayer & Treat, 1977). It has also been found to be a salient factor in drink/driving (Keane, Maxim, Teevan, 1993).

Impulsivity is also one of the hallmarks of other antisocial individuals. It is one of the most widely recognized characteristic of those individuals who frequently are involved in rule-violating behaviors: adolescent and adult offenders (Colder & Stice, 1998; Daderman & Klinteberg, 1997; Kolko & Kazdin, 1991a,b; Luengo, Carrillo-de-la-Pena, Otero & Romero, 1994; Lynam, Caspi, Moffit, Wikstroem, Loeber, & Novak, 2000; Osuna & Luna, 1989 a & b; Tremblay, Pihl, Vitaro & Dobkin, 1994; White, Moffitt, Caspi & Bartusch, 1994). Longitudinal research has found that impulsivity is one of the best predictors of self-reported delinquency (Tremblay et al., 1994).

Anyone who has worked with such antisocial individuals recognizes that they frequently appear to fail to stop and think before they act. Although antisocial individuals may *appear* to fail to think before they act; they actually do think. However, their thinking is likely to be both automatic and antisocial. When an idea or a desire strikes them, they tend to respond without stopping to consider *whether* they should respond or *how* they should respond. When faced with a problem, a temptation, or a conflict they may be less likely to assess the situation than to react to it. They often fail to restrain their response in order to consider the likely consequences of their behavior. They are "prisoners of the moment."

Many also fail to think *after* they act and, therefore, even when they have negative experiences they do not learn to modify their future behavior. They do not reflect back on their behavior and its consequences or the alternatives that might have been better choices.

Whereas the impulsivity of many drivers and many offenders may be well recognized, the reasons for their impulsive behavior may not be so clearly understood. The majority of the measures that have been used to assess impulsivity have tapped the individual's tendency to act on the spur of the moment without due consideration of the possible consequences of their actions. The impulsivity of risky drivers may indicate that they focus only on the immediate present rather than the future. However, impulsivity is not a simple concept. The behavior of antisocial drivers may be influenced more by their emotions or by physiological stimulation or by environmental pressures than by reason, principle, or good judgment. Impulsivity may reflect not just a failure to delay gratification, but a more pervasive cognitive style that is action-oriented rather than reflective.

The impulsive behavior of many delinquents and many drivers may not be just another example of 'the hurry sickness.' It may not be just a bad habit. It may not be just a matter of a lack of concern for the consequences of their behavior, or the result of irresistible internal forces which prevent them from using self-restraint. More likely, it may represent a lack of cognitive skill, specifically a failure to insert between impulse and action a temporal gap in which they assess the situation and their possible responses to it. Their impulsivity may also reflect that they have not learned to use verbal mediation or "self-talk" to regulate their behavior – they do not think through their responses verbally, or internally rehearse them before taking action. They do not reason, they respond.

One possible factor that may account for the apparent failure of offenders to stop and think is that they feel no need to do so because they have not learned problem-solving techniques such as alternative thinking or consequential thinking that would require them to pause to consider before acting. Moreover, they may not ponder whether they should or should not refrain from antisocial behavior because they may not be influenced by moral scruples – they may not have any to consider.

Their impulsivity may reflect that they have not learned coping techniques that would enable them to tolerate the frustration that arises from delaying gratification – frustrations that are ever-present when driving. Many antisocial individuals believe that when faced with a problem or a conflict the faster they act, the faster the problem goes away (at least for the moment).

Many of those who drive impulsively may not be impulsive in other aspects of their lives. Their impulsivity may not be a general lifestyle but a situationally-related behavior. Their habit of impulsive driving may have been acquired through considerable practice in making quick responses in driving situations in which, aided by a powerful engine and the collision avoidance skills of other drivers, they have been able to make many impulsive responses with considerable success and with little cost (to themselves). Later they do not reflect on the negative aspects of the risk they took. They reflect on their accomplishment.

Impulsivity has also been found among other antisocial individuals, including firesetters (Kolko & Kazdin, 1991a,b); aggressive adult psychiatric patients (Horesh, Gothelf, Ofek, Weitzman & Apter, 1999); pathological gamblers (Blaszczynski, Steel & McConaghy, 1997) and spectators who stimulate crowd disturbances at ice hockey games (Arms & Russel, 1997). We could find no studies of the driving behavior of such individuals.

NO-THINK DRIVING

*Thinking is the hardest work in the world. That's why
so few of us do it.*

Emerson

Many antisocial drivers fail to think about their offensive driving behavior. More than a third of all who admit speeding, and more than five
percent of those who admit drinking and driving, as well as more than
ten percent of drivers who admit driving through red lights report: "I
don't really think about it, I just do it" (Corbett & Simon, 1992).

In driving situations one seldom has time to do much thinking about
how best to react to a problem. More often one needs to respond in-
stantaneously. The driving situation seldom gives drivers time to engage
in lengthy contemplation. Driving is one of the most high-risk situations
in which a person can find oneself. It is a situation in which critical decisions must be made in seconds.

Although driving often requires instantaneous, reflexive responding,
drivers usually have sufficient time to be reflective – to think about the
wisdom of their driving behavior – *after* they have executed it. They
may not have time to thoroughly analyze problems that they encounter
at the moment they 'run into it'; but they can, and should analyze their
problematic driving experiences *afterwards* and store the knowledge in
their memory banks ready to influence them the next time they encounter a similar situation (Michon, 1989).

Drivers are unlikely to acquire effective observation and coping techniques unless they learn them by reflecting on their experiences and by
actively processing the information. They need to think about what they
observed, what they failed to observe, how they reacted, what were the
consequences and what they might have done differently. In particular,
they must consider what it was about their behavior and their thinking
that led to the problems they experienced in the first place.

Drivers who fail to engage in such mental exercises, drivers who have
limited cognitive skills, and drivers who fail to exercise such skills in the
driving situation are unlikely to learn to recognize hazards; to accurately
assess risks; or to acquire an adequate repertoire of the problem-avoid-
ance and coping skills that are essential for safe and cooperative driving.

Safe driving habits require good thinking habits, particularly habits of
reflection and introspection. Drivers, like most offenders whose cognitive and behavioral style is impulsive rather than contemplative, are

unlikely to engage in such activity. Therefore, they may not profit from their driving experiences.

Many drivers fail to apply to their driving behavior the cognitive skills that they have developed. Some may fail to do so because they believe that thinking is not required when driving technologically refined cars equipped with well advertised "safety features" and above average crash test scores.

COGNITION BEFORE IGNITION

Chance favours the prepared mind.
Louis Pasteur

Drivers need to think about their driving after their driving. However, what we think *before* we drive may be even more important. For example, we need to think about drinking and driving *before* we drink, not just *after* when the alcohol has impaired our thinking about whether or not we should drive and whether there is a better alternative.

IMPAIRED THINKING

Drivers must perform complex and higher-order tasks such as detecting and assessing hazards and risks and determining how best to avoid or react to them. The adequacy of their performance on such tasks can be compromised by "alcohol myopia" – a reduced *cognitive* capacity to attend to the features of one's environment engendered by the ingestion of too much alcohol and drugs (McMurran, 1993).

It can also be compromised by too little sleep. Sleep-deprived drivers have more collisions and more serious collisions. Approximately 100,000 car crashes annually in the U.S. are attributable to exhaustion. The American Medical Association estimates that more than 1,500 deaths annually involve "drowsy drivers." Even a few hours a week of sleep deprivation can impair judgment as much as does alcohol consumption. Sleep deprivation impairs our judgment – including our judgment of how sleepy we are.

Drivers, particularly truck drivers on overly demanding schedules, may believe (erroneously) that combining strong coffee with some of the wide variety of stimulant pills that are readily available for purchase over the counter may prevent them from experiencing the frequent micro-sleeps during which they are slumbering with their eyes closed for several seconds at a time while their vehicle continues on its way unimpeded by a controlling driver.

There is, as yet, no 'auto-pilot' for trucks or cars. Many drivers simply do not get enough sleep. "Drowsy drivers" are "lousy drivers."

Dangerous Thoughts

Thinking, however, is not always helpful in driving. The driver's cognitive task is to think about his/her driving. Many drivers spend their time behind the wheel thinking about other things – almost anything except their driving. Thinking about other matters may be hazardous to their health.

INFORMATION PROCESSING

Ineffective information processing is associated not only with at-risk driving but with other forms of antisocial behavior including delinquency and crime. Delinquents and adult offenders also tend to be imprecise in their information processing, frequently failing to attend to; monitor; or accurately assess the salient aspects of their environment including those that pose a risk (Feuerstein & Griffin, 1979; Koopman, 1983; Osuna & Luna, 1989a,b). They gather facts in an unsystematic way, fail to attend to important details, and fail to distinguish important from unimportant information.

Information processing deficits in social situations have also been associated with aggression (Akhtar & Bradley, 1991; Crick & Dodge, 1996; Fraser, 1996; Lochman & Lenhart, 1993; Pakaslahti, 2000; Quiggle, Garber, Panak & Dodge, 1993).

Whether it occurs in the car or elsewhere, inaccurate fact-finding is likely to lead to a failure to attend to potential problems and to a failure to appreciate the risks they entail. Drivers who fail to attend to or recognize potential problems, and fail to correctly evaluate them are unlikely to learn what is the best action to take to respond to them.

RISK TAKING

Risk is an integral component of all driving situations. The safe driver must continually scan the driving environment to identify and assess risky situations and then make decisions that will enable him/her to either avoid such situations or respond to them with effective risk-reducing driving behaviors. Risky driving increases the chances of a crash and increases the severity of injury in crashes (Olk & Waller, 1998; Simpson, 1996; Williams, 1997; Iversen & Rundmo, 2002). Risky driving contributes to crash risk particularly among young drivers (Evans, 1991; Guppy, 1993; Hodgdon, Bragg, & Finn, 1981; Jonah, 1986; NHTSA, 1995a,b; Summala, Kanninen, Kanninen, Rantanen & Virtanen, 1986).

Risky driving is not simply a matter of temperament. Drivers *decide* to take risks. They are not compelled to do so. They *choose* to do so. The question that needs to be asked is why they so choose.

Risky Thinking

Many drivers and many offenders are risk ignorant. They fail to recognize (or appreciate) the risks that they face. They believe that, at least for them, the risks are minimal and avoidable. Many drivers may not even consider their driving to be risky even though it undoubtedly increases their chances of crashing. They may not understand that by taking risks with their car they are risking their lives and the lives of others.

Modern cars and modern roads have become more 'forgiving.' They are so capable of enabling drivers to recover from their faulty driving behaviors that drivers may fail to learn the error of their ways. Technological advances have undoubtedly enabled drivers to get away with many driving errors and violations. Consequently, they acquire automatic driving habits that include a wide variety of poor driving habits that have had no adverse consequence for them and quickly became part of their driving repertoire. Feeling protected from risk by the power and safety features of their vehicle and the roads they travel, they may soon come to underestimate the risks of driving and become willing to take ever-increasing risks.

Risk taking and faulty risk perception is found among many other types of antisocial individuals (Ross & Hilborn, 2004). Many believe they are immune to negative consequences for their behavior such as apprehension, arrest, or conviction. Like many antisocial drivers, many offenders simply fail to think about the information that their negative experiences have yielded. There are many offenders and many drivers who fail to recognize risks; many who underestimate risks; and many who overestimate their ability to handle risks safely.

Risk Experience

Some risky driving may simply be a consequence of driver inexperience. Inexperienced drivers may drive impulsively and take risks because they have not yet experienced the magnitude and frequency of the risks that are involved in driving (Cvetkovich & Earle, 1990; Rumar, 1988). They have an underdeveloped understanding of the actual risks involved in driving and of the behaviors necessary to avoid such dangers. Young drivers are particularly prone to underestimate risk and overestimate their ability to handle risks (Brown & Groeger, 1988; Jonah, 1986; Trankle, Gelau & Metker, 1990; Deery, 1999). However, driving experience may not be an adequate teacher for those individuals whose decision-making style is such that risky driving is only one type of risky behavior in which the individual tends to engage. Such individuals take risks wherever they are (e.g., Barnes & Welte, 1988; Donovan, 1993; Evans, Wasielewski, & von Buseck, 1982; Jessor, 1987a, 1987b).

Not Learning The Hard Way

Perhaps experiencing a collision might lead risky drivers to change their behavior. The evidence is equivocal.

Echterhoff (1987) found that "accident-involved" drivers typically admit that they have learned something from their "accidents." Seventy-four percent reported that the experience had been the best teacher of safe driving habits. In one study it was found that most of those who had survived a fatal collision said that it had left an indelible impression on them (Foeckler, Hutcheson, Williams, Thomas & Jones, 1978). They claimed that the consequences included more cautious driving, an increased respect for the value of life, a greater sense of responsibility towards others, and increased religiosity.

However, research indicates that driving behavior does not necessarily become safer after a collision. Almost half of 160 drivers who were interviewed about the effects of a collision experience reported that they had not altered their driving behavior and thirty five percent said that they had not learned anything from the collision (Sheppard 1982). Being exposed to traffic in daily driving following a serious collision quickly extinguishes the cautious driving habits adopted just after the crash (Rajalin & Summala, 1997). Drivers with personal experience of accidents reported a lower-risk perception than those with no or little experience of accidents (Lancaster & Ward, 2002). Moreover, drivers with previous crashes are at much greater risk for future crashes. A previous year, at-fault crash increases the odds of an at-fault crash in the following year by nearly fifty percent (Elliott, Waller, Raghunathan, Shope, Trivellore & Little, 2000).

Collisions may fail to lead drivers to change their thinking habits or their driving habits. As in second marriages, hope can trump experience.

SENSATION SEEKING

Risky driving has also been found to be associated with a personal characteristic that has long been implicated in other forms of antisocial behavior – sensation seeking. Sensation seeking refers to a tendency to engage in high-risk activities for excitement or stimulation. Unlike other risk takers who seldom think about the consequences of their behavior, sensation seekers are actually motivated by thinking about the risk. Climbing mountains or jumping out of planes is not the only way to indulge one's craving for risk. Risk-seeking drivers can get high without leaving the ground.

Risk is something we would expect that most drivers would seek to avoid or minimize. Not so. There are many "adventurous pleasure seekers" (Andrews, 2000) who think that safe driving is boring and that fast, risky driving is 'just the ticket.' For example, approximately sixty percent of male and thirty-three percent of female students admitted that they at least occasionally engage in high risk driving "because it is fun" (Summala, 1987). Risky driving may reflect a high level of "venturesomeness" (Renner & Anderle, 2000).

High sensation seekers have been found to score higher on violation factors and involvement in collisions as a result of speeding (Horvath & Zuckerman, 1993). Sensation seekers are also more likely to run red lights (Horvath & Zuckerman, 1993). They are less likely to wear seatbelts (Bierness & Simpson, 1997; Wilson & Jonah, 1988). They are more likely to fall asleep at the wheel (Thiffault & Bergeron, 2003). They are also more likely to believe that they need less sleep (Lancaster & Ward, 2002).

The relationship between sensation seeking and antisocial driving has also been found in the case of drink/driving. It is associated with multiple convictions for impaired driving, convictions for drunk driving, and arrests for impaired driving that involves violations or collisions (Arnett, Offer, & Fine, 1997; Horvath & Zuckerman, 1993; Johnson & White, 1989; Jonah, 1996; Lastovicka, Murray, Jochimsthaler, Bhalla & Scheurich, 1987; McMillen, Pang, Wells-Parker & Anderson, 1991; 1992). A considerable number of studies have found positive relationships between sensation seeking and collisions, violations, and drinking and driving (Jonah, 1996; Jonah, Thiessen, & Au-Yeung, 2001.)

Sensation-seeking drivers may drive recklessly not only to show off or to compete with other drivers, but also to experience an increase in their physiological or cortical arousal. Thus, there appears to be a biological component in sensation seeking. However, cognitive factors are also operative. Sensation seeking may reflect a cognitive style that leads the individual to overestimate his/her ability to cope with risk (Horvath & Zuckerman, 1993; Jonah, 1996; Jonah et al., 2001). It may also reflect strivings for "hyper masculinity" among those who view danger as exciting, and aggression as 'manly.'

Sensation seeking is also associated with other forms of antisocial behavior including illegal behavior in young offenders, and drug abuse (e.g., Daderman & Klinteberg, 1997). Sensation seeking is also associated with risky behaviors such as gambling (Steel & Blaszczynski, 1996), financial risk taking, and smoking (Jonah, 1996; Zuckerman, 1994).

College students who admit to having been being involved in property delinquency and substance abuse evidence a penchant for situations and activities that involve thrill and high excitement (Pfefferbaum & Wood, 1994). They lack tolerance for repetitive, routine, or structured tasks and seek to 'cope' with boredom by engaging in high risk or illegal, but exciting activities.

The combination of sensation seeking, impulsivity, and inattention is a key risk factor for both substance abuse and other antisocial behavior including delinquency (Klinteberg, Andersson, Magnusson & Stattin, 1993). It has been established that the best predictor of being convicted of delinquent behavior as a juvenile (age 14 to 16) is having a history (at age 8 or 10) of being "daring" (Farrington & West, 1990).

Wilde (1994a) has noted that all drivers sometimes engage in some degree of risky behaviors because such behaviors offer benefits such as decreased time to destination and decreased boredom. He has argued that programs that seek to reduce collisions must be designed to persuade drivers to reduce the level of risk that they judge is necessary for them to achieve such benefits but must also teach them how to do so.

A study of the characteristics of "accident-involved" and "accident-free" drivers revealed that the "accident-free" group experienced more pleasure in anticipating goals rather than in the immediate sensations that "accident involved" drivers enjoyed. The "accident-free" drivers were also significantly less risk-taking in their behavior, more conforming, and more inclined to avoid novel sensations (Trimpop & Kirkcaldy, 1997).

Rushing Roulette

Delay due to traffic congestion, road maintenance, slow drivers, and a host of other obstructions is an often unavoidable feature of the driving environment. It is a frustration that taxes the patience of many sensation-seeking and risk-taking drivers and may propel them into taking innapropriate and ineffective reactions that not only can increase the length of the delay for other drivers (and themselves), but can also compromise safety for everyone. We doubt that their tolerance can be improved in a culture of driving where automobile manufacturers extol the virtue of their cars in advertisements such as the one that proclaimed "We've never considered patience to be much of a virtue." Ironically, that same advertisement noted that the car had received the "Safe Car of the Millenium Award" from the International Brain Injury Association.

Driving a car carefully may yield little satisfaction to the sensation seeker. For some antisocial drivers and some juvenile and adult offenders there is not enough excitement in obeying rules.

PROBLEM-SOLVING

I'm lost but I'm making record time.
A Pilot (somewhere over the Pacific)

Antisocial drivers who frequently take unnecessary risks may not simply have a biological or psychological need for excitement that impels them to impulsive reactions. Their failure to consider the possible consequences of their driving acts and their impulsive driving behavior may indicate that they have not adequately developed the cognitive skills that are required for effective problem-solving. Driving a car presents the individual with a fairly continuous and changing array of problems. Safe driving requires effective problem-solving ability.

Low levels of problem-solving ability have been found to be characteristic of a variety of types of antisocial individuals including aggressive children (Akhtar & Bradley, 1991); schoolyard bullies (Andreou, 2000); adolescent offenders (Slaby & Guerra, 1988); thieves (Greening, 1997); adolescent runaways (Denoff, 1991); and mentally disordered offenders (McMurran, Egan, Richardson, & Ahmadi, 1999). Adolescents who have engaged in aggressive offenses have been found to define problems in hostile ways; to fail to seek sufficient information; to think of few alternative solutions; to anticipate few negative consequences for aggression; and to choose ineffective solutions (Slaby & Guerra, 1988).

Inadequate problem-solving in adolescents is linked to aggression and delinquency and to other externalizing behavioral problems including reckless driving and intoxicated driving. It is also linked to being a passenger in a car with a reckless driver, and being a passenger in a car with an intoxicated driver (Jaffee & D'Zurilla, 2003.)

The driver who lacks sufficient ability in the following cognitive problem-solving skills is unlikely to respond in an effective manner to the problems we all encounter on the road.

Problem Recognition

The individual who is not aware that a problem exists is not likely to be able to solve it. The driver who is not aware that a problem may occur is not likely to be able to avoid it when it does occur.

Inadequacy in the ability to recognize the potential of driving situations to present problems may lead the driver to fail to detect or recognize hazards. Inadequacy in problem recognition may result in the driver simply not being aware of the possible danger involved in even the most hazardous driving situations. Many young drivers fail to realize the potential risk of an accident in hazardous situations (e.g., Deery, 1999).

Inadequacy in problem recognition has been found to be associated with driving violations (Parker et al., 1995a,b). It has also been found to be associated with social deviance (West & Hall, 1995), and delinquency (Ross & Fabiano, 1985; Ross & Hilborn, 2004).

Consequential Thinking

A fundamental skill in problem-solving is the ability to realize the possible consequences of one's behavior. Inadequacy in calculating the consequences of various driving acts may lead drivers to fail to realize the dangers involved in hazardous driving situations. They may fail to realize that the consequences of driving 'errors' may include police apprehension, traffic fines, property damage, increased cost of insurance, loss of one's driver's license, social censure, personal injury, or even death for the driver and others.

A lack of problem-solving skills may also lead the individual to fail to attend to the actions of other drivers or to fail to take into consideration the risks associated with inclement weather or poor road conditions. These can be 'grave' problems.

Individuals who report that they frequently make decisions without careful consideration of the costs and benefits are more likely to be involved in collisions. The failure to weigh the consequences of one's driving behavior and adjust one's speed accordingly, has been found to be a major factor in collisions (Parker et al., 1995b).

Antisocial individuals may drive faster because they focus on immediate needs without considering possible future consequences for oneself or others. Inadequacy in consequential thinking is associated not only with driving violations but also with social deviance. Shortcomings in the ability to calculate the consequences of their actions is common among delinquents. Delinquents and aggressive youths have been found to be less likely to judge the consequences of rule-breaking as important, probable, or severe (Guerra, 1989). Inadequacy in consequential thinking is also characteristic of abusing parents (Hansen, Pallota, Christopher & Conaway, 1989).

Drivers who report that they frequently make decisions without considering the consequences are more likely to abuse drugs (Block, Block & Keyes, 1988) and alcohol (Conley, 1985). They also engage in more risk taking.

Failure to consider the costs and benefits of decisions is a factor known to be associated with antisocial behavior. It is also associated with automobile collision rates (Elander et al., 1993). Violators of traffic laws have been found to be similar to offenders in their inadequate cognitive appraisal of the rewards and risks associated with violating traffic laws. The more often drivers break the law, the more likely they are to discount the risk of a collision (Corbett & Simon, 1992).

Cornish and Clarke's (1986) rational choice theory suggests that, in contemplating a criminal act, offenders weigh the opportunities, costs, and benefits. However, in doing so, their calculations are often unsophisticated, based on inadequate or inaccurate information and they often reflect limited rationality. High violators have been shown to rate the potentially adverse consequences of their driving behavior (e.g., apprehension by police or crashing) as less likely (Parker, Manstead, Stradling, Reason & Baxter, 1992). They are also less likely to think that other drivers will be upset by their driving behavior or to think that significant others will disapprove.

Alternative Thinking

Effective problem-solving whether on or off the road requires the ability to generate alternative solutions to problems. The roads are filled with the unexpected. Safe driving requires an ability to adjust quickly to a rapidly changing environment and unanticipated hazards. It is essential that drivers remain flexible and creative in their thinking if they are to be able to think of several possible solutions to a driving problem. The individual who thinks of only one solution is likely to be in difficulty when their one solution does not solve their problem. Drivers may not have to be as creative as David Beckham's hairdresser, but they must be flexible in order to deal with rapidly changing traffic situations.

It has been found that the rigid driver who fails to switch attention is likely to fail to consider or even recognize the wide range of possible hazards that he/she will encounter in driving (Michon 1989). Young drivers who are rigid in their thinking and older drivers who develop 'hardening of the categories' are unlikely to be sufficiently aware of changing circumstances to be adequately flexible in their response to changing circumstances.

One of the reasons that novice drivers fail to notice hazards may be that they are preoccupied with acquiring operational skills. Operational skills are normally acquired quickly – two-twelve months (Brown, 1982). They soon become automatic. However, automaticity can quickly 'progress' into rigidity, a characteristic that is unsuited to the complexity of driving. Drivers may come to form a 'mindset' or a kind of closed-mindedness that leads them to drive by habit rather than by circumstance.

Automatic behaviors are likely to be maladaptive when drivers experience deviations from their expectations as they are likely to do in most driving situations. Accordingly, in order that they can differentially respond to changing situations and circumstances, it is essential that drivers engage not only in continual visual scanning but also in continual cognitive appraisal of their changing environment.

Cognitive inflexibility also promotes repetitive behavior. Both chronic traffic violators and chronic criminal offenders who persist in repeating their antisocial acts, may not only be playing the odds against getting caught. Their behavior may actually reflect a basic cognitive shortcoming – an inability to think of alternative ways of accomplishing their goals. That problem may underlie their resistance to change. The shortcoming is particularly problematic among aggressive youths. They are unlikely to generate effective solutions to problems (Evans & Short, 1991).

Flexibility is required for safe driving. However, *imagination* is not. A study of 8,000 drivers by Dr. Sharon Clarke, of Manchester University's Institute of Science and Technology found that drivers who are imaginative are more likely to be involved in collisions. This may be because their thinking is focused on matters other than the road.

CARELESS DECISION MAKING

Careless and carefree decision making has long been associated with antisocial behavior (Ross & Fabiano, 1985). Both have also been shown to be related to collision history and to the likelihood of collisions (West, Elander, & French, 1993). For example, fifty percent of drivers who had broken speed limits reported "I was doing it without realizing it." Twenty-three percent of drivers who had failed to stop for red lights reported "I do it when I'm not concentrating properly" (Corbett & Simon, 1992).

West and his associates have demonstrated that a lack of what they term "thoroughness" in decision making is associated with fast driving and collision risk. Thoroughness is measured by a subscale of the *Decision Making Questionnaire* that includes such items as: "how often do you plan well ahead?"; "how often do you make decisions without considering all of the implications?"; "how often do you work out all the pros and cons before making a decision?"; "how often is your decision making a deliberate logical process?" (French, West, Elander & Wilding, 1993).

CRITICAL REASONING

The offense histories of most juvenile and adult offenders are replete with examples of their underestimating the risks involved in their illegal acts. Redl & Wineman (1951) reported that "they have a delusion of exceptionalistic exemption from the law of cause and effect."

> One of the most striking things about offenders is that they do not believe they will ever be caught or brought to justice. Even after going to jail, many believe that they will never be caught again. They have a magical belief in their own cleverness, luck, or whatever they call it. . . . One patient expressed to me, as an explanation for committing his offences, his 'sense of gloating' that he got away. I said, somewhat amazed, "But you did not get away, you got arrested several times." In his mind he had managed to deny the fact of the arrests and dwelt only on the occasions when he had escaped. Schmideberg (1955)

A considerable body of research indicates that a similar "optimism bias" is frequently found among drivers (Dejoy, 1989; Groeger & Brown, 1989). Most drivers realize that illegal or risky driving behaviors do not necessarily lead to crashes (Watson, 1997). However, many drivers overrate their ability to make risky maneuvers in safety. Accordingly, they believe they are unlikely to be involved in a collision (cf. Dejoy, 1989; Finn & Bragg, 1986; Matthews & Morgan, 1986; McCormick, Walkey, & Green, 1986; Svenson, 1981; Svenson, Fischhoff & MacGregor, 1985).

Thinking can be dangerous when it is unrealistic. Drivers who believe that they are unlikely to be involved in a collision have less motivation to protect themselves (and others) by behaving in ways that will reduce the probability of a collision (e.g., following too closely) or to take actions that will protect them if a collision does occur (e.g., wearing seat belts). Why bother to protect yourself from events that you think will never occur?

Such unrealistic optimism is particularly evident in young drivers and may, in part, explain their higher involvement in collisions (Dejoy,

1989; Finn & Bragg, 1986; Matthews & Moran, 1986). Young male drivers perceive lower likelihood of apprehension or other negative consequences with regard to speeding and driving through red lights and they also perceive lower risks of collisions (Corbett & Simon, 1992). Young males often have an exaggerated sense of their own driving competence believing that they are more skilled than their peers and the average driver. They also perceive less risk in a variety of dangerous driving behaviors.

Feeling protected from risk by the safety features of their vehicle, many novice drivers soon come to underestimate the risks of driving and become willing to take ever-increasing risks. An unintended consequence of improving cars may have led some drivers to think they have more control than they actually do. However, the unjustified confidence of many other drivers may be also based on a lack of critical and objective appraisal of the risks in driving and on a faulty assessment of their own driving skills (Brown, Groeger & Biehl, 1987). The belief that one is immune to collisions may reflect not just denial but a more fundamental shortcoming in critical reasoning skills.

"It Won't Happen to Me"

The problem is not that they do not consider driving to be a dangerous activity. The problem is that this danger is not perceived as applying to themselves personally (Berger & Persinger, 1980). Many drivers mistakenly conclude that driving is dangerous but only for other drivers.

Although they may have an accurate perception of the magnitude of the risks involved in driving for other drivers, many drivers believe that they themselves do not face the same level of risk because they think that they drive more skillfully and more safely than most other drivers (Lichtenstein, Slovic, Fischhoff, Layman & Combs, 1978).

Almost all drivers think they are better drivers than they really are (Corbett & Simon 1992; Berger and Persinger, 1980; Dejoy, 1989; Finn and Bragg, 1986; Manstead, Parker, Stradling, Reason, Baxter & Keleman, 1992; Matthews & Morgan,1986; Reason et al., 1990). Many think they are better drivers than they or anyone else ever could be.

Such thinking errors have been found among many antisocial drivers (Berger & Persinger, 1980; Corbett & Simon, 1992). For example, although sixty-three percent of drivers stopped for speeding believed there was a link between speeding and collisions, only fifty percent believed that their personal collision risk was increased by their own speeding (Corbett & Simon, 1992). Their thinking error may represent a common fallacy in critical reasoning – overgeneralization. Because so many of their previous risky driving behaviors were reinforced by the lack of a collision, they conclude that they will never experience one.

The driving behavior of many antisocial drivers is inconsistent with their attitudes and intentions. Whereas they may be motivated to drive carefully, they drive in a dangerous way because they fail to critically assess their own driving behavior in an objective and realistic manner. The same erroneous thinking may account for the tendency of many antisocial drivers to engage in traffic violations. Frequent violators have been found to have feelings of invulnerability and an illusion of control (Parker et al., 1995b).

Violators of traffic laws are similar to juvenile delinquents and criminal offenders in their overly optimistic assessment of the risks they face in breaking rules and laws. Reason et al. (1990) found that those drivers who report committing the most violations rate themselves as particularly skillful drivers. Drivers who frequently violate traffic laws may perceive themselves as skillful enough to engage in risky, illegal driving or they may believe that such driving is risky for other less skillful drivers but not for them. Some may believe that a marker of a good driver (such as themselves) is that they can successfully take risks and 'bend the rules.' As one driver stated, "I don't drive badly, I just get caught too often."

Lest Ye be Judged

High violators also lack an objective view of how other drivers view the violators' driving. For example, violators assess their driving skills much higher than others assess the skills of those violators (Reason et al., 1990).

High violators also misjudge the driving behavior of other drivers. They overestimate the number of other drivers who speed or drive too closely to the car ahead of them (Manstead et al., 1992). They also fail to consider the possibility that although risky driving may be the norm, it is not a norm that they must copy.

Similar errors in critical reasoning are regularly made by antisocial youths. Gibbs and Potter (1987) have shown that chronically aggressive antisocial youths frequently evidence an erroneous belief that most other youths act just as they do themselves and they rationalize that this fact neutralizes or excuses their own antisocial behavior. Perhaps the most serious of their thinking errors is *minimizing* – thinking that their antisocial behavior causes no harm and is even admirable. That is also a common refrain among antisocial drivers.

Interventions that aim to provide drivers with information about the dangers of driving are unlikely to change the behavior of drivers who lack the thinking skill to critically assess their own behavior and that of others. Traditional presentations of accident statistics and warnings and admonitions are not likely to be sufficient deterrents. It is not only their knowledge that needs to be improved. It is also their thinking.

Chapter 8

ANTISOCIAL DRIVING AND *SOCIAL* COGNITIVE SKILLS

Most of the studies of cognitive functioning and driving examine performance only on the physical tasks involved in driving. However, cognitive skills are required not only to effectively cope with the *impersonal* or physical problems the driver is likely to encounter on the road such as inclement weather, poor road conditions or traffic congestion. They are also required to effectively cope with *interpersonal* problems related to the behavior of other drivers. Accordingly, they need social cognitive skills.

Interpersonal vs. Impersonal Intelligence

Social cognition is not the same as general intelligence as measured by intelligence (I.Q.) tests. Whereas the ability to understand one's social world is not entirely independent of one's general intelligence, the two are not synonymous. Many otherwise highly intelligent individuals lack *social* intelligence – the ability to understand the behavior of others, and to predict their likely response to one's actions. Drivers must evidence competence not only in impersonal cognition but in interpersonal cognition – recognizing that other people exist and that their behavior can affect you; knowing what others are likely to do; knowing the alternative behaviors from which others will select; and knowing how best to respond to them.

Cars Are People Too

Driving is becoming more and more socially isolated as a result of the impressive increase in electronic gadgetry that we can load in our cars; driver-distracting devices that represent an extension of our homes. They may lead us to think we can live our own life without consideration of those around us. However, driving does not occur in a social vacuum. Drivers may be anonymous, but they are seldom alone. It does not require a great deal of abstract reasoning ability to realize that the cars one interacts with on the road are being driven by humans. However, many drivers behave as though such abstract reasoning is beyond them. They seem unable or unwilling to view the car as the embodiment of a person.

According to some plastic surgeons, car crashes were the primary cause of facial disfigurements (next to dog bites) a decade ago; but "interpersonal violence" is now the leading cause of facial injuries. It is interesting that they do not view crashes as interpersonal.

Driving is a situation in which people must pay a great deal of attention to the behavior of other people. Drivers must carefully observe the behavior of other drivers and use these as cues for their own behavior. Driving requires more than psychomotor skills or perceptual acuity. Driving is an activity that requires many of the interpersonal skills that are required for competence in any social activity.

Drivers must have the ability to anticipate the actions of other drivers. They must make rapid assessments of their intentions. Drivers who are inattentive or lack interpersonal understanding are unlikely to make such assessments either quickly or accurately. Drivers who assume that other drivers recognize risks and hazards and drive with the same concern for safety as they do themselves may live to regret their erroneous interpersonal judgment.

Driving While 'Inpairs'

Social factors include not only other people in other cars but passengers in one's own car. The necessity of examining the social factors associated with driving is underscored by various research studies such as those which demonstrate that the presence of other people in one's car can decrease speeding, risky driving, traffic violations, and seat belt violations (Baxter, Manstead, Stradling, Campbell, Reason & Parker, 1990). Research has also found that drivers with passengers in their cars drive on freeways with greater distance between them and the cars ahead than do solo drivers (Evans & Wasielewski, 1982).

Some car manufacturers are currently developing a device for solo drivers that chats with the driver, asking questions that the driver must answer. The device assesses the answers to determine whether the driver is alert or not. If not, the device sounds an alarm to awaken the driver or it turns off the radio or the CD or the cell phone. Such devices function rather like 'electronic back-seat drivers' that warn drivers when their dreaming has become more important than their driving. They may prove helpful in reducing sleep-related collisions; however, since drivers will feel a car equipped with a 'traveling alarm' will keep them awake, we can be 'rest-assured' that drivers in cars with such devices will be more likely to take the risk of driving when they are too tired to do so safely.

We should not rush to praise back-seat drivers. The social facilitation effect of passengers may be to increase rather than decrease antisocial driving (Baxter et al., 1990; Preusser, Ferguson & Williams, 1998). Much depends on the goals and values of the passenger. Many youths engage in risky driving 'under the influence' of their antisocial peers. Adolescent drivers seldom die alone. The number of adolescents in the car is correlated with the likelihood of a fatal collision. Many a teenaged driver has ended his driving career in a foolish, show-boating effort to impress his/her passengers.

Social Modeling

> *Where all think alike, no one thinks very much.*
> W. Lippmann

Many driving behaviors, both good ones and bad ones, are learned through observation of the behavior of other drivers, including the driver's peers and parents. Imitation of the behavior of other drivers can influence drivers' choices with respect to how close they follow other cars, whether they signal their intention to turn, whether they wear seat belts, how fast they drive and the level of risk they will accept. Such modeling may have a much stronger influence on the individual's driving style than does instruction in a driving school.

Parental modeling is particularly potent. It has been found that the driving records of adolescent drivers during the first years of licensure are related to the driving records of their parents. Thus, adolescents whose parents had three or more crashes on their record were twenty-two percent more likely to have had at least one crash compared with children whose parents had no crashes. Moreover, adolescents whose parents had three or more violations were thirty-eight percent more likely to have had a traffic violation compared with those whose parents had none (Ferguson, Williams, Chapline, Reinfurt, De Leonardis, 2001). The sins of one's father and mother are often repeated by the sons and daughters they teach to drive.

Drivers who fail to objectively assess the wisdom of what they observe other drivers doing may find that their social learning equips them with maladaptive behaviors. As Hutchinson, Cox, & Maffet (1969) put it, "drivers follow each other like sheep." Even when the drivers they observe are competent and careful, inexperienced or unskilled drivers must exercise good judgment lest they attempt to copy driving styles and maneuvers that are displayed by more competent or more experienced drivers who have acquired skills that are beyond the ability of the new driver (Wilde, 1994b).

Highway Humanity

Recognizing the tendency for drivers to feel they are all alone on the road, some Japanese designers and engineers have attempted to "humanize the car" by developing a "speaking car" that tells the driver it is happy to see them or that it misses them when they have been away. It also praises them for good road manners. The humanized car may help reduce the frequency of antisocial driving; however, we believe it is also necessary to humanize the driver.

The dehumanization and depersonalization of other people that can occur when driving is frequently found among violent offenders and sex offenders who think that since their victims are less than human they can be treated in a manner that is inhumane (Ross & Hilborn, 2004). Such cognitive distortions are common among many aggressive drivers (Lowenstein, 1997).

INTERPERSONAL COGNITIVE PROBLEM-SOLVING

Many antisocial individuals lack skills in interpersonal cognitive problem-solving – the thinking skills that are required for solving problems that are encountered in interacting with other people. Such skills are essential in driving situations.

Solving problems in the interpersonal sphere requires each of the problem-solving skills that are required for solving other kinds of problems; for example, problem recognition; considering consequences; and thinking of alternative responses. However, effectively dealing with *interpersonal* problems also requires the ability to understand how other people think and feel and how others might react to the various actions one might decide to take to solve the problem.

Inadequate development of interpersonal cognitive problem-solving skills has been found to be related to a variety of antisocial behaviors including substance abuse (Platt, Perry & Metzger, 1980; Ross & Hilborn, 2003). Many antisocial individuals have difficulty in calculating the consequences of their behavior on other people and do not understand the cause and effect relationship between their behavior and people's reactions to them. They blame other people instead of seeing that they themselves, by their actions or their attitudes, have caused people's negative reactions to them. Such misunderstandings or lack of understanding underlie many of the conflicts that are everyday occurrences on the road.

SOCIAL SKILLS

Safe driving requires interpersonal skill not only at the cognitive level but also at the behavioral level. It requires social skill – the ability to 'get along with others.' Many antisocial individuals behave antisocially partly because they lack the social skills to act prosocially (Hollin & Swaffer, 1993; Veneziano & Veneziano, 1988; Walker, Shinn, O'Neill & Ramsey, 1987). They lack an adequate repertoire of the interpersonal behavioral skills that would enable them to interact in social situations in such a way that they would gain acceptance and reinforcement, rather than hostility and rejection. Lack of the social skill of "agreeableness" has also been found to be related to traffic violations and collision frequency (Cellar, Nelson & Yorke, 2000). Moreover, individuals who behave in a socially intimidating manner in new social encounters have been found to be aggressive when driving (Bassett, Cate & Dabbs, 2002).

Some drivers display excellent social skills except when they are behind the wheel of a car. Many believe that such behaviors are neither necessary nor beneficial in driving situations. The socially skilled behavior of some antisocial drivers may be only superficial charm used as an instrument for personal gain in social situations. They may believe that there is little to be gained in traffic by displaying courtesy and consideration for others. They may believe that performing such behavior only slows their progress. They fail to realize or appreciate the fact that cooperation and consideration among drivers are essential to smooth traffic flow and safety.

MISCOMMUNICATION

The driver's safety is continually impacted by the often unpredictable behavior of other drivers. It is essential that each driver strive to assess the intentions of other drivers and anticipate what they are likely to do. Their safety depends on their ability to make such judgments both quickly and accurately. However, they must make their assessments of the intentions of other drivers with a minimum of information because communication, the basis of social interaction, is limited in most driving situations. Complicating their task is the fact that most of the individuals with whom they must interact on the road are strangers.

Communication among drivers is typically only non-verbal and, therefore, is frequently confusing and unreliable. Even the number of non-verbal clues is limited since we often are unable to see the other drivers, particularly if their windows are tinted to protect their air-conditioned interior (or their identity).

The non-verbal clues that may be available in driving situations are frequently difficult to interpret and often communicate contradictory messages. For example, sounding one's horn may be intended to communicate anger, but it also may express familiarity − or an uninvited offer of familiarity. Hand gestures of various kinds may communicate appreciation, but may be interpreted as denigration. A smile can be perceived as a sneer. Flashing one's lights at the car ahead may mean "get out of my way" or "your golf clubs are falling out of your trunk." Drivers may learn more about other drivers from reading their bumper stickers than from reading their body language.

Communication is particularly difficult when drivers are in heavy traffic or traveling at high speeds. In many such situations a nasty non-verbal message that was intended for one driver may be perceived by other drivers as directed at them.

Drivers who lack interpersonal understanding are particularly unlikely to make their assessments of the intentions of other drivers accurately. Drivers who are lacking in social cognition and whose communication skills are not strong are unlikely to fare well in the social world of driving.

Poor communication is a breeding ground for conflict and aggression. Automobile manufacturers have recently developed voice recognition devices that enable drivers to communicate with their own car, but no such device is currently being marketed that enables them to communicate with other drivers. Perhaps that is just as well. Hopefully, the 'wave of the future' will be some universally recognized gesture that communicates gratitude – or apology.

MISATTRIBUTION

A wide variety of factors influence our assessment of the likely behavior of other drivers. Our attributions of their intentions and their motives and values are multidetermined. Some are based on the other drivers' age, sex, race, or the cleanliness of the car they are driving. Even the color of a car can evoke stereotypical judgments of the personality, particularly the aggressiveness of its driver. Other attributions derive from our interpretation of the type of driving behaviors of those with whom we must interact on the road. Each driver's physiological and psychological reactions are continually impacted by their interpretation or misinterpretation of the driving behavior of other drivers (Knapper & Cropley,1981).

One frequent anger-engendering cognition involves the attribution of hostile intent in which ambiguous behaviors by others are interpreted as deliberately hostile acts. An otherwise innocent look from another driver may be perceived as a criticism or a put-down or a challenge or a threat, rather than just a glance. A maneuver by another driver that brings him/her into another driver's lane may be viewed as a deliberate encroachment designed to impede the other driver's progress, rather than a simple and unintended steering error.

The same kind of misattributions, particularly misattribution of hostile intent, has been found to be associated with antisocial aggression in *non*-driving situations (Dodge, Price, Bachorowski, & Newman, 1990). Such cognitions are frequently the trigger for violence (Lochman & Dodge, 1994). They are frequently found among child-abusing adults (Stern & Azar, 1998); among delinquents (Dodge & Frame, 1982; Palmer & Hollin, 2000); and among psychopaths (Serin, 1991). A wide range of deficient and distorted social cognitive processes including attribution biases have been found among aggressive adolescent boys and are even more pronounced among those who are violent (Lochman & Dodge, 1994).

Misattributions are very common in driving situations but they may be particularly prevalent among drivers who lack critical reasoning skills or inadequately developed interpersonal understanding. Incorrect inferences can kill.

Attribution And Roadway Aggression

A recently completed study of 218 male and female university students in Canada by one of the present authors examined the relationship between individuals' roadway aggression and the aggression they reported feeling or displaying in non-driving situations (Antonowicz, 2002). The study found that hostile attributional biases (the belief that another person has done something hostile or malicious to you) was associated with higher levels of self-reported roadway aggression.

There is a clear similarity between antisocial drivers and offenders who make unwarranted attributions of hostility to the behavior of others and react aggressively. In both cases, the misattribution can become a self-fulfilling prophecy when the individuals who are the targets of their retaliatory aggression respond in kind with their own aggressive behavior. Such a reaction appears to confirm the initial attribution of hostility and, thereby, unintentionally reinforces the misattributing behavior. Moreover, a cycle of escalating aggression may be engendered by the initial misattribution – the initial misattribution leads the individual to express aggression that triggers retaliatory aggression that, in turn, increases the initial aggression that, again in turn, increases retaliatory aggression.

STRESS AND COPING SKILLS

The research literature on driving is replete with studies demonstrating a link between collisions and stress (e.g., McGuire, 1960; Matthews, 2001; Matthews et al., 1991; Norris et al., 2000; Legree, Heffner, Psotka, Martin, & Medsker, 2003; Simon & Corbett, 1996). Driver stress may manifest itself physiologically, as in increased heart rate and blood pressure; cognitively, as in frustration, anxiety and worry; or behaviorally, as in aggression.

Individuals who experience driving as highly stressful have more incidents of driving errors and violations (Simon & Corbett, 1996; Westerman & Haigney, 2000) including speeding (Matthews et al., 1991). They also have more minor collisions (Gulian, Glendon, Matthews, Davies, & Debney, 1990). Stress has also been found to be related to "aggressive driving" (Lowenstein, 1997).

Most research has viewed stress as the outcome of a negative appraisal of driving situations (e.g., Gulian 1987; Hennessy & Wiesenthal, 1997; 1999). Several factors have been identified that frequently lead to such negative interpretations of driving situations and are likely to engender stress. They include poor roads, poor weather, and traffic congestion. Such factors impact ninety percent of Americans on their daily commute to and from work (Gulian, Debney, Glendon, Davies & Matthews, 1989a; Hennessy & Wiesenthal, 1997; Novaco, Stokols & Milanesi, 1990). Stress is also frequently experienced when drivers find themselves in situations where they must drive slowly over long distances; where they must merge with fast moving traffic; where they are unable to overtake slow moving cars; and in many other circumstances when their progress is delayed, or denied.

Stress may be created by an *over*load of stimulation such as drivers experience on corkscrew roads or on a busy high-speed highway or when they encounter aggressive drivers. However, stress may also arise from stimulation *under*load that can be experienced when stuck in traffic; or traveling on a very familiar route such as the one the driver takes each day on the way home from work (Hancock & Warm, 1989). Underload that leads to drowsiness and hypovigilance is frequently experienced when driving on the long, straight, boring highways that cover much of our driving world.

Stimulation overload may require the driver to attend to too many stimuli and to respond too quickly. However, stimulation underload may lead drivers to become inattentive to their driving behavior. That can occur when, for instance, their boredom leads them to engage in thinking about their personal concerns or worries or other matters unrelated to the task at hand.

Unwelcome Passengers

Driver stress may be created not only by events encountered on the road but also by life events beyond the driving situation (Dorn & Matthews 1992; Glendon, Dorn, Mathews, Gulian, Davies & Debney,

1993; Gulian et al., 1989, 1990, Matthews et al., 1991). The 'passengers' in our cars often include the professional, familial, and personal stresses we bring along for the ride.

Disruptions in the driver's personal life has been found to be related to his/her collision involvement (Norris et al., 2000). Many drivers killed in collisions have experienced significant stresses in the preceding twenty-four hours. Pre-collision stressors include financial, interpersonal, marital, and other problems such as losing a job or a girlfriend (Mizell, 1997; Selzer, Vinokur & Wilson, 1977; Zelhart, 1972). Collision rates have been found to be twice the average during the seven years preceding divorce and to rise significantly during the year of the divorce.

As many as eighty percent of drivers in fatal crashes have been found to have been involved in serious interpersonal conflicts before the crash compared to eighteen percent of controls. Lowenstein's (1997) review of research on drivers who are aggressive to other drivers indicates that stress at home and work often underlies such attacks.

Even relatively minor daily hassles that were not effectively resolved can create stress that is carried with drivers into the driving seat. Such unresolved conflicts can continue to arouse them, or depress them, or distract them, or make them fatigued even when the original source of the conflict is no longer present (Flannery, 1986; Gulian et al., 1990; Johnson & Stone, 1987; Lazarus, 1981; Taylor, 1991).

A common, but hidden source of stress are emotions such as anger that individuals may not even be aware of, or anger that they may be unable to effectively express. Both the unrestrained expression of anger and its suppression can contribute to antisocial driving.

Stress Home Delivery

Driver stress can also carry over from the driving situation and create difficulties within the work or home environment which may later, in a vicious circle, create more stress for the driver when he/she resumes driving (Novaco et al., 1990).

Stress-prone Drivers

Driver stress may produce a general propensity toward interpreting driving as stressful (Glendon et al., 1993; Gulian et al., 1990). Those who repeatedly experience driving as stressful may develop a generalized negative view of driving which may increase their tendency to experience a broad range of driving situations and driving tasks as stressful (Hennessy & Wiesenthal, 1997; Matthews et al., 1991). Such individuals have been found to have heightened levels of tension, arousal, and unpleasant mood states that can compromise their driving competence.

Driving Away Stress

Many individuals use driving as their way of coping with stress. Driving (particularly fast and risky driving) is used by many drivers to express their emotions, to reduce tension, to feel powerful, or to let off steam. Some use driving as a way of expressing acute or chronic anger (Donovan et al., 1983).

Coping Skills

There are marked individual differences among drivers both in their vulnerability to conflict and stress and in their ability to cope with such conflicts and stress. Ineffective coping skills make the individual more vulnerable to stress. Many early studies indicated that drivers who had experienced a collision were those who were unable to effectively cope with external stress (McGuire, 1976).

Drivers with a history of collisions have been found to be more rebellious and anti-establishment. Such antisocial attitudes and behavior may be a result of a lack of coping skills and a cause of the family and marital conflicts and other stresses that they experience and with which they cannot effectively cope.

Their review of the research literature led Donovan and his colleagues to propose a cognitive-behavioral model that suggests that the drivers at highest risk of involvement in collisions are young males who evidence hostility and aggression, heavy drinking, and inadequate skills in coping with stress and frustration (Donovan et al., 1983). They argue that such drivers are likely to experience stress as a loss of personal control and to believe that alcohol, cars, or both, provide them with a means of decreasing their tension. Such beliefs may engender high-risk driving and an increased probability of violations and collisions.

Many antisocial drivers have maladaptive coping skills (Matthews, Sparkes & Bygrave, 1996). The preferred, and in some cases, the only method of coping for them is antisocial behavior such as horn honking, swearing or yelling, flashing headlights, purposefully tailgating, and making rude hand gestures (Gulian et al., 1989 a). One study found that eighty percent of drivers used inappropriate coping behaviors, such as yelling and swearing in congested traffic, that are unlikely to reduce driver stress (Gulian et al., 1989, b). Another study found that many drivers used another coping behavior that is more than just inappropriate – daydreaming (Hennessy & Wiesenthal, 1997).

Individuals differ in how they deal with the anger we all can experience while driving. Some cope by increasing their concentration on the driving task or by trying to relax. Others curse at other drivers or engage in dangerous maneuvers such as cutting off other drivers. Some stop their car and verbally berate other drivers or even physically assault them. Research has indicated that drivers whose anger response is not adaptive also tend to be risky drivers (Deffenbacher, Lynch, Oetting & Swaim, 2002). Among university students, lower levels of skills in coping with anger were related to higher levels of self-reported roadway aggression (Antonowicz, 2002).

Many other antisocial individuals have limited competence in coping with stress and conflict. Criminal offenders evidence a hasty and unsystematic approach to problems that exacerbates rather than decreases the problems they encounter (Zamble & Porporino, 1988). A meta-analysis of the research literature has identified poor coping skills as a major deficit among offenders (Gendreau, Little & Goggin, 1988). High risk youths tend to rely on asocial (depressive) and antisocial (aggressive) coping strategies (Blechman & Culhane, 1993).

Poor coping skills are prevalent among many other types of antisocial individuals. They include delinquents (e.g., Ruchkin et al., 1999); caregivers who abuse elderly patients (Rahman, 1999); child-abusing parents (Cantos, Neale, O'Leary, & Gaines, 1997; Rahman, 1999; Stern & Azar, 1998); spousal-abusing males (Copeenhaver, 2000); partners in violent dating relationships (Bird, Stith & Schlade, 2001; Gyrl, Stith & Bird, G.W, 1991); bullies (Andreou, 2000); and substance-abusing pregnant women (Blechman, Lowell, & Garrett, 1999).

Inadequate coping skills have also been found to be common among substance abusers (Annis & Davis, 1989; Dimeff & Marlatt, 1995; Marlatt & Gordon, 1985). Many individuals use alcohol in attempting to cope with their stress and consequently drive while impaired (Johnson & White, 1989; Stacy, Newcomb & Bentler, 1991).

Thankfully, research also demonstrates that adaptive coping can be taught by cognitive-behavioral methods (Deffenbacher, Filetti, Lynch & Dahlen, 2002).

EMOTIONAL MANAGEMENT

He flung himself from the room, flung himself upon his
horse, and rode madly off in all directions.

S. Leacock

Heightened physiological and emotional arousal is frequently experienced when driving (Hennessy & Wiesenthal, 1997; Stokols & Novaco, 1981). Emotional volatility and high arousal can lead to impaired driving performance. Emotionally distressed drivers are more likely to behave impulsively, tempestuously, and aggressively, and to overreact to the innumerable frustrations that are encountered on the road.

Many drivers become inordinately emotional when driving (Harre, Field & Kirkwood, 1996). Such arousal can lead to the expression of strong reactions to even minor irritations (Heimstra, 1970). For example, Hauber (1980) has argued that drivers experience a form of territoriality about their cars and the space around them within which they feel safe. Competition for space is an ever-present phenomenon on the road. Space is often limited and continually changes as drivers proceed to their destination. Infringement of their space by other drivers is seldom avoidable and elicits strong emotional reactions in many drivers (Marsh & Collett, 1987).

After repeated exposure to adverse experiences on the road, emotional arousal may become conditioned to driving such that even the simplest act of driving can trigger negative emotions (Novaco, 1991).

One of the symptoms of emotional distress or heightened emotional arousal may be high speed/risky driving. Similar to the 'rush' that many offenders experience when committing their criminal acts, violating of traffic laws often leads antisocial drivers to experience immediate, strong, and positive emotions (Parker et al., 1995a). However, emotional distress may also be engendered by inattentiveness and a slow or inadequate response to hazards, particularly when the driver is depressed.

Emotional volatility is one of the personal characteristics that has most often been found to be related to driving risk (Donovan et al., 1983). Emotional instability, irritability, and oversensitivity to criticism has frequently been found to be a characteristic of antisocial drivers (Chliaoutakis, Demakakos, Tzamalouka, Bakou, Koumaki & Darviri, 2002; Deery & Fildes, 1999; Mayer & Treat, 1977; McGuire, 1976; Selzer et al., 1977; Tillman & Hobbs, 1949). Many drivers report that their antisocial driving is stimulated by their mood. Unusually good moods as well as bad moods can increase the likelihood that drivers will make errors or commit violations.

Emotional control is clearly a requirement for safe driving (Wells & Matthews, 1994). Drivers must be able to control both their cars and their emotions. Drivers must have enough emotional control to prevent their arousal levels from climbing higher than the red zone on their car's temperature gauge.

ANTISOCIAL ATTITUDES AND VALUES

Since driving is a social activity, it is reasonable to expect that one's sentiments, beliefs, attitudes, and values relative to other people and to social rules and conventions would influence how one drives. Supporting that general assumption is research that has established that risky drivers tend to lack psychosocial and behavioral 'conventionality' (Jessor et al., 1997). Antisocial driving is, for many drivers, only one of a constellation of antisocial problem behaviors that they evidence whether they are on or off the road. Their antisocial driving is linked to their antisocial attitudes, values, and beliefs.

Drive Free

Several early studies indicated that the frequency of both violations and collisions was related to deficits in "social conscience." Drivers with good driving records reported that they viewed themselves as responsible individuals who had respect for the law and identified with societal values (McGuire, 1976; Williams & Malfetti, 1970). High collision-involved adolescents were found to be more likely than other young drivers to evidence a disregard for social morals and defiance of authority (McFarland, 1968). High collision-risk drivers of various ages evidenced pronounced antisocial attitudes (McGuire, 1976).

Recent studies have supported those conclusions. For example, Arthur and Graziano's (1996) review of the research on driving indicates the importance of regard for authority and the law. Drivers who lack respect for the law are more prone to "accidents" than drivers with the opposite characteristics (Clark, 1976). The driver's attitude to law-breaking is closely associated with a history of convictions for driving offenses (Furnham & Saipe, 1993). Undersocialization distinguishes problem from non-problem drivers (Donovan et al., 1985).

Research also indicates that drivers whose antisocial driving style includes frequently violating traffic laws have attitudes, beliefs, and values that enable them to condone or actually stimulate their antisocial driving. For example, many high violators justify their antisocial behavior by overestimating the number of other drivers who drive as they do – including speeding and tailgating (Manstead et al., 1992). Many believe that the potential adverse consequences of their actions such as collisions or apprehension by the police are less bad (Parker et al., 1992). Many think that they will feel no regret after violating. Moreover, frequent violators are also more likely to believe that trying to refrain from their violating behaviors would be difficult for them (Parker et al., 1995a). Many think that other drivers will not be very upset by their bad behavior (Stradling, Manstead & Parker, 1992).

There is a large body of evidence that attests to the relationship between the lack of prosocial values and other forms of antisocial behavior including aggression (Crane-Ross, Tisak & Tisak, 1998); delinquency and adolescent substance abuse (Carlo, Koller & Eisenberg, 1998; Lee & Prentice, 1988; Palmer & Hollin, 1998;); and a number of other behavior problems such as risky sex (Ludwig & Pittman, 1999).

A lack of identification with adult values has also been found among "at risk" adolescents who self-report delinquency and drug abuse (Allen, Leadbeater & Aber, 1990). "Immature moral reasoning" has been found in studies of delinquents in many countries (Palmer & Hollin, 1998). Two meta-analyses of such studies have confirmed that inadequately developed moral reasoning is characteristic of many delinquents (Nelson et al., 1990). Antisocial behavior has also been found to be associated with self-serving, hedonistic values and a lack of interest in conventional values (Palmer & Hollin, 2000; Halpern, 2001).

It must be noted that many antisocial individuals are able to verbalize prosocial values but fail to act on them (Ross & Fabiano, 1985; Valliant, Gauthier, Pottier & Kosmyna, 2000).

Conscientiousness

One aspect of values that has frequently been studied is conscientiousness. Conscientious individuals are conforming and dependable, report that they are law-abiding, assert that they seldom engage in risk taking; and are less liable to be involved in collisions (Tomlinson-Keasey & Little, 1990). Conscientious individuals are more likely to follow social rules and laws (e.g., Digman & Inouye, 1986; Graziano & Ward, 1992).

Research has found that drivers who are self-disciplined, responsible, reliable, and dependable are less likely to be involved in collisions and violations than those who do not consider themselves to have such attributes (Arthur & Graziano, 1996; Arthur & Doverspike, 2001). In contrast, the highest risk young drivers have been found to lack social responsibility (Rolls & Ingham, 1992).

Conscientious individuals are more thorough in their decision-making – a cognitive characteristic that is inversely related to collision rates. They are better able to resist temptation in provoking situations such as those that are frequently encountered in driving (Ahadi & Rothbart 1994; Digman & Takemoto-Chock, 1981). Drivers who lack conscientiousness are more likely to fail to wear seat belts and fail to adequately maintain their car's brakes, steering, and tires. Mechanical defects often reflect personal defects.

EGOCENTRICITY

From zero to sixty in the blink of an "i."
Automobile advertisement

Another social cognitive factor that is associated with antisocial driving is selfishness. Antisocial driving is associated with egocentricity and the tendency to pursue personal goals over cooperative driving practices. Prosocial driving requires both the ability and the inclination to consider, appreciate, and respond not only to one's needs but also to the needs of others. Egocentricity is incompatible with cooperative driving.

One might expect that drivers would accommodate their behavior to the needs of others just as they do in other social situations because they are concerned about the needs of other people or because they wish to avoid having others think badly about them. However, it would be naive to expect that drivers who are egocentric, non-empathic, and concerned only for themselves would accommodate to the needs of other drivers. Indeed, research has found that egocentric individuals are more "accident liable" (Robertson, 1998). Drivers who evidence 'i strain' may drive as poorly as those who suffer from 'eye strain.'

Socially acceptable and safe driving requires at least a modicum of social perspective taking and concern for other people. We are all born egocentric. Too many drivers remain that way.

Egocentricity and deficits in empathy are associated with other forms of antisocial behavior such as delinquency (Kaplan & Arbuthnot, 1985); vandalism (Luengo, Otero, Carillo-de-la-Pena & Miron, 1994); sexual offending (Ward, Keena & Hudson, 2000); and aggression (Akhtar & Bradley, 1991; Bjoerkqvist & Oesterman, 1999; Ohbuchi & Kambara, 1985; Parke & Slaby, 1983). Egocentricity is associated with a history of social difficulties. Egocentricity and a lack of empathy are reflected in an exaggerated sense of entitlement and has even been found to be characteristic of cyber-saboteurs (Shaw, Ruby & Post, 2001).

Group Think

Drivers are exposed to a variety of value-laden messages from media presentations of driving (e.g., high-speed chase scenes) and from automobile advertisements extolling the speed potential of their product. One car manufacturer recently published an advertisement for their car that proclaimed, "We've never considered patience to be much of a virtue." Ironically, the same advertisement noted that the car had received the "Safe Car of the Millenium Award" from the International Brain Injury Association.

Such messages communicate not only how fast cars *can* be driven but also (intentionally or not) how fast they *should* be driven. Such messages, and simple observation of the driving of many other drivers, yield informal norms that strongly influence drivers' perceptions of social expectations regarding driving style (Parker et al., 1992). It has been found, for example, that drivers are more likely to drive faster when accompanied by young male passengers than when alone because they feel obliged to comply with what they perceive as a norm of risky driving (Baxter et al., 1990).

Observing other drivers teaches them how they should behave. They are more likely to learn how to misbehave.

If drivers are to resist the press to conform to norms of antisocial driving they must have well-developed and internalized social values in order that their personal norms for safe and courteous behavior can withstand the pressure to adopt the less prosocial norms to which they are frequently exposed on the road. They must have strong social values to withstand the temptations of violating traffic laws and to reject the message that high-speed, risky driving is *de rigueur*.

That there are such individuals is indicated by Corbett & Simon's (1992) study that found that low offending drivers who had decided never intentionally to break traffic laws often referred to their moral commitment to the law. There are some drivers who believe that adherence to traffic rules is worthwhile because the rules are designed for safety and efficient traffic flow and, therefore, maximize the benefits for everybody. There are some drivers who believe that they should consider the needs of other drivers and, whenever possible, accommodate their driving to the needs of others. There are some drivers who believe that they should drive in relation to other drivers in the same way they would want other drivers to behave in relation to them.

In driving, as in other social activities, prosocial attitudes, values and beliefs can serve as a prophylactic against antisocial behavior. However, prosocial values that are not firmly entrenched can readily be put aside. Drivers must possess strong prosocial values. They must also exercise them on the road.

Chapter 9

THINKING WHILE IMPAIRED

The research we reviewed in Chapter 5 indicated that the relationship between substance abuse, antisocial driving, and other antisocial behaviors has been well established. A host of physiological, social, cultural, situational, behavioral, and emotional factors must be considered in attempting to understand the complex relationship. However, cognitive factors play an important role.

Many of the individuals in each group evidence the same cognitive shortcomings that are characteristic of members in the other groups: impulsivity; sensation seeking; risk taking; attentional disorders; and inadequate ability to identify prosocial alternatives to their maladaptive behavior (Beck et al., 1993; Hawkins, Catalano & Miller, 1992; Hedlund, 1994; Klinteberg et al., 1993; McMurran, 1993; Ross & Lightfoot, 1985). The key risk factors, particularly impulsivity and sensation seeking, are remarkably similar.

The effect of alcohol and various drugs on cognitive functions such as inhibition, impulse control, and judgment is well known. It can increase faulty decision making and increase individuals' willingness to enter risky situations even when their blood alcohol level is well within legal limits (Burian, Liguori, & Robinson, 2002). Alcoholics Anonymous refers to the reasoning of many of its members as "*stinkin thinkin.*"

The impairment of cognitive skills by alcohol ingestion has particularly severe effects on the judgment and behavior of individuals whose cognitive skills were not well developed in the first place. Alcohol may severely impair the reasoning of individuals who have inadequately developed cognitive skills even when their drinking is less than excessive. Alcohol may lessen even further their limited cognitive skills and may compound their poor driving behaviors. Cognitive inadequacies in such individuals may also be an important factor in their injudicious, inappropriate, or excessive drinking. Alcohol and critical reasoning do not mix, although listening to conversations between drinkers might lead one to think that they think it does.

As we indicated earlier, many drunk drivers drive badly not only when they are drunk but also when they are sober. It is not only that they *drink* badly. They also *drive* badly. They drive badly whether they have been drinking or not. Their bad driving and their bad drinking may be because of their bad *thinking*.

ALCOHOL AND SOCIAL COGNITION

Alcohol consumption can lead individuals to misread social situations such as conflict situations that often occur in social situations and are frequently encountered in driving. Alcohol can impair judgment. It can increase the frequency of antagonistic behaviors that lead to interpersonal friction and inconsiderate behavior (Pernanen, 1976). It can reduce the inhibition to aggression and prevent the recognition of the potential consequences of acting aggressively (Taylor & Chermack, 1993).

Alcohol ingesting can increase rule violating. It can also decrease the ability to appreciate the steps necessary to avoid detection or apprehension and make drivers more likely to receive citations for the violations they commit. However, since the vast majority of drinking occasions are not followed by arrest or collision, the reality of the connection between drinking and negative consequences is seldom confirmed for many drinkers and many drivers.

Alcohol consumption can impair judgment, particularly *social* judgment including judgment of the risk of violence in interpersonal situations. It can lower individuals' ability to perceive or understand important social cues and lead them to misconstrue people's intentions. Whether they have been drinking or not, many delinquent and adult offenders often misinterpret innocuous non-verbal cues as threatening and their misattribution can lead to violence. The implications for such thinking errors on the highway are apparent.

CHEMICAL THINKING

Similar cognitive impairments may also be engendered by the ingestion of a variety of other substances that are frequently found in victims of collisions (Addiction Research Foundation, 1992). These include morphine, barbiturates, meperidine (e.g., demerol), cocaine, cannabis (marijuana & hashish), tranquilizers, sedatives, sleeping pills, and cocaine. Many drugs used for the common cold and drugs used to combat allergies or prevent motion sickness or prevent nausea have depressant effects that slow down the central nervous system, make drivers drowsy, slow their reaction time, and limit their ability to concentrate and pay attention to potential hazards. Mixing such chemicals with alcohol may magnify their deleterious effects.

Stimulants (including coffee, tea, and cola drinks) may help to keep the driver more alert, but they also may make them overconfident and may increase risk taking. Amphetamines also increase risk taking and may make some drivers hostile and aggressive. Marijuana and hashish may impair skills in hazard perception and recognition and their effects can last for hours after the "high" has gone. Cocaine may make drivers feel they have greater mental and physical abilities than they actually do. It also may affect their vision.

The acronym "AOD" has come to be used to express the fact that there are many chemical agents in addition to alcohol that can impair driving. However, the bulk of the research has focused on alcohol — the most widely used drug and the one most frequently linked to collisions.

THE ALCOHOL ABUSE EXCUSE

Blaming alcohol and drugs for their criminal behavior is common among offenders. Many attempt to excuse or rationalize their criminal behavior as behavior that was "caused" by alcohol. Many firmly believe that it was the alcohol and not they themselves, which was responsible for their antisocial behavior.

Many impaired drivers also use this 'neutralization' technique as a way of denying responsibility. Some convince themselves (and others) that while under the influence of alcohol they had no control over their behavior. Many fail to accept, or even consider their own role in the decision to ingest alcohol or their role in deciding to engage in the antisocial act of drinking/driving. Their view is unintentionally reinforced by many who condemn drink/driving but in so doing blame the alcohol rather than the driver who has consumed it.

IMPLICATIONS FOR INTERVENTION

Informing drivers about the effects of consuming alcohol and other drugs on their driving ability is important, but it is not enough. Even having them experience the impairment in their perception that occurs with alcohol consumption by having them drive while wearing the thick goggles designed by the Mayo clinic that simulate the "impaired" vision associated with drunk driving may have little impact on the driver who has not acquired thinking skills and prosocial values.

Programs for repeat DWI offenders should teach them not only how to control their *drinking*, but also how to control their *driving*. First, they should teach them how to control their *thinking*.

They need to be taught the technical skills of operating vehicles. However, they also need to be taught the cognitive/emotional skills and values that will enable them to operate them safely.

Think Before You Drink

Social-cognitive skills training may help alcohol-abusing offenders not only to improve their thinking and their driving but also to curb or moderate their drinking.

Chapter 10

COGNITIVE DEVELOPMENT AND ANTISOCIAL DRIVING

Young drivers are disproportionately represented in statistics on collisions. Among sixteen to nineteen year-olds, the collision rate is four times as great as the rate for all other ages combined (Williams, 1996). Traffic crashes are the leading cause of death and of spinal cord injury among teenagers. Approximately five thousand teenagers are killed in car crashes annually in the U.S. alone. Two thirds of those dead teenagers were not wearing seat belts. Twenty-five percent had blood alcohol concentrations of 0.08 or more (NHTSA, 1997).

Novice drivers experience serious crash losses far beyond their representation in the driver population (e.g., Evans, 1987; Smith, 1994; Traffic Injury Research Foundation, 1991). That is the case internationally (Wilde, 1994b). Thankfully, however, there is a marked decline with increasing age. The odds of an at-fault crash have been found to decrease about six percent per year of licensure (Waller, Elliott, Shope, Raghunathan & Little, 2001.) Within five to seven years after they commence driving, the average risk level of young drivers reaches that of mature drivers (Lonero, Clinton, Wilde, Laurie & Black, 1995).

Youths are also overrepresented among traffic violators. For example, a study of 13,809 young adult drivers in Michigan found that during the seven years since they had been licensed, seventy-three percent committed an offense that resulted in a conviction and forty-two percent had committed an offense classified as "serious" (Waller et al., 2001). However, as in the case of collisions, the research found a marked decline with increasing age.

Involvement in antisocial driving (e.g., violations and risky driving) declines with age even among the highest risk drivers (Evans &

Wasielewski, 1982; Jessor et al., 1997; Wasielewski, 1984; Yu & Williford, 1993).

The age-related decline in antisocial driving is mirrored in the age-related decline in other forms of antisocial behavior. One of the most firmly established facts about *non-driving* antisocial behavior is that it also is primarily a phenomenon of youth (e.g., LeBlanc, 1993). Although the majority of youths commit some delinquent acts, the antisocial behavior of most does not continue into adulthood. At least half of the youths convicted as juveniles never appear in court again. Among those who do, most do not continue offending beyond early adult life. Moreover, the antisocial behavior of those who do persist into early adulthood also declines with increasing age (e.g., Farrington, 1986).

The age-related decline in individuals' antisocial driving is related to their decreasing involvement in problem behaviors in general (Jessor et al., 1997). This "burn-out" phenomenon is so reliable that we might well conclude that the most effective approach to decreasing traffic violations and collisions is aging. However, the public appears to be more interested in having researchers develop means of delaying the aging process than accelerating it.

AGING AND DRIVING

A variety of factors have been suggested to explain the age/risk relationship in driving (Lonero et al., 1995; Mayhew & Simpson, 1995). Most explanations focus on factors such as poor driving skills and inexperience.

Age and Driving Skill

New drivers lack important skills, particularly those involved in recognizing potential hazards. They tend to underestimate the danger of some risky situations and overestimate the danger in others. However, the high risk for collisions among novice drivers is a consequence not only of their lack of skill but also of inappropriate driving behaviors. They include, but are not limited to, deliberate risk taking; stimulation seeking; driving at excessive speeds; failing to wear seat belts; following other vehicles too closely; running yellow lights; and driving while impaired. Violating traffic laws is a major factor in their high collision rates

(Eby, 1995a,b; Eby & Hopp, 1997; Eby, Hopp, & Streff, 1996; Jonah, 1986; NHTSA, 1997; Wasielewski, 1984).

Age And Experience

Age is obviously highly correlated with experience, but age and experience are so closely intertwined that it is difficult to determine the relative importance of each (Catchpole, Cairney, & Macdonald, 1994; Eby, 1995b; Hodgdon et al., 1981; West & Hall, 1995). Teenagers face a substantially higher crash or citation risk during the first miles and weeks of licensure (McCartt, Shabanova & Leaf, 2003). However, the fact that older novice drivers have fewer "accidents" than young novice drivers (Keskinen, 1996) indicates that it is not simply lack of experience that is the culprit. It is lack of maturation. Moreover, the fact that many older drivers with many years of experience have more than their expected share of collisions and fatalities indicates that factors other than age and experience must also be considered in explaining the relationship (Owsley et al., 1991).

Is Experience the Best Teacher?

Most people do eventually learn to drive safely as a result of experience and maturation. However, experience alone may not be an adequate teacher. Experience can, in fact, have a deleterious effect on one's driving by teaching undesirable behaviors. Although experience eventually teaches most drivers to stop making immature mistakes, it may also teach them to make mistakes that are more typical of 'mature' drivers (Fuller 1988, 1990).

Their lack of experience can lead young drivers to underestimate risk (McKenna, Stanier & Lewis, 1991; Trankle, Gelau & Metker, 1990). However, increased experience can also engender overconfidence in one's driving ability that can lead to risk taking (Summala, 1985). The young driver's risky driving is unlikely to be discouraged by occasional near-misses or even isolated collisions because the adverse consequences of their antisocial driving are so infrequent that they think they can ignore the safe driving behaviors they were taught in driving schools and the messages they frequently hear from safety campaigns (Fuller, 1984; McKenna et al., 1991; Summala, 1988; Summala & Pihlman, 1993).

As they gain experience, drivers tend to judge their skills as higher and to consider their risks as lower than do inexperienced drivers. Many experienced drivers commit violations and undertake driving maneuvers for which they have inadequate skills (Hartley & Hassani, 1994). Many think they are skillful enough to take risks that less skillful drivers cannot take. The research has indicated that the drivers who report the most violations rate themselves as particularly skillful drivers and they believe that a skillful driver is someone who can 'bend the rules.' Some think they are good drivers because they get away with the risks they take. A lack of experience or a lack of age may not be as important as a lack of judgment and a lack of maturity.

Experience might be a good teacher if its pupils were motivated to learn. However, young drivers may feel they have more personal and social rewards to gain from risky driving than from safe driving in terms of the expression of independence, tension reduction, sensation seeking, showing off, and peer approval (Summala 1987; Wilde, 1994a).

Social Maturation

The aging-out phenomenon in both driving behavior and other forms of antisocial behavior may be associated with the development of social maturity. Such a possibility was suggested as early as 1949 by the research of Tillman and Hobbs who concluded that:

> Impulsiveness and unwillingness to accept responsibility are rather characteristic of youth and immaturity. There is a moderate disdain towards the boundaries set down by childhood life. Youth expresses a desire to lead rather than to be led. He wishes to make his own decisions and formulate his own plans. He resents and often reacts antagonistically to discipline and routine. His desire for recognition and individuality makes him act impulsively. He seeks adventure and in doing this he considers himself impervious to harm. A steady job, routine, monotony, long deliberated decisions, accepting advice, etc. are considered by youth to be old fashioned. He drives as he lives and where is there a better place for him to attempt thrills and experience adventure than behind the wheel of an automobile? As he matures emotionally his impulsiveness becomes more controlled. He usually formulates proper attitudes towards the importance of law and authority. He tends to develop an awareness of the rights and privileges of others and in consequence blends his individuality to conform with the standards of the mode. Thinking, now tempered by observation and foresight, becomes more deliberate and less impetuous. Everyday living habits become impregnated with proper, flexible attitudes, attention, and foresight. These three characteristics of emotional maturity lead to safe driving.

Experience is probably most helpful for young drivers who have already achieved social maturity. Experience may be a very poor teacher for the immature.

REGULATING MATURATION

In terms of interventions to promote driving safety one must wonder what one can do about the age/collision relationship. Most approaches have focused on imposing external controls on the driver while waiting for them to gain experience and grow older. Many program interventions have focused on increasing the drivers' experience and practice in the mechanics of maneuvering the vehicle, in the perception and judgment of risk, and in the acquisition of appropriate reactions to perceived risk. However, it is not possible for such abilities to be learned in driving school alone or in supervised practice alone because such experiences do not and cannot provide exposure of the student drivers to the many and varied situations that they will come to experience in everyday driving (Duncan, Williams & Brown, 1991; Groeger, 2000). Moreover, there are a number of problems associated with interventions designed to increase young drivers' driving experience:

- The *Young Driver Paradox:* While they are increasing their driving experience, young drivers are at the same time increasing the opportunities for their unskilled driving to cause collisions. If experience is 'the best teacher,' we must resolve "Brown's dilemma" (Brown, 1982): how can we provide young drivers with the experience they need to learn safe driving without exposing them to real hazards?
- *Perceptual Immunity:* Overconfidence and unrealistic optimism may increase with increasing experience. The safe driving behaviors that drivers may acquire in driving schools tend to drop out when the drivers' experience leads them to believe that they are not necessary because they have been successful in coping with most potential threats without them (Fuller, 1984; Summala, 1988; Summala & Pihlman, 1993).
- *Motivation:* Driving experience alone does not ameliorate the antisocial attitudes and values or the behavior problems that many youths evidence both when they are driving and when they are not.

So what can we do while we patiently wait for young drivers to grow up while keeping our fingers tightly crossed that they will not be among the many who are killed or maimed in accidents, or the ones who kill or maim other people? It seems that almost all our efforts thus far encompass only two possible alternatives: legislating or suffering. A third alternative is legislating *and* suffering.

Nearly every jurisdiction in the developed world has experimented with increasing the age requirements for licensing drivers. The success of such efforts has been improved by such interventions as graduated licensing in which youths are required to demonstrate their ability to handle driving in a responsible way before matriculating to more freedom and independence in driving. Graduated licensing helps, but it is by no means a panacea (Simpson, 2003).

Such measures are designed to control and deter. Provided they are adequately enforced, they may be necessary in order to delay the occurrence of collisions among many youths while they are gaining more experience and, hopefully, more maturity. However, such efforts often are knee-jerk, politically expedient, simplistic solutions that respond to the correlation between age and collisions, but fail to consider the reasons for that correlation.

Such legislation may be effective in reducing the antisocial driving of many young drivers while they are under their control. However, they may have little impact on those youths whose lifestyle is such that they are impervious to, or oppositional to, rules and regulations designed to deal with their youthful lifestyle. Rather than simply waiting for the young people to "grow out of it," we need to speed up their acquisition of attitudes, values, and behaviors that are incompatible with antisocial behavior on the road.

Experience may enable drivers to acquire strategies for dealing with potentially dangerous driving situations. The acquisition of such strategies requires drivers to assess the actual risk of certain behaviors, process the information, predict the outcomes of their behaviors, and think about the consequences of their behaviors (Eby & Molnar, 1998). However, no matter how much experience they gain, drivers who have not developed competence in cognitive skills are unlikely to acquire such strategies.

SOCIAL COGNITIVE DEVELOPMENT

There is a growing realization that the key factors in the similarity between the age-related decline in delinquency and in antisocial driving are a number of psychological characteristics that are known to be age and experience-related (Russo , Stokes, Lakey, Christ, McBurnett, K. & Loeber, 1993; Stradling & Parker, 1996). The 'maturing-out' phenomenon in both antisocial behavior and antisocial driving may be partly the result of a common underlying factor: the development of social cognitive skills and values.

The decline in the frequency of traffic violations and collisions is correlated with increasing involvement of the individual in conventional adult social roles. The developmental decline in risky driving, from age 18–25, is related to increases in psychosocial and behavioral conventionality (Jessor, Turbin & Costa, 1997). The assumption of marital, parental, and employment roles has also been associated with the reduction or discontinuation of involvement in a variety of other antisocial behaviors including criminal behavior (Sampson & Laub, 1993) and the use of alcohol and illicit drugs (Yamaguchi & Kandel, 1985).

Involvement in adult social roles may reflect the adoption of more conventional attitudes, values, beliefs, and behaviors that are incompatible with antisocial behavior. The development of social ties to individuals, family, workplace, or community may serve as informal social controls that influence behavior both on and off the road. They constitute social bonds that motivate the individual to avoid antisocial behaviors.

Unfortunately, many individuals fail to adapt to adult roles because they lack the skills and values that underlie social and emotional competence. Other individuals do develop such skills and values in sufficient strength to achieve an adequate prosocial adjustment in most aspects of their lives but not in sufficient strength to overcome the cultural, social, and situational factors that encourage egocentric, risk-taking antisocial driving.

More Than Enough

Driving is a complex social activity that requires more than just a modicum of social skills, interpersonal understanding, and empathy. Drivers have countless opportunities to behave both egocentrically and illegally. Doing so requires little planning, little skill, and little effort. Temptations abound in the form of quicker progress to destination; excitement; opportunities to express aggression; disdain for the law; and exhibitionism; and the freedom to indulge in selfishness. Safe and courteous driving requires drivers who have sufficiently well-developed social cognitive skills and values to enable them to withstand such temptations.

Drivers who are genuinely caring, empathic, socially skilled, and socially responsible may drive as though such qualities should apply wherever they are. Unfortunately, many drivers have social cognitive skills and values that are strong enough to motivate and enable them to cope in most *non*-driving situations but not in driving situations. Drivers who are lacking in social cognitive skills and values, particularly empathy and social perspective-taking, are not likely to be paragons of courtesy when driving.

However, as we discuss in Chapter 14, such skills and values can be taught. It is possible to teach even high-risk antisocial individuals to acquire a high level of the social cognitive skills and values that are required for prosocial competence and that can serve as a prophylactic against antisocial behavior. Before discussing how that can be accomplished, we wish to present further evidence of the link between cognition and antisocial driving that was found in an original study that was conducted for this book in a country where antisocial driving is a major social problem.

Chapter 11

ANTISOCIAL DRIVING IN THE UNITED ARAB EMIRATES

M. I. Barhoun and A. Abdennur
Sharjah University
In collaboration with
R. R. Ross and D. H. Antonowitz
University of Ottawa

The bulk of the research we reviewed in the foregoing chapters was conducted in Europe and North America. We wanted to determine whether our conclusions about the relationship between cognition and driving could be generalized to another country with a different culture. In this chapter we present the results of our study of the relationship between social cognitive factors and driving behavior in the United Arab Emirates. In the Islamic culture of the Emirates social and legal attitudes to antisocial behavior and to the use of alcohol are very different from those in Europe and North America.

Automobiles began to replace camels not many years ago as the principal means of transportation in the United Arab Emirates. Vehicular traffic has increased exponentially in recent years. The number of vehicles and the number of miles they travel has more than doubled over the last twenty years (UAE, 1994).

The rate of collisions per 100,000 cars is the highest by far of twenty developed countries despite the UAE having a motor-vehicle density below thirty percent of the average of those countries. The collision rate is twice the average rate of those other countries (Norman, El-Sadig & Lloyd, 1999).

Collisions are the second most frequent cause of serious injury, disability, and premature death among adults in the United Arab Emirates (Al-Quabasi, Al-Mofareth, Al-Bunyan, Al-Karion, & Hague, 1989; Baker, Oppenheimer & Stephens, 1980; Bener, Abouammoh, & El-Khalout, 1992). Although the collision rate markedly declined during the 1981–1995 period, the rate of injuries and fatalities resulting from collisions more than doubled. In 1995 alone, in a population of less than 2.6 million, 9,820 people were injured in automobile collisions and 543 of them died from their injuries (Norman, et al., 1999).

Major improvements have been accomplished in the United Arab Emirates in roadway design during the 1990–1995 period. However, analysis of collisions that occurred over that period indicates that environmental factors such as vehicle conditions and road conditions were relatively unimportant (Norman et al., 1999).

Drinking/driving was also not a significant factor in roadway collisions during those years, as might be expected given the Islamic disapproval of alcohol.

The most common cause of collisions remained constant throughout the 1990–1995 period – individual factors reflected in excessive speed and carelessness. Researchers have concluded that the frequency of collisions is primarily a function of factors such as "a lack of judgment" (Norman, et al., 1999). The salience of such individual factors has remained constant in spite of major improvements that have been achieved in roadway design, driver education, traffic management, enforcement efforts, and the introduction of seat belt legislation. Antisocial driving continues to be a major social, legal, and public health problem in the United Arab Emirates.

THE UAE STUDY

A study designed to explore the role of social cognitive factors and driving behavior in the United Arab Emirates was conducted through the auspices of Sharjah University. One hundred and forty-six, male and female, undergraduate students in the Faculties of Social Science, Business Administration and Law were asked to anonymously complete a battery of measures assessing their history of traffic violations and collisions; their driving style; and their social cognitive functioning – specifically, empathy; social perspective-taking; problem-solving; and impulsivity.[10] The majority of drivers (84%) had driven over 500 miles in the three months prior to the study.

Correlational analyses were conducted with the overall sample of male and female students. More specifically, correlations were computed between driving behaviors and (1) empathy, (2) social perspective-taking, (3) impulsivity, and (4) selected problem-solving measures.

RESULTS

The significant correlations found in this study indicate that the same social cognitive factors that the research literature that we reviewed in previous chapters had found to be associated with antisocial driving among European and North American drivers are found in an Arab population. Drivers who reported having committed various acts of antisocial driving evidenced a number of specific cognitive characteristics that our literature review indicated are characteristic of antisocial drivers.

Among our sample of drivers in the UAE, significant correlations were found among measures of antisocial driving and each of the following cognitive characteristics: impulsivity; careless decision-making; lack of empathy; rigid thinking; and social perspective-taking.

A significant association was also found between antisocial driving and an overall measure of rational problem solving as well as a number of particular problem-solving variables such as problem identification and problem conceptualization.

Impulsivity

Consistent with the evidence of the relationship between antisocial driving and impulsivity, drivers in the United Emirates study who reported that they were impulsive in their general behavior were more likely to admit that they liked driving fast. They also acknowledged that they would like to be racing drivers. Although they reported that they sometimes felt that they were going to lose control of their car, they confessed that they had driven fifty kilometers over the speed limit.

---

10. Empathy and social perspective-taking were assessed by subscales from the Davis General Attitude Survey (Davis, 1980); impulsivity by the Barratt Impulsiveness Scale (Patton et al., 1995); and problem solving by subscales of the Social Problem-Solving Inventory-Revised (D'Zurilla et al., 1997). Driving behavior was assessed with items derived from a variety of self-report questionnaires.

They also believed that "in order to arrive on time, one sometimes has to take risks." They were more likely to report that they would rather overtake a vehicle and cut back in sharply than not overtake it. They would prefer to accelerate than to brake to get out of a difficult situation.

More broadly, they believed that "one cannot always drive very carefully" and that "the faster other people drive, the faster they find themselves driving." They were more likely to endorse the view that penalties for driving convictions are too severe.

The impulsive drivers were also more likely to believe that they can drive perfectly well holding the steering wheel with only one hand. They believed that good drivers do not need seat belts. They reported that they seldom look at the fuel gage while driving. They were also more likely to report that they thought each person is only thinking of himself on the road and that "if you are ever to get anywhere you cannot show consideration for other drivers."

They admitted that they are usually impatient at traffic lights and find it difficult to control their temper when driving. They also admitted that they had flashed their headlights at another driver in anger, had deliberately cut off another driver, and liked to compete with other vehicles on the road.

Although they reported that the thought of having a collision sometimes worries them when they start out on a journey, they were more likely to believe that "one cannot always obey traffic laws" and that "one cannot drive for one year without slight damage to the vehicle."

Decision-Making

Careless decision-making in the drivers' general life was reflected in careless decision-making in their driving. Drivers who admitted that they were frequently careless in their decision-making were more likely to report that they overtake other cars even when they are not sure they can do so safely. They were less likely to report that they are usually careful when changing lanes in traffic or that the thought of having a collision or being injured worries them.

Careless decision-makers were also less likely to believe in the value of safety measures such as sixty kilometer speed limits in towns. Indeed, they even reported that they "did not believe there should be rules and regulations in driving."

Careless decision-makers also differed from more careful decision-makers in their attitude to pedestrians. They were significantly less likely to believe that "pedestrians are no bother." Careless decision-makers were also less likely to believe in the value of pedestrian crossings (where drivers have to stop and pedestrians have the right of way).

Empathy

Drivers who scored lower on the measure of empathy were significantly more likely than high empathy drivers to report that they like taking corners as fast as possible; that they like to compete with other vehicles on the road; that they "would not mind breaking a traffic law if it means getting out of a difficult situation"; and that they had engaged in both drinking/driving and drunk driving. Moreover, they were *less* likely to report they never overtake unless they are sure they can pass safely, or that they are usually careful when changing lanes in traffic.

Low empathy was also associated with rejection of the view that there should be certain rules and regulations in driving or the view that even good drivers should wear seat belts. Reflecting their egocentricity, low empathy drivers were more likely to believe that "if you are ever to get anywhere you cannot show consideration for other drivers." They were also less likely to accept the view that pedestrian crossings where they are supposed to stop for pedestrians are a good idea.

Problem-Solving

The study indicated that antisocial drivers in the United Arab Emirates are similar to those in Europe and North America in terms of their approach to problem-solving. Drivers in the United Arab Emirates who reported that they used *good* problem-solving techniques were significantly less likely to report driving behaviors or attitudes to driving that were antisocial. Differences were also found in the following problem-solving skills:

- *Identifying Problems And Thinking Of Alternative Solutions:* Drivers whose performance on the problem-solving measure indicated a *good* approach to problem definition and formulation and a habit of considering alternative solutions to problems were more likely to recognize that they are usually impatient at traffic lights and to think that drivers take their lives in their hands on the roads. They were more likely to report that they believe that drivers should be sensitive to road conditions (for example, that they should worry about skidding on wet roads). They were more likely to report that they never overtake unless they are sure they can do so safely and that they carefully assess the driving environment when changing lanes in traffic. Good problem-solvers were less likely to report having driven while drunk.

- *Total Rational Problem-Solving:* In terms of a measure of their total rational problem-solving, drivers with low scores were significantly less likely to believe there should be certain rules and regulations in driving, that speed limits in towns and pedestrian crossings are a good idea, that seat belts are necessary even for good drivers, or that they are concerned about skidding when roads are wet. Low scores on *general* problem-solving were also associated with antisocial driving behaviors and attitudes. Thus, lower scores were more likely to be found among those who reported that they would not mind breaking a traffic law if it meant getting out of a difficult situation; those who admitted that they pass even when they are not sure they can do so safely; those who are less likely to be careful when changing lanes in traffic; and those who admitted having driven while drunk.

Social Perspective-Taking

Drivers who reported that they tended not to engage in social perspective-taking were more likely to reject the idea that pedestrian crossings and speed limits in towns are a very good thing. They were less likely to believe that even good drivers do not need seat belts and believed that one cannot avoid taking risks on the road. They admitted to having driven while drunk. They did not subscribe to the view that one should not overtake unless they can be sure they can do so safely. Moreover, they felt that "each person is only thinking of himself on the road."

Limitations

It must be emphasized that this study was exploratory. Our sample of drivers in the United Arab Emirates was small and limited to a university population of relatively young drivers. Moreover, we were unable to assess the psychometric properties of our measures when they were translated and made culturally appropriate for an Arab population.

The similarity of the findings to the results of other studies on the relationship between cognitive factors and driving behavior suggests that further study should be conducted to examine the personal factors, particularly the social cognitive characteristics of drivers in the United Arab Emirates. The present study indicates that at least some of those social cognitive factors may be associated with antisocial driving behavior and attitudes.

IMPLICATIONS

The behaviors and attitudes indicated by the responses of many of the drivers we studied raise questions about the wisdom of relying exclusively on increasing recognizance and prosecution and improving highway design and traffic management for reducing the frequency of collisions in the United Arab Emirates. The development of the social cognitive skills and values that are essential for prosocial competence and prosocial values on the road requires more than engineering and management.

In the following chapters we describe research that led to the development of a program that has achieved success in improving the social cognitive skills and attitudes that appear to be associated with antisocial driving in Europe and North America and in the United Arab Emirates. The materials for this program have previously been translated into Arabic and modified to make them more appropriate for an Arab culture (Ross & Abdennur, 1996). A new form of the program that specifically targets driving behavior will be described in Chapter 16.

Chapter 12

DETERRING ANTISOCIAL DRIVERS

There are three primary approaches to preventing and reducing antisocial driving: driver examinations, driver training programs, and deterrence programs. We will indicate in Chapter 14 the major conclusions of evaluation studies of how effective driver examinations can be in identifying antisocial drivers and how effective driver training can be in dissuading novice drivers and experienced drivers from driving antisocially. The focus of the present chapter is the efficacy of attempts to reduce antisocial driving by deterrence.

A Principle In Search of a Method

Catching, arresting, convicting and punishing transgressors is the oldest and most popular approach of society to preventing antisocial driving. The deterrence model is based on the assumption that drivers would choose not to drive antisocially if their risk of being caught and convicted was high and the severity of the punishment they would receive would outweigh the possible gains their antisocial behavior might yield.

Deterrence advocates recommend increasing the frequency and intensity of police surveillance activity in order to increase the probability of apprehension. They also propose toughened prosecutorial and judicial response to increase the probability that being caught will lead to a conviction, and to increase the probability that convictions will lead to punishment. They also urge politicians to increase the severity of punishment for driving misbehaviors so that antisocial drivers who violate a traffic law might live to regret it.

Deterrence *can* be effective. There is evidence that convictions for traffic violations can significantly reduce traffic fatalities. A recent study examined the driving history of more than ten million Canadian drivers for longer than a decade (Redelmeier, Tibskirani & Evans, 2003). It was found that convicting drivers for traffic offenses reduced the rate of subsequent fatal crashes by thirty-five percent in the month following conviction. Moreover, the risk of a fatal car crash in the month following a conviction for a traffic offense was found to be thirty-five percent lower than in a comparable month with no conviction for that driver.

Regretful But Forgetful

Apprehension and prosecution may make traffic violators regret. However, many of them quickly forget. The large-scale Canadian study found that the beneficial effect of prosecuting violators lessened substantially at two months following their conviction. The effect was no longer statistically significant by three to four months (Redelmeier et al., 2003). We wonder whether the effect would be sustained if enforcement were maintained.

Another study indicates that drivers who have been convicted for traffic offenses are at even greater risk for future offenses or crashes. A previous-year offense doubles the odds of another serious offense during the subsequent year (Elliott, Waller, Raghunathan, Trivellore & Little, 2000).

Where Are The Cops When You Need Them?

Deterrence *could* work. There is very little doubt that if we could position police officers in patrol cars every few yards along the millions of miles of roads and highways in our country we might make a dent in the frequency of driving violations and collisions. However, research (and common sense) makes it pretty clear what would be required if we wanted to maintain the reduction.

We would have to have cops everywhere. We might also have to keep them there because research indicates that only large-scale enforcement has a measurable effect on "road accidents," whereas small-scale enforcement has no apparent effect and the effect of enforcement rapidly dissipates soon after the large "dosage" of enforcement is reduced (Beenstock, Gafni & Goldin, 2001).

The effects of increasing police enforcement on one part of the highway is unlikely to generalize to other parts of the highway. There is little spill-over (Beenstock, Gafni & Goldin, 2001). Traffic offenders are mobile. Crackdowns on violations of speed limits, for example, yield 'accident migration' as drivers choose other locations for their speeding. When the police move they take their deterrent effect with them.

Perhaps we might rely on "virtual policemen" in the form of speed cameras. Unfortunately, even speed cameras (if they are visible) positioned at various locations along the road may have little deterrent effect on risk-taking antisocial drivers. Knowing that only some of the cameras are likely to be operating at any one time, some antisocial drivers play 'Hollywood' – flashing their most photogenic smiles at the camera as they speed by. Others slam on the brakes when they spot a camera, then slam down the accelerator until they spot the next one. Pity the drivers behind them.

However, photo monitoring that does not allow drivers to discern photo-free from photo-present segments of a highway has been shown to change driving behavior not only at the camera locations, but also along the entire enforcement segment of the highway (Chen, G., Meckle, W. & Wilson, J., 2002). Would our politicians allow the entire highway system to be under camera? Could they afford the costs? Would they risk the political fallout?

Police surveillance can have a marked effect on driver behavior. A police car at the side of the road ahead of us can have a remarkable effect on how we drive. We slow down; fight our fear-induced rush of adrenalin; take a deep breath (or stop breathing momentarily); put both of our hands on the wheel; check that our seat belt is fastened; put on our best poker face; and stare intently ahead, trying to portray ourselves as the ultimate safe driver. We slowly and carefully pass the police car making sure that our foot does not touch the brake pedal for fear of the brake light informing the police officer that we had been driving faster before we spotted the patrol car. We check our rearview mirror to ensure that we are not being pursued by the police cruiser. Then we relax our stranglehold on the steering wheel and press down on the accelerator. Our poker face gives way to a wide grin as we begin to breathe normally once more and resume our excessive speed.

Spot The Cop

Surveillance may lead drivers to think that their responsibility is to watch for police, not to watch their driving. There are many car drivers who frequently drive with their eyes focused on the road behind them rather than on the road ahead of them.

Surveillance provides a way to improve one of our driving skills: the skill of spotting police cars before the police spot us. Many drivers have experienced the plaudits of their companions as they demonstrate their ability to pick out unmarked police cars and radar traps on the road ahead. Passengers are even expected to contribute to this 'game' by acting as human radar detectors. Performing well in this assignment is perceived as a sign of their competence as passengers.

Deterrents to Deterrence

Major and long-term increases in surveillance, apprehension, and conviction *could* have a marked deterrent effect. They could if they could be adequately operationalized. However, the achievement of a substantial deterrence effect would require substantial increases in the powers and technological resources of police with impacts on police and court budgets that would be staggering. The perceived threat to civil liberties precludes the possibility that surveillance could even approach the required intensity. Moreover, the car is a symbol of individual freedom and many citizens would strongly object to such police control of their "rights" to freedom of expression in their driving style. When it comes to their driving, many citizens are likely to agree with John Stuart Mill who argued:

> Neither one person, nor any number of persons, is warranted in saying to another human creature of ripe years that he shall not do with his life for his own benefit what he chooses to do with it. All errors he is likely to commit against advice and warning are far outweighed by the evil of allowing others to constrain him to do what they deem his good.

There were no cars around when Mills made that declaration.

No Pain, No Gain

Deterrent measures are unlikely to have much impact on antisocial driving if drivers think there is little risk of apprehension (e.g., Makinen & Zaidel, 2002; Ostvik & Elvik, 1990). From a psychological perspective, deterrence has little reality or meaning if deterrence programs only promise to punish drivers who happen to be caught breaking the rules, but only now and then.

THE POSITIVE PUNISHMENT EFFECT

The fact that cops can't be everywhere means that many, perhaps most, traffic offenses and acts of antisocial driving can be committed without legal consequence. It is only on rare occasions that a driver is likely to be caught. Even a small number of experiences of 'apprehension avoidance' can lead us to believe that apprehension is unlikely. We soon come to believe that we can get away with it. The intermittent punishment effect may serve to increase rather than decrease the chances that we will offend again. Moreover, for many antisocial drivers, getting away with it is just as enjoyable as the risky driving that they get away with.

Deterrence advocates tend to believe that individuals who have been caught and punished will be less likely to offend again. However, there is some research that indicates the opposite. Drivers who have been punished may believe that lightning only strikes once. They believe that their punishment experience insulates them from future apprehension. Such a "positive punishment effect" has been found in several studies (Paternoster & Piquero 1995; Piquero & Pogarsky, 2002; Pogarsky, 2002; Pogarsky & Piquero, 2003). For example, Piquero and Paternoster (1998) found that drivers who had been stopped at a roadside drink/driving checkpoint were *more* likely to offend in the future. The drivers believed that the certainty of future punishment was lower for them than for drivers who had been less frequently punished before. This is similar to the gambler's fallacy in which lottery players (for example) believe that because their favorite number has not come up for a long time it is bound to come up soon. It is a very common error in critical reasoning to think that the occurrence of an unlikely event makes its reoccurrence even more unlikely.

Deterrence is also unlikely to be effective for driving violators when they believe that there is little likelihood of their punishment being either immediate or severe (Summala, 1988). Immediate administrative sanctions such as suspending drivers' licenses on the spot are much more likely to be effective than delayed complex, expensive, and uncertain criminal proceedings. However, rapid processing frequently raises the hackles of the driving public and of lawyers who prefer due processing. Rapid processing also raises the anxiety of government accountants who have to tally the court costs for successful appeals of convictions.

Deterring the Undeterrable

The research we present in this book indicates that many antisocial drivers seldom consider the consequences of their acts of illegal or offensive driving. Many underestimate the risks. Some are indifferent to the risks. Some thrive on risks. Many are sublimely optimistic; they believe that they will not be caught; if caught, not convicted; if convicted, not sentenced; if sentenced, not imprisoned; if imprisoned, quickly released. Are their beliefs unrealistic?

The likelihood of antisocial driving leading to an aversive legal consequence is so low that expecting to be caught and convicted may be as irrational or unrealistic as thinking that one is immune. For example, it takes between 200 and 2,000 repetitions of drunk driving to produce one arrest (Canada Safety Council, 2000). Approximately twenty-eight percent of offenders (in the U.S.) admit to drinking and driving within the previous year but for every drink/drive offense there are 200–300 that do not lead to an arrest (Wanberg & Milkman, 1998). It is not a simple matter to convince drivers that "we mean business."[11]

Police blitzes that temporarily and situationally increase the likelihood of negative consequences for offensive driving are hardly likely to affect antisocial drivers who seldom consider consequences. Moreover, many of the punishments for traffic violations are only mildly aversive to many drivers.

The efficacy of deterrence is also compromised by the impulsivity of many of those we might wish to deter (Nagin & Pogarsky, 2001; Piquero & Tibbetts, 1996). This is particularly the case when drivers' concern for the possible consequences of their behavior as well as their judgment of the aversiveness of the penalties and the risks involved have been temporarily or permanently impaired by their ingestion of alcohol.

There are also many sober but antisocial drivers who fail to recognize risks; many who underestimate risks; and many who overestimate their ability to handle risks safely. It may be that the drivers we most want to deter are the ones who are least likely to respond to the punishments we often promise but seldom deliver.

---

11. According to the Canada Safety Council, approximately eighty-four percent of impaired driving trips are accounted for by fewer than five percent of drivers. The five percent appear to be hard-core offenders who are alcohol dependent. Limiting drink/driving interventions to those that penalize social drinkers for drinking and driving is unlikely to be effective in deterring such hard-core drunk drivers.

Many antisocial drivers will also not learn much from license suspension. Many will simply continue to drive antisocially without a license. It is unrealistic to assume that while their license is suspended, antisocial drivers will learn their lesson without some additional intervention.

Experience Is Not The Best Teacher

Even "accidents" appear to have little deterrent effect. "Near-accidents" are generally forgotten extremely rapidly, with an estimated eighty percent of incidents being no longer reported after a delay of less than two weeks (Chapman & Underwood, 2000). Moreover, an at-fault crash in the previous year *increases* the odds of subsequent-year at-fault crashes by nearly fifty percent (Evans et al., 2000).

Is Deterrence Only A Mirage?

In short, research has indicated that deterrence is difficult to operationalize, inordinately expensive, and questionably effective. Traffic rules are essential but there are not enough police to enforce them on a steady basis. Simply implementing "get tough" programs now and then will not suffice. Our methods must be consistent, powerful, and economical. Passing tough laws is easy; enforcing them is not.

Off The Road

Research on the efficacy of deterrence in preventing other forms of antisocial behavior also does not justify optimism for such a *single* approach to antisocial driving. Very low correlations have been found between antisocial behavior and punishment. Deterrent effects are typically unreliable and weak (Gendreau & Ross, 1981).

Deterrence effects, when they are achieved, are typically only temporary. Deterrence effects may only serve to change the kind of antisocial behaviors displayed to other kinds that have not been made a focus of attention. One example of how antisocial drivers will attempt to thwart efforts to control their driving is the "Go-box Traffic Light Switcher" that changes the color of lights from red to green when pointed at the pole from a moving vehicle.

Deterrence programs often serve only to shift crime to another geographic location. Many attempts to achieve crime control by surveillance of particular locations where crime is frequent have been effective only in moving crime around the block. Just like antisocial drivers, criminal offenders are mobile.

As is the case for many antisocial drivers, offenders consider the amount of gain their behavior can bring them as the primary motive for their antisocial behavior and report that the likelihood or even the certainty of apprehension and punishment is the least likely consideration in their decision to offend (Carroll, 1982).

Adolescents often commit offenses for "expressive" reasons such as excitement, hostility, revenge, or because of peer influence (Shover & Henderson, 1995). Their decision to offend is more often haphazard and emotional rather than considered and rational (Wright & Decker, 1994). They seldom engage in calculating the potential consequences of antisocial acts over the potential gains. They engage in risky activities with little appreciation and often with little realization of the dangers (Shover & Henderson, 1995).

Not Sufficient, Just Necessary

Before we rush to bury deterrence along with the remains of the victims of antisocial drivers, we must note that in terms of *general* deterrence the *total* actions of the justice system communicate standards of acceptable behavior and have a very substantial *overall* deterrence effect (Cook, 1980).

Anarchy on the Road

Although the research on deterrence cannot convince us that it is the answer to antisocial driving, we shudder to think what our roads would be like if there was no deterrent to such driving. Hospitals and funeral homes would be very busy as would insurance companies (at least the ones that could survive).

Positive Deterrence

The threat of punishment is effective for at least one subgroup of drivers – those who are not likely to misbehave on the highway because they hold beliefs, values, and sentiments that support prosocial driving (Pogarsky, 2002). Punishment may be most effective for those who need it the least – the ones whose behavior is sufficiently prosocial that they are never likely to encounter the punishment.

Although the benefits of convictions found in the large-scale study of the consequences of convictions for violations among Canadian drivers were short-lived and not statistically significant beyond two months, their personal benefits to the individuals who were not killed by those drivers in the short period of time since the drivers' convictions were certainly not insignificant in the personal or social sense. Moreover, the social, economic, and health benefits of the reduction in traffic deaths associated with convictions for traffic violations were substantial. The researchers suggest that their data indicated that one death was prevented for every 80,000 convictions, one emergency hospital visit for every 1,300 convictions, and $1000 in societal costs for every thirteen convictions. The thirty-five percent reduction in fatalities yielded by convictions is significantly greater than the risk reduction from *all* mandatory vehicle improvements of the past fifty years that has been estimated to be approximately twenty percent (Evans, 1991; Waller, 2002).

DETERRING DRINKING AND DRIVING

A systematic review was conducted of 125 studies reported from 1960 to 1991 on the effects of DWI interventions including license suspension, jail sentences, mandatory community service, license suspension, fines, selective enforcement patrols, regular police patrols, sobriety checkpoints, and breath testing. The review led to the conclusion that all of the DWI interventions were associated with reductions in drink-driving and collisions. However, that conclusion must be questioned given that the reviewers reported that the preponderance of studies employed weak designs and many provided inadequate reports of basic data (Wagenaar, Zobeck, Williams & Hingson, 1995).

Another review found that no specific form of punitive legislation had a measurable effect on fatalities. However, these reviewers found suggestive evidence that a multifaceted approach involving multiple laws and interventions designed to increase the certainty of punishment (e.g., sobriety checkpoints, and breath testing) had "some" deterrent effect (Evans, Neville & Graham, 1991).

Many countries have increased surveillance and enforcement and instituted severe penalties for impaired driving, yet many individuals continue to drink and drive and alcohol-related deaths still occur as often as one every thirty minutes. One in seven road deaths (in the U.K.) is the result of a drink/drive related "accident." Drunk driving remains the 'No. 1' most frequently committed violent crime. There still are an extraordinary large number of individuals who allow their driving ability to be compromised by their drinking ability.

COMBINING DETERRENCE AND EDUCATION

Although a single approach such as increased deterrence is unlikely by itself to yield long-term improvements in driving behavior, research has demonstrated that traffic law enforcement programs combined with public education campaigns can reduce the frequency of some unsafe driving practices. The effectiveness of several such programs has been shown in studies of drinking and driving (e.g., Kinkade & Leone, 1992; Streff & Eby, 1994). The double-barrelled approach has also been found to be effective in some studies of safety belt usage (e.g., Eby & Christoff, 1996; Jonah, Dawson, & Smith, 1982; Ulmer, Preusser, & Preusser, 1994; Piquero & Paternoster, 1998; Williams, Wells, McCartt & Preusser, 2000).

Media reports of the frequency and severity of collisions in which the driver was under the influence of alcohol have made the public more aware that drinking impairs driving. Public education 'crusades' and the efforts of victims groups coupled with increased surveillance and roadside breathalyzer blitzes by the police have had another impact – they have helped make the public realize that drinking/driving is an antisocial behavior (Kinkade & Leone, 1992; Streff & Eby, 1994). Efforts to challenge the social acceptability of drinking and driving are essential to the achievements of reductions in the frequency of alcohol-related collisions and there is evidence that they have been successful in yielding significant reductions (e.g., DETR, 2000; Yanovitzky, 2002).

CONCLUSION

A review of the research literature on interventions to increase driving safety among teenagers by John Mattox, II, of the University of Memphis supports our view that informing individuals about good driving behavior and traffic safety is not enough to change their bad driving.

His review indicated that threat of penalties is also an essential requirement for keeping teenagers safe behind the wheel. However, safety also requires self-enforcement.

An essential component of effective programs for reducing antisocial behavior is training antisocial individuals to consider the consequences of their behavior. It is difficult to train anyone or motivate anyone to drive in such a way that they will avoid negative consequences if there are no such consequences.

Chapter 13

EXAMINING, TRAINING AND RETRAINING

Given the practical difficulties in deterring antisocial drivers, perhaps a better approach – or an additional approach – to preventing or reducing antisocial driving is to identify drivers who are likely to become antisocial drivers before we license them; to train novice drivers to become prosocial rather than antisocial drivers; and to retrain drivers who have been driving antisocially.

THE DRIVER EXAMINATION

A core element in society's armamentarium in its fight against unsafe driving is the Driver Examination. In most countries it involves two tests; (1) a written test of the applicant's knowledge of the rules of the road; and (2) a brief road test of his/her ability to competently maneuver a car without breaching traffic rules; without damaging the car, or other cars; without causing traffic jams; and without injuring pedestrians (or the Examiner). How reliable are such tests in screening out potential drivers who are likely to be unsafe drivers?

Applicants who lack the basic skills in operating a vehicle may be quickly identified by their performance in the Driver Examination. However, whereas the short sample of their driving performance may indicate that the applicants have the skills to drive around a few city blocks without crashing and can manage the task of parallel parking without the aid of a tow truck, it is questionable how well such assessment of their driving behavior can reliably predict how well they will perform in other situations such as when driving at high speeds on the nations' expressways.

The driving test can help to weed out the incompetent but it may not provide us with much reliable data on the probable future driving behavior of the others. Research casts serious doubt on the value of driver testing in differentiating between those who are *able* to drive safely and those who are likely to *choose* to drive unsafely when they no longer have an Examiner looking over their shoulder (Evans, 1991; Lester, 1991).

There is very little evidence that the factors known to be associated with driving safety are related to the information acquired through driver examinations (West & Hall, 1995). Nevertheless, such examinations may be the best measure we currently possess. Unfortunately, we are much better at predicting past events — identifying unsafe drivers after rather than before they have established a record of unsafe driving.

Driver Examinations may have limited predictive value because they measure only some aspects of the safe driving equation. They assess knowledge of traffic regulations, road signs, parking signs and the like and they assess driving skills that are essential for safety. However, they do not measure safety motivation or the social skills, cognitive skills, and values that determine driving style. A Driving Examination is not a Driver Examination. Almost anyone can become a driver — no matter their character or their social competence.

DRIVER TRAINING

Driver education is a multimillion dollar industry that prospers on the basis of an assumption that has rarely been adequately tested — training individuals how to drive will lead them to drive safely.

It boggles the mind to think how our traffic system (and our emergency health system) would cope if drivers did not have some training before they acquired a license. However, serious questions have been raised about whether they need professional training. The vast majority of drivers have had some professional training — more than ninety percent in the U.K. (Forsyth, 1994). Unfortunately, the most common conclusion of reviews of research on the efficacy of driver education has been that the results are equivocal. Few programs have been found to have much of an influence on subsequent collision frequency (e.g., Brown, Groeger & Biehl, 1987; Hall & West 1996; Horneman, 1993; Koppa & Banning, 1981; Lynn, 1982; Struckman-Johnson et al., 1989).

Even defensive driving courses which teach anticipatory, safe driving habits do not appear to reduce drivers' collision involvement (Lund & Williams, 1985).

There are many driver education programs that undoubtedly improve the initial driving skills of their students. However, the initial benefits may be offset by the fact that the provision of driver education may encourage more young persons to drive at an early age thereby exposing them to more risk and leading them to crash at an earlier age.

It is not possible at this stage to identify the kinds of driver training programs that are most likely to be successful. Many programs focus on giving information about traffic laws and seat belt usage. One might wonder whether we should expect drivers to pay much attention to information aimed at improving their safety if they quickly come to believe, as most do, that they are better than the average driver. Moreover, although both necessary and appropriate, information-giving is unlikely to prove beneficial to the many drivers whose antisocial driving does not derive from a lack of information. There is little evidence that the ignorant driving behavior of antisocial drivers is related to their ignorance of safe driving practices. Perhaps that is because the driving behavior of antisocial drivers reflects not a lack of *knowledge* about how to drive safely, but a lack of *motivation* to do so (Koppa & Banning, 1981).

There is also little evidence that driver education programs have been successful in persuading students of the merit of courteous driving. However, rather than dismissing the value of professional driving instruction, we should be directing our attention to how such training could be improved such that its goal becomes not simply equipping students with knowledge and skills that enable them to operate a vehicle sufficiently well to obtain a license, but also on ways of equipping them with skills, values, and motivation to operate their cars prosocially.

DRIVER RETRAINING

Another approach in society's efforts to produce safe drivers is driver retraining. Hopefully, driver retraining and advanced driving courses yield drivers who violate traffic regulations less often and crash less often. However, reliable evidence of such benefits is still lacking (Lund & Williams, 1985; Lonero et al., 1995; Mayhew & Simpson, 1995;1997). Overall, studies of such programs have yielded mixed results. Some find no improvement (e.g., Koppa & Banning, 1981; Lynn, 1982). Others report fewer collisions and fewer traffic violations but only for a discouragingly short period of time following program completion (e.g., Finigan, 1996; McKnight & Tippets, 1997; Wark, Raub & Reischl, 1998). There may be benefits over the first six months of driving, but the positive effects tend to quickly vanish (Mayhew & Simpson, 1997). Drivers who obtain training in emergency control procedures quickly revert to their pretraining behaviors when faced with an emergency after training (Watson, 1997).

A large number of driver retraining programs have been developed and there are many proposed models for improving such programs (e.g., Lonero et al., 1995; Young, 1993). However, there are many questions about the likely success of such programs. The content of programs is highly varied and research has yet to identify the program ingredients that determine the likelihood of success or failure (Waller, 1983).

Driving skill can improve with training and practice but there is a ceiling effect beyond which further experience and training may encourage novice drivers to overrate their driving ability. Overconfidence can be dangerous because it can desensitize the driver to fear and thereby encourage risk taking (Job, 1990). For example, in Norway, "slippery road car handling training" made drivers more likely to crash after having been "successfully" trained (Glad, 1988). Similar findings have been reported in Oregon (Jones, 1992). In Germany, the graduates who reported that their course had helped them the most had the *worst* subsequent records (Siegrist & Ramsier, 1992). Some driving schools put beginning drivers in situations where they are out of control so they can learn how to regain control or avoid such situations in the future – however, the training may lead them to think they are invulnerable (something they already 'know').

Beyond the Core Curriculum

Such findings do not indicate that driving courses or advanced driving courses are inherently harmful. However, they do suggest that instructors must ensure that the acquisition of driving skill is accompanied by their students understanding the limitations and dangers associated with the application of such skills. They must also ensure that the students are motivated to apply their acquired driving skills in the service of safety rather than making them feel that they now are able to take greater risks.

Attendance

A major problem with most driver retraining courses and treatment programs for DWI offenders is poor attendance. Many who are assigned either fail to enroll or drop out well before completing the program – even when they have been assigned by court order. McKnight & Tippett's (1997) study found that of the violators assigned to instructional programs, more than fifty percent failed to complete the eight hours to which they were assigned. Most never even enrolled. Moreover, in some courses those who do not attend do better in terms of both violation frequency and collision frequency than those who do attend and complete the course.

Studies of experimental rehabilitation courses in the U.K. for drunk drivers have found that attenders are almost three times less likely to reoffend than those who do not attend (DETR, 2000). One concern about such findings is the possibility that those who attend are the ones who are most motivated to change their driving behavior and are the ones who are least likely to need the course. Those who do not attend may be the ones with the lowest motivation and the ones who may need the program the most.

GOOD DRIVER PROGRAMS

Rewarding prosocial driving has often been suggested as an approach to discouraging antisocial driving but few such programs have been implemented, or if implemented, sustained. However, there is some evidence that the approach can "work."

A meta-analysis of thirty-four studies supports the assertion that incentive programs can yield improvements in seatbelt use (Hagenzieker, Bijleveld & Davidse, 1997). They can also help prevent collisions. For example, incentives for collision-free driving were found to yield reductions in collisions in California by as much as twenty-two percent in the first year and thirty-three percent in the second year (Harano & Hubert, 1974). More recent evidence has been found in studies of the reduction in collisions when youths are promised reimbursement of the surcharge on their insurance (with interest) – a thirty-five percent reduction in collisions was found in Norway (Vaaje, 1991). Collisions among truck drivers in Germany have also been reduced by offering them bonuses for every six months of collision-free driving (Gros,

1989). The use of incentives to reward safe driving has often been recommended and just as often rejected as unworkable (Wilde, Robertson & Pless, 2002).

Unfortunately, researchers have demonstrated the efficacy of only a limited number of practical methods that can be implemented to reward responsible and courteous driving and there appear to be few incentives for politicians to implement those that might be effective.

Some parents have installed devices on their cars that function like the black box used on airplanes. They monitor the car's computers to indicate how it has been driven. Teaching drivers to drive safely is likely to require more than "automotive whistleblowers." It remains to be seen whether the combination of such devices with training in the social skills and values of safe driving and rewarding drivers for the absence of negative reports on their driving or for recorded evidence of rule-complying driving behavior rather than punishing them for driving misbehaviors can reduce violations and collisions among drivers.

CHANGING DRIVING BY CHANGING ATTITUDES

Intermittently punishing acts of antisocial driving and/or rewarding acts of prosocial driving is not likely to change the behavior of antisocial drivers who seldom perform such acts. Drivers must also be taught the skills and attitudes that make prosocial driving both possible and palatable. Teaching driving skills is important, but it is not enough. Driver training programs must not only teach potential drivers how to drive but also influence how they are likely to *choose* to drive. Driver training programs must teach drivers not only how to control their cars, but how to control themselves.

Drivers must learn not only the skills that are required for competent driving but the thinking and emotional skills and values that are required for *prosocial* driving. Effective programs must target attitudes, beliefs, and values (Groeger & Clegg, 1994; Wilde, 1994, b). Some driver improvement programs that include counseling efforts to lead participants to think about their driving style and attitudes have yielded improvements in recidivism (e.g., Bartl & Stummvoll, 2000; Utzelmann & Jacobshagen, 1997). We cannot afford to continue to assume that a reduction in antisocial driving will be automatically achieved by driver skill training or even by advanced driving skill training. Research suggests that programs designed primarily to reduce repeat traffic violations are more effective in reducing both violations and collisions than instruction that is solely directed toward collision prevention (McKnight & Tippetts, 1997). Perhaps that is because the former programs convey some message about respect for the law. As Wilde (1994b) suggests, we must not only aim to teach practical perceptual, decisional, and motor skills; we must also seek to instill more mature views, beliefs, and values. Teaching *defensive* driving may be essential but it is not sufficient. We also must teach drivers to refrain from *offensive* driving.

We must discourage antisocial beliefs, attitudes, values, and behavior and teach the social/emotional skills and values that foster prosocial driving. How can that best be done? Indeed, can it be done? In the next chapter we present evidence that the behavior of antisocial individuals can be changed – it can be done, it has been done, and it is now being done in many countries.

Chapter 14

THE MODIFICATION OF ANTISOCIAL BEHAVIOR

The approach to the modification of antisocial driving that we propose in this book is based on a research project that involved a series of empirical research studies conducted over the past forty years. The project was designed to determine whether antisocial behavior can be changed, to identify how such change might be achieved, and to develop programs to reduce the frequency of antisocial behavior.

The project, and many other studies conducted by researchers in Canada; Britain; Germany; Spain; and the U.S.A., demonstrated that some rigorously evaluated programs have yielded significant reductions in antisocial behavior even among some of the most antisocial individuals. The research has also identified the principles and program practices that are required for program success.

The success of almost all programs that have been effective in changing antisocial individuals has been achieved by applying training techniques which foster the development of the same cognitive skills, emotional skills, social skills, and values that the research we reviewed in previous chapters has identified as being associated with antisocial driving.

RESEARCH IN SEARCH OF A PROGRAM

The long-term project led to the development of a program for the modification of antisocial behavior, the *Reasoning and Rehabilitation Program (R&R)*, that is based on more than one hundred studies that have been demonstrated to be effective in the amelioration of antisocial

140

behavior. Its efficacy has been established through several independent, international, controlled evaluations that are described in the next chapter. The program content and practice of *The Prosocial Driver Training Program*, a version of *R&R* that is specifically targeted at antisocial drivers, are described in detail in the final chapter.

The research project was conducted in sequential stages in a field-theoretical design. The results obtained at each stage suggested refinements in the understanding of antisocial behavior, in the nature of the program and in the program model which were then tested in subsequent stages of the project.

STAGE 1 – ANTISOCIAL ADOLESCENTS

The first stage of the research began in the early 1960s in Canada at the Department of Psychology, University of Waterloo. Stimulated by Department Chairman, Richard Walters' interest in adolescent aggression (Bandura & Walters, 1963), a large-scale research program was initiated that aimed to develop effective programs for the treatment of adolescents whose chronic antisocial behavior had led them to be admitted to an institution. Their admission followed a long history of antisocial behaviors such as alcohol and drug abuse, or chronic disruptive behavior at home, in school or in other institutions. An affiliation was established between the institution and the clinical psychology department of the university to enable treatment of the youths to be guided by research and supported with the assistance of faculty and graduate students in the doctoral program. The institution came to function as the equivalent of a "teaching hospital" for the study and treatment of antisocial behavior (Ross, 1967).

Evaluation studies conducted during the ten-year project found that a wide variety of treatment techniques including individual and group psychotherapy and several behavior modification programs failed to reduce the adolescents' antisocial behavior. Most programs actually increased their antisocial behavior both in the institution and in the community following their release (Ross & McKay, 1979).

An effective program was finally developed when traditional treatment programs for the antisocial youths were terminated and an unorthodox program was implemented. The adolescents were taught in this program how to analyze the antisocial behaviors of their peers and then trained in a social skill that enabled them to encourage prosocial behavior among their peers.

The results of the program were remarkable. In a well-controlled evaluation it was found that among the adolescents who were trained, major behavior problems in the institution (e.g., assault, vandalism, flagrant disobedience) were virtually eliminated. Their post-institutional adjustment was also exceptional. During a nine-month follow-up period their rate of return to the institution for antisocial behavior was only six percent. In contrast, the rate for a matched group which received only the regular institution program was thirty-three percent.

The peer group program led the adolescents to change their values from egocentric thinking to a concern for others, and equipped them with a social skill that enabled them to improve their interpersonal interactions with peers and adults both while in the institution and after they returned to community living. The program constituted an early version of a cognitive behavioral approach to the amelioration of antisocial behavior.[12]

Confirmation of the efficacy of similar training in social skills and social perspective training in engendering prosocial behavior has since been found in two residential settings in the U.S.A. for antisocial adolescents with a history of aggressive, disruptive, and antisocial behavior (Chalmers & Townsend, 1990; Gibbs, 1995).

Based on close to twenty years of research, the program has since been refined into a highly structured, multifaceted, cognitive-behavioral program that has been successfully implemented internationally with a wide variety of adolescent and adult antisocial individuals. New editions of the program have recently been developed that are responsive to more recent research on the relation between cognition and antisocial behavior. The new versions of the program are specifically designed for various groups, including antisocial drivers.

STAGE 2 – BIBLIOTHERAPY FOR CYNICS

Stage 2 of the long-term project was conducted at the University of Ottawa in Canada. It was stimulated by widely publicized reports in Britain and U.S.A. of the failure of almost all programs designed to

---

12. We are indebted to Dr. Andy Birkenmayer for this explanation of the success of the program.

change the behavior of antisocial individuals (e.g., Martinson, 1974). According to those reports, attempts to reduce antisocial behavior by educational or therapeutic programs have been long on promise and short on achievement.

The typical conclusion of such reports was that in the prevention of antisocial behavior and in the reformation of antisocial individuals, success is rare – prevention programs do not prevent, rehabilitation programs do not rehabilitate, correctional programs do not correct.

The highly publicized conclusion that "almost nothing works" contributed to a widespread view that antisocial behavior could not be changed. However, that conclusion was based on reviews of research on the efficacy of programs for the rehabilitation of antisocial adolescents and adults that were conducted before 1967.

In Stage 2 of the project a new review was undertaken which examined more recent research. The review examined studies of the efficacy of programs that were published in refereed journals between 1973 and 1978 (Gendreau & Ross, 1979; Ross & Gendreau, 1980). The new review, in marked contrast to the ones that yielded the "nothing works" zeitgeist, identified a number of controlled studies which had been found to be highly effective in reducing the frequency and severity of antisocial behavior. More than one hundred successful studies were found.

Many studies involved a substantial number of subjects (2,000 in one study) with follow-up periods as long as three to fifteen years after treatment. Positive outcomes had been achieved in some programs for antisocial "at-risk" youths, some programs for "high-risk" adolescents, some programs for recidivistic adult offenders, some programs for violent offenders, and some programs for substance abusers. Additional studies of effective programs were found in a later stage of the project that involved a review of studies published between 1981 and 1987 (Gendreau & Ross, 1987).[13]

However, the research indicated that not all programs "work." In fact, successful programs are well outnumbered by interventions that failed to reduce antisocial behavior. Effective programs are exceptional. They are exceptional both in their results and their program principles and methods.

---

13. Descriptions of some of the best of those programs are presented in the book, *Going Straight* (Ross, Antonowicz & Dhaliwall, 1995).

STAGE 3 - SUCCESS VS. FAILURE

Research conducted in Stage 3 of the long-term project addressed the question: what is the difference between programs that succeed and programs that fail?

The research indicated that fundamental to the success of programs is the conceptualization of antisocial behavior on which the program is based (Gendreau & Ross, 1981). The conceptual model of antisocial behavior determines the goals of the intervention and the intermediate targets on which the program should focus in order to achieve these goals. It also serves as a guide for practitioners in terms of the techniques they must employ.

Many programs were based on a disease model that views antisocial behavior as symptomatic of some underlying psychopathological condition that requires "cure" through some form of "therapy." Research in Stage 3 revealed that among the many effective programs described in the literature between 1970 and 1987, not one was based on such a disease model (Gendreau & Ross, 1987). Rather than assuming that antisocial behavior is a symptom of psychopathology, effective programs viewed it as a consequence of a variety of social, situational, cognitive, and behavioral factors which are known to be functionally related to antisocial behavior.

The effective programs did not employ therapy to cure diseases, but used training and education to teach new skills and attitudes. They fostered the development of prosocial competence by teaching skills and values that enable individuals to achieve success without having to resort to antisocial behavior.

A wide variety of intervention modalities had been used in effective programs. However, analysis of the studies indicated that almost every successful program shared one characteristic: they included some technique which could be expected to have an impact on their clients' *thinking*. Almost every treatment effort which had been successful included some technique which would influence their thinking and reasoning skills, their problem-solving skills, and their attitudes and values (Ross, 1980).

Effective programs included as a target of their intervention not only their behavior, feelings, and social skills, but also their cognition: their information-processing, their reasoning, their attributions, their understanding and appraisal of the world, and their values. The research suggested that attending to how antisocial individuals *think* is at least as important as focusing on how they *behave*.

Effective programs included some technique which could enhance the offenders' impulse control; increase their reasoning skills; improve their sensitivity to the consequences of their behavior; improve their ability to comprehend the thoughts and feelings of other people; increase their interpersonal problem-solving skills; and help them to develop alternative interpretations of social rules; and social obligations. They fostered the development of cognitive-behavioral skills that underlie prosocial competence and serve as alternatives to antisocial behavior. As the research we have reviewed in this book indicates, shortcomings in those skills and values are also associated with antisocial driving.

STAGE 4 – ANTISOCIAL BEHAVIOR AND COGNITION

The results of the analysis of successful programs led to another research question – improving the social-cognitive functioning of antisocial individuals improves their behavior. Does that mean that there is something wrong with their cognitive functioning in the first place? Do antisocial individuals differ from prosocial individuals in their cognitive functioning, in the way they think? That question was addressed in Stage 4 of the project.

A search of four decades of research literature revealed a considerable body of empirical evidence that many antisocial individuals lack an adequate repertoire of the specific cognitive skills and values which are essential for prosocial competence (Ross, 1980; Ross & Fabiano, 1985). We now know that the skills and values that the research reviewed in this book indicate are lacking in antisocial drivers are the same as those that earlier and current research indicate are characteristic of other antisocial individuals. Those characteristics have been the targets of programs that have been successful in the rehabilitation of antisocial individuals – impulsivity; impatience; risk-taking; rigid thinking; egocentricity; shortcomings in critical reasoning and interpersonal problem-solving; and antisocial attitudes, values and beliefs.

STAGE 5 – PROGRAM ANALYSES

The importance of training in social cognitive skills in programs for antisocial individuals was first recognized in 1980 through informal analysis of successful programs (Ross, 1980). The "cognitive model" was subsequently supported by quantitative component analysis of effective and ineffective programs and by two meta-analyses (Garrett, 1985; Izzo & Ross, 1990) and later through a statistical analysis of forty of the most rigorously evaluated programs (Ross & Antonowicz, 1994). Those analyses confirmed the conclusion that most programs which included a cognitive component "worked"; most which did not, failed.

SOME THINGS WORK

Since the research conducted in the 1970s that indicated that some programs work, a solid body of criminological research has developed that clearly and convincingly demonstrates that antisocial individuals can be rehabilitated. Positive results have been demonstrated in rigorously evaluated research studies including several international meta-analytic analyses of several hundred independent studies (e.g., Andrews, Zinger, Hoge, Bonta, Gendreau & Cullen, 1990; Izzo & Ross, 1990; Lipsey, 1992; Losel & Koferl, 1989; Redondo, Sanchez-Mecca & Garrido, 1999).

There is now an extensive body of empirical research that demonstrates that some cognitive-behavioral programs are effective in reducing antisocial behavior. The evidence is both persuasive and clear. Antisocial behavior can be changed. However, in order to change how people behave we must equip them with skills and values that will enable them to behave in a prosocial manner and motivate them to choose to behave in a prosocial manner.

The Cognitive Model

The peer group program that was successful in the rehabilitation of the institutionalized antisocial youths program in the 1960s was an early precursor of a wide variety of "cognitive behavioral" programs that have been identified in more recent research as the key to the effective rehabilitation of antisocial individuals. The basic assumption of the cognitive model is that antisocial individuals lack the cognitive/emotional skills required for prosocial competence, and hold beliefs, attitudes, and behaviors that lead them into antisocial behavior. The model suggests that their *rehabilitation* requires changing these antisocial thoughts and beliefs and fostering their development of prosocial values.

A Cautionary Note

Our social cognitive model of antisocial driving is not an explanatory model of the cause of collisions. The causes of collisions are much too complex for an explanation that focuses only on driver behavior. The cause of many collisions include risk factors such as faulty vehicle or road design or maintenance, weather conditions, poor lighting, and a host of other situational and transient factors (including the behavior of other drivers). Not all collisions involve cognitive incompetence. Collisions can and do happen to anyone. However, drivers whose cognitive skills and values are not well developed are particularly vulnerable.

The model we present is an intervention model for changing the thinking of drivers and potential drivers so as to increase the frequency of safe, courteous, and cooperative driving practices. Its aim is to teach social/emotional skills and values that are associated with prosocial driving. Such skills and values can be taught.

Chapter 15

PROGRAM DEVELOPMENT AND
EVALUATION

Stage 6 of the long-term project was designed to develop a program that could effectively teach the cognitive skills and values that research had found to be lacking among antisocial individuals. The program was created by selecting the best training techniques from those rehabilitation programs that had been demonstrated to lead to major reductions in antisocial behavior and combining them with additional techniques which other research had indicated were effective in teaching social cognitive skills. These techniques were then refined and blended into a multifaceted small group program, the *Reasoning and Rehabilitation (R&R) Program.*[14] The program was based on more than a hundred rigorously evaluated programs that a variety of researchers in North America and Europe had found to be effective in preventing or reducing antisocial behavior.

The efficacy of the R&R program was then tested in Stage 8 in a controlled study of high-risk, antisocial older adolescents and adults. Subsequently, in Stage 9, it was independently tested with large numbers of the most severe antisocial adults – inmates in Canadian prisons. It has since been successfully tested in several independent, international evaluations with a variety of antisocial populations in both community and institutional settings.

The evaluations of R&R are discussed in this chapter following a brief description of the program. A detailed description of the version of the program specifically designed for antisocial drivers is presented in the following chapter.

---

14. "R&R" was never intended to be an acronym for "Road Rage." It is also 'accidental' that "R&R" is also the initials of its authors: Robert Ross and Roslynn Ross.

STAGE 6 – THE *R&R* PROGRAM

The R&R program is a multifaceted, cognitive-behavioral group program for teaching cognitive skills and values that are essential for prosocial competence. The major components of the program are:

- **Self-Control**. Participants are taught to stop and think before they act; to consider all the consequences before making decisions; and to use thinking techniques to control their emotions and their behavior.
- **Meta-Cognition**. Many antisocial individuals seldom reflect on their behavior or think about what they are thinking about when they take risks. In R&R they are taught to tune into and critically assess their own thinking – to realize that *how* they think determines *what* they think, how they *feel* and how they *behave*.
- **Social Skills**. Many antisocial individuals act antisocially because they lack the skills to act prosocially. Utilizing a modification of Goldstein's technique (e.g., Goldstein, 1988; 2000), the participants are taught a number of skills which will help them achieve positive reinforcement and avoid the antagonism that is engendered by antisocial behavior.
- **Interpersonal Cognitive Problem-Solving Skills**. Using the techniques that were employed in a successful rehabilitation program for heroin abusers, participants learn how to analyze interpersonal problems; how to understand and consider other people's values, behavior and feelings; how to recognize how their behavior affects other people; and to realize why others respond to them as they do (Platt, Perry, & Metzger, 1980).
- **Alternative Thinking**. To combat their conceptual rigidity a number of techniques developed by deBono (e.g., 1985) are utilized to teach antisocial individuals to think of alternative, prosocial rather than antisocial ways of responding to the problems they experience.
- **Critical Reasoning**. Participants are taught how to think logically, objectively, and rationally without distorting the facts or externalizing the blame.
- **Social Perspective-taking**. Participants are trained to consider other people's views, feelings and thoughts. In effect, the program emphasizes the development of empathy.
- **Values Enhancement**. A number of group discussion techniques are used to teach values; specifically, to move participants from

their egocentric world view to a consideration of the needs of others.

- **Emotional Management**. Recognizing that success in social adjustment depends on the individual's ability to control their emotions, anger management techniques were adapted so that they could be used in the R&R program to teach control not only of anger but of other emotions such as excitement, depression, fear, and anxiety which may be equally or even more problematic for many antisocial individuals.

STAGE 7 – HIGH RISK OFFENDERS

The first in a continuing series of controlled evaluations of R&R was conducted in 1986 in Stage 8 of the project (Ross, Fabiano, & Ewles, 1988). It involved a rigorous test of the program's value in reducing the recidivism of adults who had a history of antisocial behavior and convictions for illegal behavior. Each had been assessed by a reliable risk-predicting instrument as being at high risk of persisting in such behaviors (Andrews, 1989).

The program was conducted by probation officers who were trained in program delivery. The evaluation consisted of an experimental study entailing random assignment of the high-risk individuals to *R&R* or to control groups that did not receive *R&R*.

Police data revealed that only eighteen percent of those trained in R&R were convicted of an illegal act during a nine-month follow-up period from program entry compared to an average of fifty-nine percent of those in the control groups.

STAGE 8 – THE CANADIAN PRISON PROJECT

A version of the original R&R Program was developed in 1988 for application in institutional settings operated by the Correctional Service of Canada (CSC) (Ross & Ross, 1988) and the program's efficacy was subjected to a test with the most serious antisocial individuals in Canada – prisoners in Canadian prisons who were serving sentences from two years to life.

In a series of studies, the outcomes for program participants who had been randomly assigned to R&R were compared with those of inmates who had been randomly assigned to a no-treatment (waiting list) control group (Porporino & Robinson,1995; Robinson & Porporino, 2000).

Study 1

The initial study found that R&R participants made improvements in a number of cognitive skills and in attitudinal targets known to be associated with persisting antisocial behavior. Significant improvements were found in problem-solving skills, impulsivity, social perspective taking, and attitudes toward the law. Significantly lower reoffending was also found during an eighteen month follow-up.

Study 2

In a 2.5 year post-release follow-up of the sample examined in Study 1, only twenty-two percent of the offenders who had participated in the R&R program were reconvicted compared to fifty percent of comparable offenders who had no exposure to the program. This constituted a recidivism reduction of fifty-six percent associated with participation in R&R relative to no treatment.

Study 3

Subsequently, outcome data with a larger sample of 255 offenders was studied. It was found that in a one year, post-release follow-up, approximately half as many R&R participants (7%) were reconvicted compared to untreated controls (13%).

Study 4

A later study was based on a large sample of offenders (1,444) who had completed the R&R program between 1989 and 1994. A 20 percent reduction in reconvictions was found for those who had completed R&R training compared to offenders who had been randomly assigned to R&R and were on a waiting list, but never received the program.

The reduction in reconvictions were much greater among offenders who received R&R in the community. They evidenced a 66.3 percent reduction in convictions during the one year follow-up.

R&R is the core curriculum for the rehabilitation programs of the Correctional Service of Canada which operates forty-seven prisons and community residences across Canada for the nation's most serious antisocial individuals.

STAGE 9 – INTERNATIONAL
DISSEMINATION

We estimate that by the end of the year 2002, the *Reasoning &*
Rehabilitation Program has been delivered to more than forty thousand
antisocial individuals around the world. It is being conducted with
high-risk adolescents and adults as an integral component of probation services in many countries including Canada, England, New
Zealand, Scotland, U.S.A., and Wales. It is also being delivered in
various institutions for juveniles in Canada, Scotland, and the U.S.A.;
in adult prisons in Canada, England, Estonia, Latvia, and Scotland;
and in county, state and federal prisons in the U.S.A. It is also being
conducted in Australia, the Canary Islands, Denmark, Estonia,
Germany, Hong Kong, Latvia, Lebanon, New Zealand, Spain, and
Sweden.

R&R is currently being delivered in various settings in thirty-two
states in the U.S. including Alaska, Arizona, California, Colorado,
Connecticutt, Massachusetts, Michigan, Minnesota, New Jersey, New
Mexico, Ohio, Oregon, Texas, Utah, Vermont, and Washington. A culturally modified program has been implemented for antisocial individuals in the urban ghettoes in the Bronx, Mid-Manhattan, and Harlem in
New York City.

R&R has also been conducted with illiterate adolescents from the
slum barrios of Caracas, Venezuela; with high-risk probationers in
impoverished coal-mining towns in Wales; with probationers in Day
Centres and Probation Hostels in many parts of England (including
those from high crime rate areas in Liverpool, London, and Manchester); with offenders in various prisons and community correctional settings in Scotland; and with antisocial adolescent gangs in
Texas.

R&R has been successfully delivered to a wide range of individuals including "at risk" children in schools; child and spouse-abusers;
juvenile gang members; families of antisocial adolescents; alcohol
abusers; drug abusers; chronically unemployed individuals; and even
mentally disordered forensic patients. It has also been widely and
successfully implemented with chronically recidivistic adult offenders; violent offenders; car thieves; sex offenders and white collar
criminals. Many of those treated had extensive histories of convictions for driving offences.

STAGE 10 – INDEPENDENT INTERNATIONAL EVALUATIONS

Many of the international applications of R&R have been conducted independently of the program authors within controlled evaluation research projects.[15]

R&R in Texas

A controlled evaluation of an abridged version of the R&R program found significant improvement in antisocial behavior among high-risk felons (Kownacki, 1995).

R&R in Georgia

During a sixteen month follow-up, thirty-nine percent of adolescent offenders in Georgia who received R&R training were rearrested compared to seventy-five percent of randomly assigned controls who did not receive the program.

Those who received R&R performed better on outcome measures including return to prison, rearrest/parole revocation rates, and reoffending (Spruance, Van Voorhis, Johnson, Ritchey, Pealer & Seabrook, 2000).

R&R in Wales

A controlled study of the efficacy of R&R was conducted in 1991 with high-risk probationers in impoverished mining communities in MidGlamorgan, Wales. The study found that R&R led to lower than predicted conviction rates during a one year follow-up. However, the improvements did not continue beyond the first year suggesting the need for continuing treatment or booster sessions (Raynor & Vanstone, 1996).

R&R in Spain

The social adjustment of antisocial adolescents in an institution in Barcelona, Spain was found to be significantly improved by their participation in an R&R program (Garrido, 1995).

---

15. Descriptions of the evaluations are presented in *Thinking Straight* (Ross & Ross, 1995).

R&R in the Canary Islands

Significant improvement in the post-institutional success of prison inmates in Tenerife was obtained through an abbreviated version of the program combined with social work services (Martin & Hernandez, 1995).

R&R in England

A study of the efficacy of R&R in prisons in England and Wales examined the post-institutional performance of 667 prisoners who were trained in R&R compared to matched prisoners who had not received the program. It was found found that R&R led to "a fifty-five percent reduction in the chances of being reconvicted within two years after discharge" (Friendship, Blud, Erikson, Travers & Thornton, 2001).

A second study compared the reconviction rate for 670 offenders who were serving sentences of two or more years and had committed a sexual, violent, or drug offense with the reconviction rate for a group of 1,801 offenders who had not participated in the program. Significant reductions in reconvictions were found over the two-year follow-up: "up to fourteen percentage points lower than matched comparison groups" (Friendship, Blud, Erikson & Travers, 2002).

However, later, when the quality of the program delivery became suspect, another study found no significant differences, indicating that program integrity is essential to program efficacy (Falshaw, Friendship, Travers & Nugent, 2003).

R&R was the first program to be accredited by the British Prison Service's panel for the Accreditation of Offending Behavior Programmes.

R&R with Substance Abusers in California

Although the implementation and supervision of R&R was somewhat lacking in program integrity, substance-abusing probationers in California who were trained in R&R were found to be less likely to be arrested during follow-up (25.3%) than those who were involved in a multiphase drug treatment program (32.3%) (Austin, 1997).

R&R with Substance Abusers in Colorado

R&R was implemented within a large state-wide community service in Colorado and was independently evaluated within an experimental design involving random assignment of substance abusing probationers to R&R or to a specialized drug program or a no-treatment control condition.

A small improvement in revocation rates for the R&R group (25.5%) was found compared with the drug program group (29.5%). Both groups fared considerably better than the no-treatment controls (43%). However, a substantial benefit in terms of lower recidivism was found among those who had the most severe drug/alcohol problems when R&R was added to the specialized drug program (18% with R&R vs. 43% without R&R) (Johnson & Hunter, 1995).

Related Studies

- R&R was found to improve the problem-solving abilities and the social adjustment of mentally disordered forensic patients in Scotland (Donnelly & Scott, 1999).
- An analysis of evaluations of R&R using the *Maryland Scale for Scientific Rigor* concluded that R&R is a successful program for reducing recidivism (Allen, MacKenzie & Hickman, 2001).

A Handbook For Teaching Cognitive Skills

A Handbook of instructions and materials for conducting R&R was created in 1986 (Ross, Fabiano & Ross, 1986). A slightly revised version of the Handbook was created in 1988 for use in institutions and community settings operated by the Correctional Service of Canada (Ross & Ross, 1988).

A second edition of the Handbook, *Reasoning & Rehabilitation 2 (R&R 2)*, is being developed to update the program in accord with new research that has been published since the original R&R was developed fifteen years ago: research on the relationship between cognition and antisocial behavior; and research on the characteristics of effective programming for the prevention of antisocial behavior and the rehabilitation of antisocial individuals (Ross & Hilborn, 2004). The research on which the new edition is based has been described in a book, *Time To Think Again* (Ross & Hilborn, 2004). The new edition of R&R is also based on lessons learned from fifteen years of experience in program delivery and from the many evaluations of the program's efficacy.

STAGE 11 – SPECIALIZED R&R2 PROGRAMS

The 1986 versions of the R&R program Handbook were designed for use in applications with all types of antisocial individuals. However, based on analysis of the literature on the needs of specific groups of antisocial individuals, *Reasoning and Rehabilitation 2* programs have been designed such that specific versions of the program can be used that are appropriate for application with particular client groups, including adolescents (Ross & Hilborn, 2003); children with conduct problems in school; antisocial individuals with learning disabilities; and families of antisocial youths (Ross, Hilborn & Greene, 2003). The version for antisocial drivers which we describe in the next chapter is the *Prosocial Driver Training Program* (Ross, 2004).

Chapter 16

THE *PROSOCIAL DRIVER TRAINING PROGRAM*

The *Prosocial Driver Training Program* is a multifaceted educational program designed to teach potential drivers, novice drivers, and experienced drivers the social cognitive skills and values that are essential for prosocial competence when driving. This chapter provides an overview of the program. The content of the program is described along with discussion of the program's goals, targets, and procedures. We also discuss the characteristics of those individuals who are most likely to effectively deliver the program.

The Prosocial Driver Training Program teaches the cognitive and social skills and values that are prerequisites to prosocial driving competence and that are antagonistic to antisocial driving. The program is designed to teach drivers that prosocial driving is a skill.

It must be emphasized that although the program focuses on driving, the skills, and values it teaches are generic. They are essential for prosocial competence in any situation. The skills are the building blocks for all interpersonal activities, including driving an automobile. The program aims to change driving behavior; but it also seeks to equip drivers with skills and values that can improve their general social behavior such that they are less likely to experience conflict in their homes, at work, and in other social situations that can indirectly impact their driving. It aims to equip drivers with skills that will enable them to become better able to cope with interpersonal stresses wherever they are encountered.

The Prosocial Driver Training Program version of R&R includes all of the major components of the original R&R program. However, the content of each has been refined for specific application to driving situations. Each component is based on techniques developed and tested by psychologists and educators. Many of these specific components can provide a vehicle for teaching specific cognitive skills. However, our particular combination and blend of the selected techniques and our recommended adaptations of them for drivers constitutes a more efficient approach and one which is designed to ensure that participants learn all of the cognitive skills required for social competence on the road.

The Prosocial Driver Training Program can be delivered as a stand-alone program; but it can also be conducted as an integral part of or in tandem with programs that teach driving skills, including training programs for novice drivers; school-based driver education programs; advanced driving programs; and driver retraining programs.

It should be noted that the Prosocial Driver Training Program and all of the other R&R programs qualify as "cognitive behavioral" programs in that they are designed to modify antisocial beliefs, attitudes, and behaviors that are associated with antisocial behavior. However, all R&R programs are designed not only to teach prosocial beliefs, attitudes, and values but also to teach the cognitive skills that make the acquisition of such beliefs, attitudes, and values possible. The programs are more than cognitive/behavioral programs. They are cognitive/emotional *skills training* programs that are designed to teach the social/cognitive/emotional skills that make the acquisition of prosocial competence possible. Their focus is on modifying *how* people think, not just on modifying *what* they think.

Program Materials

Program materials and a detailed description of the program are presented in a trainer's manual: *PROSOCIAL DRIVER TRAINING: A Handbook for Teaching Prosocial Driving Skills and Values* (Ross, 2004). The Handbook provides most of the materials for teaching the program and detailed step-by-step instructions for the Trainer. Volume 1 is a manual of instructions for Trainers. Volume 2 contains materials for delivering the program. Volume 3 is a Participant's Workbook which includes a brief explanation of each of the skills taught in the training sessions along with self-administering tests of personal driving behaviors, and out-of-class exercises that participants are required to complete for practice in applying the skills.

Trainers

A basic assumption of our long-term research project was that in order to have a major impact in reducing antisocial behavior, an effective program must be developed that does not require the services of highly specialized mental health professionals. There are simply not enough psychiatrists, psychologists, or social workers (or enough funds to support them) to enable a program which requires their services to be provided to enough individuals to have a major impact in reducing antisocial behavior. All of the R&R programs can be delivered by a wide variety of individuals regardless of their educational background. The Prosocial Driver Training Program can be delivered by driving instructors, by teachers, by parents and even by graduates of the program provided they have the requisite social skills and values, have a solid grasp of the program principles, and have been trained in program delivery.

Program Content

The program consists of seven interrelated modules:

• PROBLEM SOLVING
• SOCIAL SKILLS
• NEGOTIATION SKILLS
• ALTERNATIVE THINKING
• EMOTIONAL MANAGEMENT
• VALUES ENHANCEMENT
• CRITICAL REASONING

Each module contains a number of sessions each of which includes exercises that are structured opportunities for participants to learn and practice a particular skill. The program has been designed in modular fashion in order that maximum flexibility can be achieved and the various modules can be used on an 'as needed' basis. Factors such as time availability and group characteristics which require emphasizing some modules, or adding other activities can be accommodated.

The program has been designed in such a way that Trainers can deliver it in any schedule they wish. The total program can be taught in twelve, two-hour sessions delivered two to three times a week – a total of 24 hours of in-class training. However, shortened programs and more compressed or more distributed scheduling of sessions can be readily available.

Techniques were selected that lack the appearance of therapy or school activities which might be aversive to some participants. Most are intrinsically motivating and the program is both highly enjoyable and highly demanding. Trainers are advised to select from the program materials the content which appears best suited to the particular sociocultural setting and the particular participants they are training. Changes in content can be readily made without changing the process of teaching the skills.

PROBLEM-SOLVING

As the research we reviewed in earlier chapters indicated, many antisocial drivers lack adequate skills in interpersonal cognitive problem-solving – the thinking skills which are required for solving problems in interacting with other people:

- They often fail to recognize that a problem exists or is about to occur.
- They do not consider alternative solutions to such problems but continue to drive in ways that are ineffective or inappropriate.
- They have either failed to determine – or have not even thought about – the driving responses they can and should take to cope with problems they encounter when driving.
- They fail or are unable to calculate the consequences of their driving behavior on other people.
- They do not understand, or they fail to think about, the cause and effect relationship between their driving behavior and other drivers' reactions to them.

The problem-solving module is designed to teach drivers a number of the cognitive and behavioral skills which are required for identifiying and coping with the variety of problems, hazards, and conflicts that are likely to be experienced every time one ventures into traffic.

In order to cope well with problems they are likely to encounter when driving, individuals need to obtain as much information as possible about such potential problems. The information may be gained through driving training, but is more likely to be acquired through driving experience. However, individuals may fail to profit from either instruction or experience unless they have acquired an approach to problem solving in their everyday life that includes an attitude which recognizes that they are likely to encounter problems wherever they are and that they can cope with most of them by applying effective problem-solving techniques. Such attitudes are taught in the program as are problem-solving techniques that can be effectively applied to a wide variety of problem situations, not only those that are encountered on the road.

There are a large number of problem-solving training programs. In the Prosocial Driver Training Program, problem-solving training is not limited, as it is in many other programs, only to teaching specific solutions to specific driving situations. It aims, instead, to teach cognitive and behavioral skills which will enable the individual to develop a *general* and *principled* approach to problems. The Problem-Solving module consists of six sessions:

1. Problem Recognition
2. Problem Identification
3. Conceptualizing
4. Alternative Thinking
5. Consequential Thinking
6. Assertive Behavior

Participants are taught to continually observe their environment in order to foresee hazardous situations and are taught to recognize the potential consequences of such situations. They are also taught to reflect upon problems they have encountered on the road and to consider their cause and all of the alternative solutions they might have chosen. They are taught to think of all of the possible consequences of such options, then carefully decide the best action they might have taken to avoid or solve the problems while taking the perspective of others into account.

Emphasis is placed throughout the problem-solving module on teaching drivers to recognize in driving situations the value of trying to understand how other people feel and how those feelings might lead them to react. Participants are taught how to consider how other drivers are likely to respond to the driving actions the participants might take to deal with various problem situations they encounter. This includes teaching them the consequences (for themselves and for other drivers) of aggressive as opposed to assertive reactions they might take in trying to cope with driving problems.

Included in many of the examples and exercises are problems related to time management. Many drivers create problems for themselves (and other drivers) by failure to anticipate problems and by engaging in risky, high-speed driving because they have failed to manage their activities in such a way that they can reach their destination without succumbing to "*temper fugit.*" Lack of skill in time management may also be reflected in the failure of drivers to learn how to anticipate speed and safety margins in driving (van der Hulst, Meijman & Rothengatter, 1999). Individuals who are chronically late are particularly susceptible to collisions.

SOCIAL SKILLS

Many of the drivers who offend us on the road behave in an antisocial manner simply because they lack the skills to behave in a prosocial manner. Many lack the skills to interact positively with others wherever they are. The behavior of such drivers is unlikely to be significantly changed by programs that are limited to emphasis on the legal consequences of their antisocial driving or even by fines for their traffic violations, or the costs of repairs to their damaged cars, or the related costs in terms of increased insurance premiums. Teaching drivers to be aware of such consequences is unlikely to be a sufficient lesson for the driver who lacks the social skills to drive in a more socially acceptable manner. Such drivers must develop an adequate repertoire of thinking and social skills so that they learn to interact in social situations, including driving, in such a way that they avoid such adverse consequences.

Other antisocial drivers may have social skills that enable them to relate well off the road but fail to apply them on the road. They need to be taught several things:

- Driving is a social situation that involves other people; not just cars.
- The driver's safety and well-being, and that of other people with whom they share the road, depends on their practicing the social skills that are expected of prosocial individuals wherever they are.
- Behaving in a socially skillful manner on the road yields many benefits such as less conflict; less retaliatory aggression; less emotional arousal; more relaxation and comfort; better traffic flow (that reduces time to destination); and increased self-respect.

Many skills can be taught in this module. Among those, the ones we emphasize for drivers are sensible, objective, effective, and socially acceptable ways of doing the following:

• Assessing your skill
• Expressing appreciation
• Expressing a complaint
• Responding to complaints
• Concentrating
• Setting your priorities
• Determining responsibility
• Identifying and labeling your emotions
• Relaxation
• Self-control
• Helping others

NEGOTIATION SKILLS

Many drivers, when faced with conflict with other drivers, react in a manner that antagonizes the drivers with whom they must share the road. Their reactions often magnify the problem and may lead to difficulties with the law or to a collision.

Many other antisocial drivers, do not respond to the conflict in a direct way but retaliate by engaging in manipulative driving tactics that are equally antisocial and dangerous. For example, they may slow down to inconvenience the other driver; make a quick turn without signaling their intention to do so; or hog the center line or the passing lane to block the progress and engender the frustration of drivers behind them with whom they are in conflict. Either of those reactions – aggressive confrontation or indirect manipulation – may represent the individual's lifestyle response to interpersonal conflict and not just his/her driving style. Both represent maladaptive responses which are likely to create problems, rather than solve problems.

Participants in the program are taught an alternative response to conflict: *negotiation.* Negotiation is a "no-lose" strategy through which both parties are able to satisfy their needs in a manner that ends the conflict in a way that is mutually satisfactory.

Negotiation is seldom a viable alternative in driving situations. However, negotiation skills training is taught in the Prosocial Driver Training Program for two reasons. First, it is an important social skill that many antisocial drivers can benefit from acquiring since it teaches them that there is an alternative to aggression in interpersonal conflict – an alternative that may involve compromise but is far more likely to yield personal gain for both parties, rather than increased antagonism with no gain for either party. Second, negotiation skills training can stimulate antisocial individuals to think about their aggressive behaviors both on the road and off the road and, in particular, to think about the consequences of their response style for themselves and others.

The Negotiation Skills module used in the Prosocial Driver Training Program relies heavily on role-playing, practice and feedback. Participants are taught in four steps:

• How to clearly identify a problem situation;
• How to identify options (possible responses);
• How to identify consequences of the various options;
• Simulation – behavioral rehearsal (role-playing) of the options.

EMOTIONAL MANAGEMENT

The purpose of thinking is to arrange the world so that our emotions can be applied in a valuable manner.
                                        Edward de Bono

Decades of research have documented that effective programs for modifying antisocial behavior must be multi-faceted. Although the Prosocial Driver Training Program may be described as a cognitive program, cognition is only one part of the program. Our emphasis on drivers' cognition does not mean that we believe their emotions are not important.

Undoubtedly, how and what one thinks can have a major effect on one's behavior, values, and feelings, and even on one's physical health. However, how individuals behave socially depends not only on their cognition, but also on their feelings, goals, needs, purposes, values, and all of the situational factors that impinge on them. It is not possible to understand social behavior strictly from the analysis of the individual's cognitive processes. Individuals function effectively in many social situations without relying on cognitive processes. Unlike Mr. Spock or Data in Star Trek, humans are not simply analytic, information-processing machines.

There is convincing evidence that participants in R&R programs who have acquired social cognitive skills do apply these skills in social situations outside of the group and thereby improve their ability to solve many interpersonal conflicts which previously would have led to antisocial or deviant behavior. They also learn to avoid many such situations before they develop. However, neither they nor us can avoid all conflict. There are countless times when the problems we encounter on the road will engender heightened emotional and physiological arousal in all of us. A moderate level of arousal in conflict and problem situations is both natural and essential since it energizes and can serve to motivate problem-solving activity. However, very strong feelings and very high levels of arousal may interfere with the individual's application of cognitive skills which he/she has no difficulty using when calm. Drivers who allow their emotions to become more overheated than leaky radiators on a mountain road are unlikely to think clearly or objectively. Accordingly, the Prosocial Driver Training Program includes a module on "The Management of Emotions" in which trainers teach participants how to deal with anger and other emotions.

The success of drivers in successfully coping with the problems, conflicts, and stresses in driving will depend in large measure on their ability to:

- Respond in a manner which prevents them from becoming emotionally aroused.
- Reduce their level of arousal to a moderate level in emotionally provoking situations.

The Prosocial Driver Training Program provides training in relaxation and other cognitive and behavioral techniques that enable drivers to control their level of arousal and to recognize and moderate it before it becomes too high.

Participants are asked to practice the application of the cognitive skills under conditions which correspond as closely as practical to the emotionally charged conflicts they are likely to encounter in driving. Trainers engage participants in practicing the cognitive skills while they are imagining highly arousing problem-driving situations. In constructing the program, we selected sample problems and role-playing scenarios which are designed to engender strong emotional reactions. Participants are asked to image these situations vividly and to respond in role-playing as though they were actually in those situations.

Anger and Other Emotions

> *Anybody can become angry – that is easy; but to be angry*
> *with the right person, and to the right degree, and at the right*
> *time, and for the right purpose, and in the right way – that*
> *is not within everybody's power and is not easy.*
>
>   Aristotle

In the Emotional Management sessions the participants are taught how to effectively control one strong emotion: anger. That is the emotion that is most often the focus of programs to combat 'road rage' and 'aggressive driving.' Anger is frequently triggered among antisocial drivers often by minimal provocation. How the driver attempts to control the level of his/her anger, and how he/she expresses it, frequently engenders even greater problems than the one that triggered the anger in the first place.

Evidence of the efficacy of both cognitive and relaxation techniques in the reduction of driving anger was found in the research conducted by Deffenbacher and his colleagues (e.g., Deffenbacher, Huff, Lynch, Oetting & Salvatore, 2000). However, anger is by no means the only emotion that can be problematic for drivers. There are other emotions that can also engender antisocial driving behaviors: fear, anxiety, sadness, and excitement. The management of emotions module in the Prosocial Driver Training Program was designed to enable trainers to teach drivers how to manage not only anger but also other motions that may be particularly problematic for them.

Teaching the management of emotions in the Prosocial Driver Training Program involves four elements:

- Recognizing the cues which signal that anger is about to be experienced. Participants are taught to realize under what kinds of situations or circumstances they are most likely to feel angry so that they can take action to avoid or be prepared to effectively deal with such situations. The situations are not only those they encounter when driving but also those they encounter at other times. Emotions such as anger that are not effectively managed off the road may travel with drivers on the road and compromise driving safety.

- Taking action to reduce the likelihood that such situations will engender anger. Drivers are taught to begin applying their cognitive skills at the earliest possible opportunity in order to cope with the problems they encounter and thereby prevent or reduce the level of the emotions they might otherwise experience.
- Recognizing the physiological and psychological signs of arousal. By accurately monitoring their level of arousal, individuals can acquire some degree of control over it and often can prevent it from escalating. More important, they become aware of when their anger is beginning to "get-out-of-hand" so that they can take appropriate action to reduce it.
- Finally, they are taught relaxation techniques and cognitive-behavioral techniques which they can use to lower their arousal.

The Management of Emotions module is an adaptation of various techniques long used by psychologists in Anger Management programs. We modified these so that they can be quickly and effectively delivered by Trainers without training in psychology. However, the module is not intended to be a substitute for a more comprehensive anger management program which may be required by drivers who have severe, chronic problems with anger.

The Management of Emotions module is only one aspect of the total program that is directed to teaching drivers how to combat stress.

ALTERNATIVE THINKING

Many antisocial individuals evidence cognitive rigidity – they stubbornly cling to their ideas regardless of contrary evidence. Many antisocial drivers persist in risky driving practices and/or in violating traffic rules in spite of repeated adverse consequences such as apprehension, convictions, and court warnings or more severe forms of punishment. Their perseveration may actually reflect a basic cognitive deficit – they fail to profit from their negative experiences because they view their driving style from a fixed perspective that considers only the immediate, the egocentric, or the macho.

Many of the exercises throughout the program are designed to expand the driver's horizons and move them beyond narrow or restricted thinking. In the Alternative Thinking sessions, some of the techniques developed by de Bono (1985) are used to teach what he refers to as "lateral thinking" – creative thinking that enables the generation of new ideas in contrast to more conventional thinking which tends to inhibit the production of ideas by its dependence on fixed cognitive patterns. The program teaches drivers to think of alternative, prosocial rather than antisocial ways of responding to the problems they experience while driving or anywhere else.

de Bono's techniques are described in an impressive quantity of publications. They can be effectively used to help antisocial individuals to understand the social, legal, and economic consequences of their offensive behavior. The Prosocial Driver Training Program adapted these techniques for antisocial drivers to teach them to consider the consequences of their driving not only in terms of its immediate effects but also in relation to its long-term effects for themselves, for their families, and for society at large.

Training involves the following steps:

- Presenting the group with examples of antisocial beliefs about driving laws and regulations. Examples are: "*On the road it is every one for him/herself*"; "*All traffic lights should be abolished*"; "*Drivers should be allowed to drive at whatever speed they wish*"; "*No one should be allowed to drive until they have demonstrated that they can weave in and out of traffic on the highway.*"
- Asking them to express their thoughts on it;
- Introducing them to a tool which enables them to consider it in a way that enables them to go well beyond their previous thinking. The tools are used to stimulate them to engage in brainstorming activities designed to teach them to consider both the positive and the negative aspects of traffic rules and regulations and of various driving styles; to consider all the factors involved in creating driving laws and in choosing a driving style; to consider the short-term consequences and long-term sequels of such choices; to consider their aims, goals, and objectives in choosing how they drive; to determine their first important priorities in various driving situations and to consider their merit; and to think about the points of view of other drivers.

One goal of this module is to teach drivers to make their thinking deliberative rather than responsive; reasoned rather than reactive; open rather than closed-minded; and responsive to a broad rather than a narrow perception of the world of driving. However, in the Prosocial Driver Training Program, we use de Bono's thinking tools for another purpose: to give drivers a technique for examining the thinking of others.

Once they have learned the tools and have applied them to their own thinking they are asked to observe whether the thinking that other people use (both in the group and elsewhere) is adequate – i.e., whether other drivers are considering matters as broadly, carefully and systematically as the participant has been enabled to do by using the tools. By getting them to examine other's thinking, the drivers' awareness of their own thinking and the development of their social perspective-taking are fostered.

VALUES ENHANCEMENT

The important thing is to persuade drivers that to Violate is antisocial even when they get away with it, that Violating is just not on, and that decent citizens feel bad if they do it.
DETR (2001)

There is little sense in teaching driving skills, cognitive skills, social skills, or any other kind of skill to antisocial drivers unless one also teaches values. Otherwise one's program may only produce more skilled antisocial drivers.

However, we must ask: what values should we teach? That is a highly controversial matter. Many would argue that in our complex society there is no longer any universally accepted system of values. There is considerable disagreement even about fundamental principles or morality and ethics. Values which are "correct" for one group may be repudiated by other groups. Values are, indeed, relative to subgroups and even to individuals within subgroups. Values are also relative to time, place, and circumstance and change frequently in a rapidly changing world.

There is one value which is universally endorsed: concern for other people. It is this value which we believe must be acquired by antisocial drivers and must guide and control their social behavior on the road; it is this value which is a major target of all the exercises in our program and the primary focus of our *Values Enhancement* module.

Virtually all moral perspectives would endorse the position that consideration of the needs of others is a basic requirement for safe and courteous driving. In driving, as in any other social activity, one should be concerned with and behave in such a way as to accommodate the legitimate rights and needs of other people. One does not have to be a religious zealot to appreciate that the Rules Of The Road are based on the principle that driving in a considerate manner is the most likely way to yield the greatest benefit for everyone on the road and is essential for ensuring efficient traffic flow and everyone's safety. Unfortunately, many antisocial drivers do not adequately grasp the principle and thus may not respect those Rules.

Rules Of The Road booklets are required reading for driving license applicants in most countries of the world. Unfortunately, such booklets seldom mention courtesy; cooperation; manners; or concern for others. Moreover, there are few rewards for displaying such behavior when driving. The feeling of satisfaction that can ensure from driving courteously and safely is not likely to be viewed by antisocial drivers as being of equal value to the feelings of excitement and power that can ensue from risky driving.

Many antisocial drivers view traffic rules and informal principles for safe and courteous driving only as restrictions on their personal freedom. Many fail to understand or appreciate the purpose of such rules and conventions. Accordingly, it might be helpful if the underlying principles and values involved in safe driving practices were taught to drivers before they obtain their license. However, many might not grasp the value of such values because they lack basic social perspective-taking skills or empathy.

Some antisocial drivers lack empathy either at the emotional level or the cognitive level. They may be unable to *feel* what other individuals may be experiencing (emotional empathy), and/or they may be unable to *understand* what others are feeling (cognitive empathy).

Many antisocial drivers may have developed empathy but not in sufficient strength that would lead them to express it in driving situations when overwhelmed by stress. Many stop being empathetic when it is safe to be selfish and there seems to be little immediate benefit to be gained by being empathetic. Others may have acquired empathetic ability and express it in their everyday life but fail to do so when they are driving because they do not perceive driving as an interpersonal activity in which empathy is necessary. Many may feel that on the road empathy is neither necessary nor appropriate.

It is unlikely that anyone can feel what another person is feeling unless they first have some understanding of what the other person is experiencing. If one cannot understand what others are feeling it is unlikely that one will have concern for them. The Prosocial Driver Training Program is designed to teach interpersonal understanding, to teach antisocial drivers to understand how other drivers may be thinking and to understand how other drivers are feeling.

A Values Enhancement module was developed in which participants are engaged in activities which require that they think about the feelings of others. This is done by exposing them to social and cognitive conflict – by creating situations in which they find that they are in conflict about what they believe and in which their ideas are in conflict with those of others. In such situations the participants are required to seriously question and examine their ideas about the laws of driving and the *morality* of their own and others' driving styles. More important, they are impelled to consider the legal and moral perspectives of other drivers and of society at large.

It is an assumption of the program that it is both possible and essential to lead drivers to think beyond their egocentric world view and develop a broader social perspective of their driving behavior and their driving responsibilities. The message that is conveyed in the Prosocial Driver Training Program is that rules and regulations, accommodation to the needs of others, and good manners are an essential precondition for cooperation in all human activities, including driving, and have value in helping everyone achieve shared goals.

The Prosocial Driver Training Program approach to values enhancement is not character education or indoctrination. We reject any attempt to inculcate values by preaching, moralizing, or sermonizing. We do so primarily because we do not believe such approaches will be effective with antisocial drivers. Participants are likely to ignore or summarily reject attempts to tell them what values they should or must adopt. Installing signals on the roof of cars that can flash "THANK YOU" or "SORRY" messages will not suffice.

As an alternative, we recommend challenging drivers to examine their beliefs, raising questions which stimulate them to reconsider their views, and consider alternative perspectives. Trainers are instructed how to challenge the participants' egocentric thinking and how to persuade them to try to understand and appreciate the views, wishes, attitudes, and feelings of other drivers.

Our approach to improving the values of offenders is multifaceted. There are several major methods by which trainers can improve their participant's values:

- The specific Values Enhancement sessions;
- All of the other techniques in the program. All have been designed to teach some specific cognitive skill, but they have also been designed to create situations which stimulate participants to think about their values. No single item in the program is value-free.
- Trainers ensure that in all exercises and activities throughout the program; (1) participants are aware of the values issue; (2) participants consider carefully how their values influence both their thoughts and their actions; and (3) participants are aware of the value implications of their driving style.
- Modeling – whether they like it or not, trainers serve as a model for participants. They must not only be models of the social cognitive skills they are teaching; they must also be models of the values they hope the participants will acquire. Trainers are required to frequently reinforce participant's prosocial talk and actions. That is, they take as many opportunities as possible to support and encourage (by word or gesture) the behavior and verbalizations of participants which reflect prosocial attitudes. Moreover, they also respond to participants' antisocial driving talk by *questioning* the participants about the personal and social implications and consequences of such positions.
- Current Events and Personal Anecdotes: Participants are required to bring to the sessions news articles, advertisements, and anecdotes which are drawn from current newspapers, TV, etc. which exemplify the values that are reflected in both antisocial and prosocial driving behaviors.

CRITICAL REASONING

As indicated earlier, cognitive skills training that is provided in R&R programs is not the same as cognitive therapy or cognitive behavior modification. Such programs are designed to modify *what* a client thinks. In contrast, cognitive skills training is designed to teach a client *how* to think. Antisocial individuals need to learn *how* to think before they can be taught *what* to think.

An essential aspect of learning how to think is learning how to think critically. Critical thinking does not mean finding fault with something or someone. Rather, it refers to a particular quality of thinking – thinking carefully, logically, and rationally.

The adjective, "critical," is meant to indicate that individuals who use such thinking can and do judge or evaluate their thinking and the thinking of others in order to ensure that it is logical and rational; that their conclusions and those which are presented to them by others have been arrived at without flaws in logic, and are based on sufficient and correct information rather than on biases; unwarranted assumptions; distortion of facts; or untested opinions.

The thinking of many antisocial drivers tends to be emotional rather than rational. As a result, they often evidence erroneous beliefs and unreasonable attitudes about driving. For example, many risk driving through traffic at excessive speed, or risk passing other drivers in unsafe circumstances thinking that passing will enable them to get to their destination more quickly. They do so even though their savings in time is minimal at the best of times and negative at the worst of times (e.g., when they are stopped by the police or are involved in a collision). They think that their hurry represents 'time well spent' but actually is 'time wasted.'

Many drivers fail or are unable to critically evaluate their own opinions or the views of others. This is most frequently seen in the behavior of adolescent drivers who are overly responsive to the risky driving modeled by their peers and fail to critically assess the wisdom of copying it. The Prosocial Driver Training Program teaches them critical reasoning so that they will not be easily misled into complying with norms that are inappropriate (such as riding as a passenger in a car driven by a driver they know has been drinking). They must learn the fallacy and folly of *argumentum ad populum.*

Cognitive Exercises

The program includes a variety of problem-solving exercises and games which provide challenging and highly entertaining exercises for stimulating participants to think and to practice some of the social cognitive skills being taught in training. The games and exercises are used not just for recreation but for teaching social cognition.

Process vs. Content

The program's exercises and activities aim to teach basic problem-solving, conflict-resolution and interpersonal skills and values. They are designed to take the participants beyond a narrow, concretistic mode of thinking, to help them develop abstract reasoning skills, and to broaden their view of the driving world beyond the immediate, the obvious, and the egocentric. Accordingly, most sessions deal with matters of principle and value in interpersonal and social interaction. However, the program is not limited to philosophical or intellectual discussions on abstract issues. The discussions focus on practical driving matters.

Group Size

The ideal group size for cognitive training varies with the characteristics of the members of each particular group, but generally the aim should be to have eight to fourteen participants. Groups can function with less than six members, but they are limited in the number of subgroup techniques one can use and the variety of different perspectives to which individual participants are exposed. Groups composed of more than fourteen limit the opportunities for individual members to express their views and some larger groups may be difficult to control given the intensity of discussion which is desired. Individual applications can also be conducted by experienced trainers.

Facilities

The program requires no special facilities or equipment except an overhead projector, a flip-chart, and video recording and playback equipment. The Prosocial Driver Training Program can be conducted in any setting that can accommodate a group of eight to fourteen participants in such a way that each is in full view of the others and the trainer. There must be sufficient room to enable two participants to role-play in full view of the video camera and the other participants.

Training vs. Informing

Very few concepts are taught in the program through didactic presentations. The exception is the material on the effects of alcohol and other substances. The teacher is more of a process facilitator and less a source of factual information. The Trainer is also a model of the prosocial skills and values he/she wishes to impart.

The primary vehicle for teaching the cognitive skills is small group discussion with particular emphasis on Socratic dialogue. Trainers seek to establish a group atmosphere which is informal, thought provoking, stimulating, lively, and debate-like. The sessions are often loud and emotional but controlled. They are also deliberately frustrating and unsettling. The goal is to challenge participants to think about questions and issues rather than to give them answers. The sessions are conducted at a brisk pace both to maintain interest and to stimulate a high level of cognitive activity.

Social-cognitive theory suggests that cognitive development requires that "individuals face others who contradict their own intuitively derived concepts and points of view, and thereby create cognitive conflicts whose resolutions result in the construction of higher forms of reasoning" (Bearison, 1982).

The Prosocial Driver Training Program also accords with the theory of planned behavior (Ajzen, 1985) which proposes that in small group discussions reasoned action can be engendered through the group process in which group norms are made more explicit. A study in Sweden found that group discussion was the most effective of four strategies in reducing collision rate over a two year period (Gregerson, 1996). Further evidence of the value of engendering reasoned action in small group sessions in improving driving behavior has been indicated by the work of Parker, Stradling, and Manstead (1996); and that of Anthony (1996).

Program Length

The program was designed to be taught in twelve sessions, each session comprising two hours. Thus, the program is twenty-four hours in length. However, where time does not permit application of the entire program, a shorter (6 session) program is available. The shorter program may serve to whet the appetite of participants and motivate them to seek further training through the complete program regimen. It may also help participants begin the process of cognitive development by encouraging them to examine their thinking (and that of others) and to realize how their thinking affects their feelings and behavior and, consequently, their driving.

There is no maximum number of hours for the Prosocial Driver Training Program. It is possible, by following directions in the program Handbook, to extend the program into a long-term program where appropriate.

Program Schedule

The sessions can be delivered in almost any schedule that suits the requirements of the agency and the availability of the participants. The ideal is between two to four sessions a week. More compressed and more extended schedules are possible but compressed schedules limit the time available for participants to digest the material and to practice the skills they have acquired in the sessions. Distributing the sessions too widely may result in reducing the participants' motivation and in their forgetting previously taught materials.

Motivation

An underlying assumption of the program is that the participant's motivation for change is not only his/her responsibility, or that of the trainer, but is the responsibility of the program. Few antisocial drivers are likely to arrive at the trainer's door eager to become involved in driver retraining or cognitive skills training.

Most will arrive expressing hostility and resentment about restrictions to their freedom and thinly-veiled opposition to a program that aims to challenge the adequacy of their driving behavior. Because it was assumed that participants would not be well motivated, care was taken to maximize the likelihood that in both content and process the program would be enjoyable for participants (and trainers) and would motivate them to realize that they need what the program has to offer.

Prochaska, Norcross, and DiClemente (1982) have proposed a model of the change process which suggests that behavior change should be thought of as a process involving a series of stages. The Prosocial Driver Training Program accords well with that model. Most participants will be in the initial stage – they have not yet personally identified a need for change in their driving behavior because they consider it unnecessary or because they believe that their driving style provides valuable outcomes that far outweigh its possible negative consequences.

We view the Prosocial Driver Training Program not just as a training program but as a motivational program which stimulates individuals with low motivation for change to move through the stages of change. A primary goal of the early sessions of the program is to stimulate the participants to realize and think about the fact that, although their approach to driving may make them feel better temporarily, it significantly affects their well-being both on and off the road. It also leads them to realize and appreciate that there are alternative ways of thinking and behaving which would yield them fewer conflicts and more personal satisfaction in their interactions with other drivers. It then helps them to become aware that a change may be desirable and teaches them social cognitive skills which enable them to take effective action to achieve change. The reinforcement which is yielded by their newly-acquired skills can serve as a motivator to help them maintain their changed behavior.

Initial Meeting

An initial, preprogram individual meeting is used for orienting and motivating the participants. In this meeting the purpose of the program is explained. The explanation varies with the individual needs of the participant and the trainer's personal style, but often approximates the following:

> Research has shown that an individual's skill in driving depends on his/her thinking or reasoning skills. A high I.Q. is no guarantee that the individual will become a successful or a safe driver. Skill in maneuvering a car is important but is no guarantee of safe driving – many of the most 'competent' drivers have collisions. They include professional drivers, bus drivers, and even racing car drivers. *All* drivers need something else. They need skills that will enable them to anticipate the actions of other drivers, skills in recognizing hazards, skills in controlling their emotions, and skills that enable them to avoid conflict with other drivers.
>
> Research has found that all of those skills require that drivers must first have skills in reasoning, thinking, and problem-solving. These skills are called 'cognitive skills.' They can be learned. You may already have some of them and you can help us teach them to others. You can learn more skills in the Prosocial Driver Training Program.
>
> The skills are relatively easy to learn and you will find learning them enjoyable, but also hard work. It requires that you attend the sessions regularly, that you participate seriously and fully in each of them and that you practice the skills you learn in each session as often as you can between sessions.
>
> Your group will meet approximately X times for two hours each time. Often I will ask you to work on some assignment between sessions. The assignments will usually consist of practicing the skills we have worked on in the group. These will be opportunities for you to test your ability to apply the skill learned in the group. Practice is essential.

The initial meeting is also designed to give the Trainer an opportunity to develop rapport with the participant using motivational interviewing techniques.

Individual Differences

The initial interview also provides the Trainer with an opportunity through a structured series of questions and with measures of the participant's driving history, attitudes, and behavior to assess the individual's characteristics and provide feedback to him/her as to both why they need the program and how it can benefit both them and the other drivers with whom they must interact on the road.

The program provides modular flexibility to accommodate staggered entry and differential intervention according to the characteristics of the participants. Not all antisocial drivers evidence cognitive difficulties, but a considerable number do. Moreover, those who evidence inadequate competence in some cognitive skills may be fully competent in other social cognitive functions. A number of typologies for differentiating drivers in terms of their characteristics have been proposed (e.g., Beirness & Simpson, 1988; Deery & Fildes, 1999; Donovan et al., 1985). However, well-standardized and reliable tests that would enable specific allocation of subgroups of antisocial drivers to differential treatment are not yet available. Accordingly, trainers are instructed to screen their prospective clients in the initial interview and to continually monitor their performance in the program activities in order that they can tailor the program to their specific needs.

Helper Therapy

It is not easy to change the driving behavior of antisocial drivers by attempts to convince them that their over-rating of their driving skills and their unwarranted optimism about their chances of being involved in collisions is unrealistic and jeopardizes their personal safety. It is much easier to get them to change their behavior by persuading them to be concerned about the safety of *others*.

Throughout the program the antisocial drivers are encouraged to share teaching tasks such as helping other participants, leading discussions, or even conducting part of a session (provided they have sufficient competence). There are enough tasks to be performed in the program that most participants can be assigned responsibility for some. They are asked to be teachers for each other, and to exercise the skills that they are being taught when they are assuming such roles. We also recommend that Trainers enable drivers who are graduates of the program to serve as Assistant Trainers in subsequent groups. By encouraging antisocial individuals to act in prosocial roles, they often come to appreciate the value of prosocial behavior, to recognize the awards it can bring them, and to acquire social skills which can serve as alternatives to their antisocial behavior. Individuals who are placed in such roles often come to see themselves in a very different light and begin to attribute to themselves positive, prosocial characteristics which were foreign to them.

Our emphasis on involving participants as co-teachers is based on the adage that "the best way to learn anything is to teach it." One can become attached to an idea by advocating it. Moreover, research in social psychology indicates that individuals tend to attribute to themselves characteristics of the roles they play. Thus, if we can subtly get people to behave in ways in which they do not normally behave, they come to attribute to themselves the characteristics of people who usually behave in those ways.

We recommend, wherever practical, that agencies engage participants in voluntary activities such as auxiliary helpers of police, or as volunteer support givers for accident victims and their families at hospitals, or as volunteer participants in school programs on driving. We encourage them when appropriate, to become members of such groups as "Highway Watchers"; "Driver Watchdogs"; "Highway Angels" (the highway equivalents of Neighborhood Watch). For example, members of such groups (who currently are mostly truckers) contact the police when they spot drivers who are driving in a hazardous manner. When placed in such roles many come to see themselves in a very different light; they come to see themselves as prosocial rather than antisocial drivers. Moreover, they often come to appreciate the value of prosocial behavior as they begin to recognize the rewards it can bring them.

Homework

In order to foster the transfer of cognitive skills from the classroom to 'real-life,' each session includes specific instructions to participants to practice outside the group situation the skills they have learned in the session. They are directed to try out the skills in appropriate situations. If possible, they are asked to teach them to others. They are, in fact, encouraged to become 'prosocial back-seat drivers' for their family and friends.

Participants are asked to pay attention and observe how other drivers behave. They are often surprised to see how well they themselves do in comparison with others who have not been trained. Each session also includes some time for obtaining feedback from participants on their "out-of-class" observations and experiences including their observations of 'Random Acts of Road Respect.'

Homework assignments are also designed to lead the participants to acquire a view that driving is a skilled behavior, but that the skills include not only motor skills but also social and cognitive skills.

Training vs. Therapy

It is a fundamental premise of our cognitive model that the best approach to treatment for antisocial drivers is an educational one – directly and systematically training them in the skills needed to live and drive more effectively. We advise both trainers and participants that the program is not designed to deal with the driver's personal problems. It is not therapy. Cognitive training has been found to be therapeutic in that it fosters improved interpersonal and social adjustment. However, cognitive training is not therapy that deals directly with the driver's personal, social, or emotional problems. On the contrary, the Prosocial Driver Training Program is designed to equip drivers with skills which will enable them to deal with these problems themselves whenever possible. It teaches skills which will also help them to avoid such problems in the first place. This is not to deny the importance of such problems; it is only to suggest that they not be allowed to become the content of the discussions and thereby distract from the primary goal of the program.

It is clearly essential that the driver's personal/social/situational problems and his/her illegal behavior be effectively responded to. However, we suggest that these matters should be left out of the cognitive training sessions and dealt with elsewhere. Their participation in the cognitive skills program is likely to make the drivers more willing to accept help with their problems and their improved cognitive skills may equip them to benefit from the counseling and other assistance that other programs may provide.

We also discourage participants from discussing their driving history in the sessions. We do not want them to compete with each other in terms of who is the fastest or most daring driver or who has the most impressive record for avoiding apprehension for breaches of driving regulations. We also do not want to allow them to promote the impression that their most important characteristic is their fast or risky driving. The focus of the program is the driver's thinking, not his/her driving history.

RELAPSE PREVENTION

Strategies for extending and maintaining responsible driving and preventing regression to earlier behavior following their program participation include teaching students the principles of monitoring and modifying their own behavior. For example, since rewards for safe driving are relatively rare, the student is taught to find a source of internal reward that can be used to maintain the behavior. The relapse prevention techniques include teaching students to identify high-risk situations and problem-solving strategies that enable them to avoid or cope with such situations (Sulzer-Azaroff, 1994, 1991).

The value of relapse prevention has been demonstrated in the rehabilitation of drivers convicted of driving while disqualified (Bakker, Hudson & Ward, 2000; Bakker, Ward, Cryer & Hudson, 1997). The research of Bakker and his associates was limited to disqualified drivers who are a distinct group of antisocial drivers. Some of the components provided in the Prosocial Driver Training Program were included in their ten-week intervention with groups of eight to twelve male offenders: social skills, anger management, problem-solving, and relapse prevention.

Interestingly, the program not only reduced violations of license revocation among the 144 drivers compared to matched controls for lengths of time ranging from one month to three years. It also led to improvements on a number of social competency variables. The researchers also reported that although their program yielded no difference in the number of subsequent drunk-driving convictions, it appeared that the program may have reduced other types of subsequent criminal offending. Unfortunately, the program did not include training in alternative thinking, negotiation, or values which we consider essential in our multifaceted program.

Role Of The Trainer

The Handbook for the program is not just a cookbook that provides a recipe which anyone can follow step-by-step and expect to create an effective program. The Handbook describes the essential ingredients for a cognitive program and indicates how these ingredients should be prepared and served; but a successful program requires more than that. It requires a good cook who knows not only how to follow a recipe but also how to modify it to suit the characteristics of his clientele and how to serve it so it is optimally palatable. The success of the program depends in large measure on the quality of the trainer.

Trainers are not lecturers who are providing information, nor preachers who are inculcating values, nor therapists who are trying to counsel people, nor entertainers who are only providing stimulation and enjoyment for the participants' leisure time. Trainers are taught in Prosocial Driver Training Program training workshops to act as teachers in all the positive senses of that term. Trainers listen as well and as often as they speak. They not only stimulate, encourage, and empathize; they also challenge. They model the prosocial interpersonal skills they wish the participants to learn.

Training In Context

Cognitive training is not conducted in a vacuum, so many hours a week in isolation from the rest of the participant's everyday life. Nor is it designed to replace other programs; but wherever possible it should be integrated with or specifically paired with other programs such as driving training for novice drivers, retraining in driving skills, defensive driving courses, or advanced driving courses.

A comprehensive approach to increasing the frequency of safe and courteous driving requires not only enrolling antisocial drivers in prosocial training programs but doing so as part of a comprehensive strategy that enlists the active participation and support of other members of the community such as families, social agencies, police, automobile associations, car manufacturers, insurance companies, courts, and legislators.

The program should be implemented in such a way that significant individuals in the participant's environment – parents, spouses, friends, probation officers, etc. – understand the principles of the program, and reinforce and encourage the participant's skill acquisition. There is mounting evidence of the significant influence of friends and parents on the driving behavior of adolescents.[16] For example, low risk driving adolescents have been found to be more than three times more likely to report low parental monitoring and two times more likely to report low parental restrictions (Hartos, Eitel & Simons-Morton, 2002). However,

---

16. Beck, Shattuck & Raleigh, 2001; Beck, Hartos & Simons-Morton, 2002; Ferguson et al., 2001; Hartos, Eitel, Haynie & Simons-Morton, 2000; Jaffee & D'Zurilla, 2003; Kennedy, Isaac, Nelson, & Graham, 1997).

parents can be persuaded to adopt driving agreements and impose greater restrictions on early teen driving (Simons-Morton & Hartos, 2003).

The *R&R2 SHORT Version for Parents* has been developed to respond to the need to involve significant others in the training process. This program informs parents and other individuals such as social workers and probation officers about the skills the program teaches and, where possible, gives them assignments which will enable them to contribute to the program's effectiveness.

The program which is subtitled *Road-Proofing The Teen Age Driver*, is designed for parents of adolescents who are at that stage in adolescent development which for many parents is the most anxious moment of their lives – when their children are old enough to learn how to drive. It is a time when many parents might wish that their children could be placed in a deep-freeze until they have achieved emotional maturity. The greatest fear of many parents is that a police officer, hat in hand, will knock on their door. There is little consolation in telling them that it is likely that the same police officer has been knocking at the doors of other parents whose adolescents were killed in the same car. The program is designed to equip adolescents with the social cognitive skills and values that make it likely that they will become prosocial drivers. Parents can help.

CONCLUSION

Drivers require training in driving skills, training in hazard recognition, and training in risk assessment. They need to realistically appraise their driving skills. They need to be informed of the potential consequences of reckless and risky driving and the legal, familial, and social consequences of drinking and driving. They need to understand the effects of alcohol and other drugs and the lack of sleep on driving skill. They need to be taught how their thinking, their feelings, and their driving behaviors can be as great a hazard as the external hazards they are likely to encounter on the road. However, they also need to be taught to think, to reason, to consider, to reflect, and to care so that such lessons will be driven home. Good driving is no accident.

REFERENCES

AAA. (1997). *Aggressive driving: Three studies on road rage.* American Automobile Association.

Abdennur, A. (2000). *Camouflaged aggression: The hidden threat to individuals and organizations.* Calgary: Detselig Enterprises.

Aberg, L., & Rimmo, P. (1998). Dimensions of aberrant driver behavior. *Ergonomics, 41,* 39–46.

Addiction Research Foundation. (1992). *Alcohol, other drugs and driving.* Toronto, ON.

Ahadi, S. A., & Rothbart, M. K. (1994). Temperament, development and the Big Five. In C. F. Halverson, G. A. Kohnstamm, & R. P. Martin (Eds.). *The developing structure of temperament and personality from infancy to adulthood.* Hillsdale, NJ: Erlbaum.

Ajzen, I. (1985). From intentions to actions: A theory of planned behavior. In J. Kuhl and J. Beckmann (Eds.). *Action control: From cognition to behavior.* New York, NY: Springer Verlag.

Akhtar, N., & Bradley, E. J. (1991). Social information processing deficits of aggressive children: Present findings and implications for social skills training. *Clinical Psychology Review, 11,* 621–644.

Allen, J. P., Leadbeater, B. J., & Aber, J. L. (1990). The relationship of adolescents' expectations and values to delinquency, hard drug use, and unprotected sexual intercourse. *Development and Psychopathology, 2,* 85–98.

Allen, J. P., MacKenzie, D. L., & Hickman, L. J. (2001). The effectiveness of cognitive behavioral treatment for adult offenders: A methodological quality-based review. *International Journal of Offender Therapy & Comparative Criminology, 45,* 498–514.

Al-Quabasi, Q. D., Al-Mofareth, M. A., Al-Bunyan, A. R., Al-Karion, A., & Hague, M. M. (1989). Road traffic fatalities in Riyadh Central Hospital. *Annals of Saudi Medicine, 9,* 10–14.

Anderson, B.J., Snow, R.W., & Wells-Parker, E. (2000). Comparing the predictive validity of DUI risk screening instruments: Development of validation standards. *Addiction, 95,* 915–929.

Andreou, E. (2000). Bully/victim problems and their association with coping behavior in conflictual peer interactions. *Educational Psychology, 21,* 59–66.

Andrews, D. (1989). Recidivism is predictable and can be influenced: Using risk assessments to reduce recidivism. *Forum on Correctional Research, 1,* 11–18.

Andrews, D. (2000). *Effective practice – Future directions. In sustaining effectiveness in working with offenders.* Cognitive Centre Foundation: DinasPowys, Wales.

Andrews, D. A., Zinger, I., Hoge, R. D., Bonta, J., Gendreau, P., & Cullen, F. T. (1990). Does correctional treatment work? A clinically relevant and psychologically informed meta-analysis. *Criminology, 28,* 369–404.

Annis, H. M., & Davis, C. S. (1989). Relapse prevention. In R. K. Hester & W. R. Miller (Eds.). *Handbook of alcoholism treatment approaches.* New York: Pergamon Press.

Anthony, S. B. (1996). Modifying beliefs and attitudes to exceeding the speed limit: An intervention study based on the theory of planned behavior. *Journal of Applied Social Psychology, 26,* 1–19.

Antonowicz, D. (2002). *Hostile attributional biases, driving anger, and roadway aggression among university students: Application of a model of affective aggression.* Doctoral dissertation, Carleton University.

Antonowicz, D., & Ross, R. R. (1994). Essential components of successful rehabilitation programs for offenders. *International Journal of Offender Therapy and Comparative Criminology, 38,* 97–104.

Argeriou, M., McCarthy, D., & Blacker, E. (1985). Criminality among individuals arraigned for drinking and driving in Massachusetts. *Journal of Studies on Alcohol, 46,* 525–530.

Arms, R. L., & Russel, G. W. (1997). Impulsivity, fight history, and camaraderie as predictors of a willingness to escalate a disturbance. *Current Psychology: Developmental, Learning, Personality, Social, 15,* 279–285.

Arnett, J., Offer, D., & Fine, M. A. (1997). Reckless driving in adolescence: "State" and "trait" factors. *Accident Analysis & Prevention, 29,* 57–63.

Arthur, B., Barrett, G. V., & Alexander, R. A. (1992). Prediction of vehicular involvement: A meta-analysis. *Human Performance, 4,* 89–105.

Arthur, W., & Doverspike, D. (1992). Locus of control and auditory selective attention as predictors of driving accident involvement: A comparative longitudinal investigation. *Journal of Safety Research, 23,* 73–80.

Arthur, W., & Doverspike, D. (2001). Predicting motor vehicle crash involvement from a personality measure and a driving knowledge test. *Journal of Prevention & Intervention in the Community, 5,* 35–42.

Arthur, W., & Graziano, W. G. (1996). The five-factor model, conscientiousness, and driving accident involvement. *Journal of Personality, 64,* 593–618.

Arthur, W., Strong, M. H., & Williamson, J. (1994). Validation of a visual attention test as a predictor of driving accident involvement. *Journal of Occupational & Organizational Psychology, 67,* 173–182.

Austin, J. (1997). *Evaluation of the Drug After-Care Program and the Reasoning & Rehabilitation Program in California Probation.* Unpublished manuscript. Washington, DC: National Council on Crime & Delinquency.

Aviolo, B.J., Kroeck, K. G., & Panek, P. E. (1985). Individual differences in information processing ability as a predictor of motor vehicle accidents. *Human Factors, 27,* 577–587.

Ayres, M., Hayward, P., & Perry, D. (2003). *Motoring Offenses and Breath Test Statistics.* London: Home Office, 2003.

Baker, C. C., Oppenheimer, L., & Stephens, B. (1980). Epidemiology of traumatic details. *American Journal of Surgery, 140,* 149–150.

Bakker, L. W., Hudson, S. M., & Ward, T. (2000). Reducing recidivism in driving while disqualified: A treatment evaluation. *Criminal Justice & Behavior, 27,* 531–560.

Bakker, L. W., Ward, T., Cryer, M., & Hudson, S. (1997). Out of the rut: A cognitive-behavioral treatment programme for disqualified drivers. *Behavior Change, 14,* 29–38.

Bandura, A., & Walters, R. H. (1963). *Social learning and personality development.* New York: Holt, Rinehart and Winston.

Barnes, G. M., & Welte, J. W. (1988). Predictors of driving while intoxicated among teenagers. *Journal of Drug Issues, 18,* 367–384.

Barrett, G. V. (1968). Relationship between embedded figures test performance and simulator behavior. *Journal of Applied Psychology, 53,* 253–254.

Bartl, G., & Stummvoll, G. (2000). Description of post-licensing methods in Austria. In G. Bartl (Ed.). *DAN-Report. Results of EU- project: Description and Analysis of Post Licensing Measures for Novice Drivers.* Kuratorium fur Verkehrssicherheit.

Bassett, J. F., Cate, K. L., & Dabbs, J. M. Jr. (2002). Individual differences in self-presentation style: Driving an automobile and meeting a stranger. *Self & Identity, 1,* 281–288.

Bauer, J. (1955). The teen age rebel and his weapon – The automobile. *Traffic Safety, 518,* 10–13.

Baxter, J., Manstead, A., Stradling, S., Campbell, K., Reason, J., & Parker, D. (1990). Social facilitation and driver behavior. *British Journal of Psychology, 81,* 351–360.

Bearison, D. J. (1982). New directions in studies of social interaction and cognitive growth. In. F. C. Serafica (Ed.). *Social-cognitive development in context.* New York: Guilford Press.

Beck, A. T., Wright, F. D., Newman, C. F., & Liese, B. S. (1993). *Cognitive therapy of substance abuse.* New York: Guilford Press.

Beck, K. H., Hartos, J., & Simons-Morton, B. (2002). Teen driving risk: The promise of parental influence and public policy. *Health Education & Behavior, 29,* 73–84.

Beck, K. H., Shattuck, T., & Raleigh, R. (2001). Parental predictors of teen driving risk. *American Journal of Health Behavior, 25,* 10–20.

Beenstock, M., Gafni, D., & Goldin, E. (2001). The effect of traffic policing on road safety in Israel. *Accident Analysis & Prevention, 33,* 2001, 73–80.

Beirness, D., & Simpson, H. (1997). *Study of the profile of high-risk drivers: Final report.* Ottawa: Traffic Injury Research Foundation.

Beirness, D., & Simpson, H. M. (1988). Lifestyle correlates of risky driving and accident involvement among youth. *Alcohol, Drugs & Driving, 4,* 193–204.

Bener, A., Abouammoh, A. M., & El-Khalout, G. R. (1992). Road traffic accidents in Riyadh. *Journal Royal Society of Health, 108,* 34–36.

Berger, R.J., & Persinger, G. (1980). *Survey of public perception of highway safety.* McLean, VA: Automated Services, Inc.

Bird, G. W., Stith, S. M., & Schlade, J. (2001). Psychological resources, coping strategies, and negotiation styles as discriminators of violence in dating relationships. *Journal of Applied Family & Child Studies, 40,* 45–50.

Bjoerkqvist, K., & Oesterman, K. (1999). Social intelligence=empathy=aggression? *Aggression & Violent Behavior, 5,* 191–200.

Blaszczynski, A., Steel, Z., & McConaghy, N. (1997). Impulsivity in pathological gambling: The antisocial impulsivist. *Addiction, 92,* 75–87.

Blechman, E. A., & Culhane, S. E. (1993). Early adolescence and the development of aggression, depression, coping and competence. *Journal of Early Adolescence, 13,* 361–382.

Blechman, E. A., Lowell, E. S., & Garrett, J. (1999). Prosocial coping and substance use during pregnancy. *Addictive Behaviors, 24,* 99–109.

Block, J., Block, J. H., & Keyes, S. (1988). Longitudinally foretelling drug use in adolescence: Early childhood personality and environmental precursors. *Child Development, 59,* 336–355.

Blockley, P. N., & Hartley, L. R. (1995). Aberrant driving behavior: Errors and violations. *Ergonomics, 38,* 1759–1771.

Bradford, J., & Dimock, J. (1986). A comparative study of adolescents and adults who wilfully set fires. *Psychiatric Review of the University of Ottawa, 11,* 228–234.

Brookhuis, K., deVries, G., & deWaard, D. (1991). The effects of mobile telephoning on driving performance. *Accident Analysis and Prevention, 23,* 309–316.

Brow, R. A. (1980). Conventional education and controlled drinking education courses with convicted drunk drivers. *Behavior Therapy, 11,* 632–642.

Brown, I. D. (1982). Exposure and experience are a confounded nuisance in research on driver behavior. *Accident Analysis & Prevention, 14,* 345–352.

Brown, I. D., & Groeger, J. A. (1988). Risk perception and decision taking during the transition between novice and experienced driver status. *Ergonomics, 31,* 585–597.

Brown, I. D., Groeger, J. A., & Biehl, B. (1987). Is training contributing enough to road safety? In J. A. Rothengatter & R. A. de Bruin (Eds.). *Road users and traffic safety,* van Gorcum: Assen, Maastricht.

Buntan-Riklefs, R. (1992). *Report for NHTSA.* Washington, DC: Department of Transportation.

Burian, S. E., Liguori, A., & Robinson, J. H (2002). Effects of alcohol on risk-taking during simulated driving. *Human Psychopharmacology: Clinical & Experimental, 17,* 141–150.

Caldwell, M. (1999). *A short history of rudeness: Manners, morals, and misbehavior in modern America.* New York: St. Martin's Press.

Canada Safety Council (2000). *Personal communication.* Ottawa: Canada Safety Council.

Cantos , A. L., Neale, J. M., O'Leary, K. D., & Gaines, R. W. (1997). Assessment of coping strategies of child abusing mothers. *Child Abuse and Neglect, 21,* 631–636.

Carlo, G., Koller, S., & Eisenberg, N. (1998). Prosocial moral reasoning in institutionalized delinquent, orphaned, and noninstitutionalized Brazilian adolescents. *Journal of Adolescent Research, 13,* 363–376.

Carroll, J. S. (1982). Committing a crime: The offender's decision. In J. Konecni & E. B. Ebbesen (Eds.). *The criminal justice system: A social-psychological analysis.* San Francisco: W.H. Freeman.

Castelnuovo-Tedesco, I. P. (1977). Stealing, revenge, and the Monte Cristo complex. *International Journal of Psychoanalysis, 55,* 169–177.

Catchpole, J. E., Cairney, P. T., & Macdonald, W. A. (1994). Why are Young Drivers Overrepresented in Traffic Accidents? *ARRS Special Report # 50.* Victoria, Australia: Australian Road Research Board, Ltd.

Cellar, D. F., Nelson, Z. C., & Yorke, C. M. (2000). The five-factor model and driving behavior: Personality and involvement in vehicular accidents. *Psychological Reports, 86*, 454–456.

Chalmers, J. B., & Townsend, M. A. (1990). The effects of training in social perspective-taking on socially maladjusted girls. *Child Development, 61*, 178–190.

Chapman, P., & Underwood, G. (2000). Forgetting near-accidents: The roles of severity, culpability and experience in the poor recall of dangerous driving situations. *Applied Cognitive Psychology, 14*, 31–44.

Chen, G., Meckle, W., & Wilson, J. (2002). Speed and safety effect of photo radar enforcement on a highway corridor in British Columbia. *Accident Analysis & Prevention, 34*, 129–138.

Chenery, S., Henshaw, C., & Pease, K. (1999). *Illegal parking in disabled bays: A means of offender targeting.* London: Home Office Policing & Reducing Crime Unit.

Chliaoutakis, J., Demakakos, P., Tzamalouka, G., Bakou, V., Koumaki, M., & Darviri, C. (2002). Aggressive behavior while driving as predictor of self-reported car crashes. *Journal of Safety Research, 33*, 431–443.

Clark, A.W. (1976). A social role approach to driver behavior. *Perceptual & Motor Skills, 42*, 325–326.

Cleckley, H. (1955). *The mask of sanity.* St. Louis: C. V. Mosby Co.

Cohen, J. H., & Larkin G. L. (1999). Effectiveness of ignition interlock devices in reducing drunk driving recidivism. *American Journal of Preventive Medicine, 16*, 81–87.

Colder, C. R., & Stice, E. (1998). A longitudinal study of the interactive effects of impulsivity and anger on adolescent problem behavior. *Journal of Youth & Adolescence, 27*, 255–274.

Conger, J. J., Gaskill, H. S., Glad D. D., Rainey R. V., Sawrey, W. L., & Turrell E.S. (1957). Personal and interpersonal factors in motor vehicle accidents. *American Journal of Psychiatry, 113*, 1069–1074.

Conley, J. J. (1985). A personality theory of adulthood and aging. *Perspectives in Psychology, 1*, 81–115.

Cook, P. (1980). Research in Criminal Deterrence: Laying the Groundwork for the Second Decade. In N. Morris & M. Tonry (Eds.). *Crime and Justice: An Annual Review of Research, vol. 2.* Chicago: University of Chicago Press.

Cooper, P. J., Pinili, M., & Chen, W. J. (1995). An examination of the crash involvement rates of novice drivers aged 16 to 55. *Accident Analysis and Prevention, 27*, 89–104.

Copeenhaver, M. M. (2000). Testing a social-cognitive model of intimate abusiveness among substance-dependent males. *American Journal of Drug & Alcohol Abuse, 26*, 603–628.

Corbett, C., & Simon, F. (1992). Decisions to break or adhere to the rules of the road, viewed from the rational choice perspective. *British Journal of Criminology, 32*, 537–549.

Cornish, D., & Clarke, L. (1986). *The Reasoning Criminal.* New York: Springer-Verlag.

Cramerus, M. (1990). Adolescent anger. *Bulletin of Menninger Clinic, 54*, 512–523.

Crane-Ross, D., Tisak, M.S., & Tisak, J. (1998). Aggression and rule violation among adolescents: Social-reasoning predictors of social behavior. *Aggressive Behavior, 24*, 347–365.

Crick, N. R., & Dodge, K. A. (1996). Social information-processing mechanisms on reactive and proactive aggression. *Child Development, 67,* 993–1002.

Croake, J. W. (1982). Adolescent depression: Identification and intervention. *Individual Psychology Journal of Adlerian Theory, Research, and Practice, 38,* 123–128.

Curry, S. G., & Marlatt, G. A. (1987). Building self-confidence, self-efficacy and self-control. In W. M. Cox (Ed.). *Treatment and prevention of alcohol problems: A resource manual.* Orlando: Academic Press.

Cusson, M. (1989). Querelles d'nonneur et agressions gregaires (Disputs over honour and gang aggression). *Reviue Internationale-de-Criminologie et de Police Technique, 42,* 290–297.

Cvetkovich, G., & Earle, T. C. (1990). Decision making and risk taking of young drivers: Conceptual distinctions and issues. *Alcohol, Drugs, and Driving, 4,* 9–19.

D'Zurilla, T. J., & Nezu, A. M. (1997). Development and preliminary evaluation of the Social Problem-Solving Inventory. *Psychological Assessment: A Journal of Consulting and Clinical Psychology, 2,* 156–163.

Daderman, A., & Klinteberg, B. (1997). *Personality dimensions characterizing severely conduct disordered male juvenile delinquents.* Report from the Department of Psychology, University of Stockholm. Stockholm: University of Stockholm.

Davis, M. H. (1980). Measuring individual differences in empathy: Evidence for a multidimensional approach. *Journal of Personality and Social Psychology, 44,* 113–126.

De Bono, E. (1985). *Six Thinking Hats.* Toronto: Key Porter Books.

Deery, H. A. (1999). Hazard and risk perception among young novice drivers. *Journal of Safety Research, 30,* 225–236.

Deery, H. A., & Fildes, B. N. (1999). Young novice driver subtypes: Relationship to high-risk behavior, traffic accident record, and simulator driving performance. *Human Factors, 41,* 628–643.

Deffenbacher, J. L., Huff, M. E., Lynch, R. S., Oetting, E. R., & Salvatore, N. F. (2000). Characteristics and treatment of high-anger drivers. *Journal of Counseling Psychology, 47,* 5–17.

Deffenbacher, J. L., Lynch, R. S., Oetting, E. R., & Swaim, R. (2002). The Driving Anger Expression Inventory: A measure of how people express their anger on the road. *Behavior Research & Therapy, 40,* 717–737.

Deffenbacher, J. L., Filetti, L. B., Lynch, R. S., & Dahlen, J. (2002). Cognitive-behavioral treatment of high anger drivers. *Behavior Research & Therapy, 40,* 895–910.

Deffenbacher, J.L., Deffenbacher, D. M., Lynch, R. S., & Richards, T. L. (2003). Anger, aggression and risky behavior: A comparison of high and low anger drivers. *Behavior Research & Therapy, 41,* 701–718.

Dejoy, J. (1989). The optimism bias and traffic accident risk perception. *Accident Analysis & Prevention, 21,* 333–340.

Denoff, M.S. (1991). Irrational beliefs, situational attributions, and the coping responses of adolescent runaways. *Journal of Rational-Emotive and Cognitive Behavior Therapy, 9,* 113–135.

DETR (2000). *Tomorrow's roads: Safer for everyone.* London: Department of the Environment, Transport & the Regions.

DETR (2001). *Influencing driver attitudes and behavior.* London: Department of the Environment, Transport & the Regions.

Digman, J. M., & Inouye, J. (1986). Further specification of the five robust factors of personality. *Journal of Personality and Social Psychology, 50,* 116–123.

Digman, J. M., & Takemoto-Chock, N. K. (1981). Factors in the natural language of personality: Re-analysis, comparison, and interpretation of six major studies. *Multivariate Behavioral Research, 16,* 149–170.

Dimeff, L. A., & Marlatt, G. A. (1995). Relapse prevention. In R. Hester & W. R. Miller (Eds.). *Handbook of alcoholism treatment approaches: Effective alternatives. (2nd ed.).* Boston: Allyn and Bacon.

Dodge, K. A., & Frame, C. L. (1982). Social cognitive biases and deficits in aggressive boys. *Child Development, 53,* 620–635.

Dodge, K. A., Price, J. M., Bachorowski, J. A., & Newman, J. P. (1990). Hostile attributional biases in severely aggressive adolescents. *Journal of Abnormal Psychology, 99,* 385–392.

Donnelly, J. P., & Scott, M. F. (1999). Evaluation of an offending behavior programme with a mentally disordered population. *British Journal of Forensic Practice, 1,* 25–32.

Donovan, J. E. (1993). Young adult drinking-driving: Behavioral and psychosocial correlates. Journal of Studies on Alcohol, 54, 600-613.

Donovan, D. M., Queisser, H. R., Salzberg, P. M., & Umlauf, R. L. (1985). Intoxicated and bad drivers: Subgroups within the same population of high-risk men drivers. *Journal of Studies on Alcohol, 46,* 375–381.

Donovan, D. M., Umlauf, R. L., & Salzberg, P. M. (1990). Bad drivers: Identification of a target group for alcohol-related prevention and early intervention. *Journal of Studies on Alcohol, 51,* 136–141.

Donovan, D. M., Umlauf, R. L., & Salzberg, P. M. (1985). Derivation of personality subtypes among high-risk drivers. *Alcohol, Drugs & Driving, 4,* 233–244.

Donovan, D.M., & Marlatt, G.A. (1982). Personality sub-types among driving-while-intoxicated offenders. *Journal of Consulting Clinical Psychology, 50,* 241–249.

Donovan, D. M., Marlatt, G. A., & Salzberg, P. M. (1983). Drinking behavior, personality factors and high-risk driving. *Journal of Studies on Alcohol, 44,* 395–428.

Dorn, L., & Matthews, G. (1992). Prediction of mood and risk appraisals from trait measures: Two studies of simulated driving. *European Journal of Personality, 9,* 25–42.

Duncan, J.P., Williams A.F., & Brown, I.D. (1991). Experience does not mean expertise. *Ergonomics, 34,* 919.

Eby, D. W. (1995a). *The convicted drunk driver in Michigan: A profile of offenders.* Ann Arbor, Michigan: University of Michigan Transportation Research Institute.

Eby, D. W. (1995b). *An analysis of crash experience: Age versus driving experience.* Ann Arbor, Michigan: University of Michigan Transportation Research Institute.

Eby, D. W., & Christoff, C. (1996). *Direct observation of safety belt use in Michigan: Fall 1996.* Ann Arbor, Michigan: University of Michigan Transportation Research Institute.

Eby, D. W., & Hopp, M. L. (1997). *Direct observation of safety belt use in Michigan: Fall 1997.* Ann Arbor, Michigan: University of Michigan Transportation Research Institute.

Eby, D. W., Hopp, M. K., & Streff, F. M. (1996). *A profile of adolescent drivers convicted of felony drunk driving.* Ann Arbor, Michigan: University of Michigan Transportation Research Institute.

Eby, D. W., & Molnar, L. J. (1998). *A literature review of cognitive development.* Michigan: The University of Michigan Transportation Research Institute.

Echterhoff, W. (1987). *Sicherheitswidrige Und Sicherheitsgemasse Reaktionen Auf Den Eigenen Kraftfahrzeugubfakke.* Bundeesanstakt fur Strasswessen, Bereich Unfallforschung, Bergisch Galdbach.

Elander, J., West, R., & French, D. (1993). Behavioral correlates of individual differences in road-traffic crash risk: An examination of methods and findings. *Psychological Bulletin, 113*, 2, 279–294.

Elliott, M. R., Waller, P. F., Raghunathan, T. E., Shope, J. T., Trivellore, R. & Little, R. J. A. (2000). Persistence of violation and crash behavior over time. *Journal of Safety Research, 31*, 229–242.

Evans, L. (1987). Young driver involvement in severe car crashes. *Alcohol, Drugs, & Driving, 3*, 63–78.

Evans, L. (1991). Traffic safety and the driver. New York: Van Nostrand Reinhold.

Evans, L., & Wasielewski, P. (1982). Do accident-involved drivers exhibit everyday risky driving behavior? *Accident Analysis & Prevention, 14*, 57–64.

Evans, L., Wasielewski, P., & von Buseck,C.R. (1982). Compulsory seat-belt usage and driver risk taking behavior. *Human Factors, 24*, 41–48.

Evans, W. N, Neville, D., & Graham, J.D. (1991). General deterrence of drunk driving: Evaluation of recent American policies. *Risk Analysis, 11*, 279–289.

Evans, S. W., & Short, E. J. (1991). A qualitative and serial analysis of social problem solving in aggressive boys. *Journal of Abnormal Child Psychology, 19*, 331–340.

Falshaw, L., Friendship, C., Travers, R., & Nugent, F. (2003). *Searching for what works: An evaluation of cognitive skills programmes.* London: Home Office.

Farrington, D. P. (1986). Age and crime. In M. Torny & N. Morris (Eds.). *Crime and Justice: An annual Review of Research (Vol.7).* Chicago: U. of Chicago Press.

Farrington, D. P., & West, D. J. (1990). The Cambridge study in delinquent development: A long-term follow-up of 411 London males. In G. Kaiser and H (Eds). *Criminality: Personality, Behavior, Life History.* Heidelberg: Springer.

Fergenson, E. P. (1971). The relationship between information-processing and driving accident and violation record. *Human Factors, 113*, 173–176.

Ferguson, S. A., Williams, A. F., Chapline, J. F., Reinfurt, D. W., & De Leonardis, D. M. (2001). Relationship of parent driving records to the driving records of their children. *Accident Analysis & Prevention, 33*, 229–234.

Feuerstein, R., & Griffin, D.K. (1979). *Crime and reason.* Ottawa: Correctional Services, Canada.

Finigan M. (1996). *Societal outcomes of drug and alcohol treatment in the state of Oregon.* Oregon: Office of Alcohol and Drug Abuse Programs.

Finn, P., & Bragg, B. (1986) Perception of the risk of an accident by young and older drivers. *Accident Analysis & Prevention, 18*, 289–298.

Flannery, R. B. (1986). Major life events and daily hassles in predicting health status: Methodological inquiry. *Journal of Clinical Psychology, 42*, 485–487.

Foeckler, M., Hutcheson, F, Williams, C. Thomas, A., & Jones, T. (1978) Vehicle drivers and fatal accidents. *Suicide and Life Threatening Behavior, 8,* 174–182.

Forsyth, E. (1994). *Road User Behavior Research: Review paper.* London: Department of Transport.

Fraser, M. W. (1996). Cognitive problem solving and aggressive behavior among children. *Families in Society, 77,* 19–32.

French, D. J., West, R. J., Elander, W. J., & Wilding, J. M. (1993). Decision-making style, driving style, and self-reported involvement in road traffic accidents. *Ergonomics, 36,* 627–644.

Friendship, C., Blud, L., Erikson, M., Travers, R., & Thornton (2001). *Cognitive-behavioral treatment for imprisoned offenders: An evaluation of HM prison services' cognitive skills programme.* London: Home Office.

Friendship, C., Blud, L., Erikson, M., & Travers, R. (2002). *An evaluation of cognitive behavioral treatment for prisoners.* London: Home Office.

Fuller, R. (1984). A conceptualization of driving behavior as threat avoidance. *Ergonomics, 27,* 1139–1155.

Fuller, R. (1988). Psychological aspects of learning to drive. In T. Rothengatter & R. de Bruin. *Road user behavior: Theory and research.* New Hampshire: Van Gorcum.

Fuller, R. (1990). Learning to make errors: Evidence from a driving task simulation. *Ergonomics, 33,* 1241–1250.

Furnham, A., & Saipe, J. (1993). Personality correlates of convicted drivers. *Personality & Individual Differences, 14,* 329–336.

Galovski, T., & Blanchard, E. B. (2002). Psychological characteristics of aggressive drivers with and without intermittent explosive disorder. *Behavior Research & Therapy, 40,* 1157-1168.

Galovski, T. E., & Blanchard, E. B. (2002). The effectiveness of a brief psychological intervention on court-referred and self-referred aggressive drivers. *Behavior Research & Therapy, 40,* 1385–1402.

Galovski, T. E., Blanchard, E. B., & Veazey, C. (2002). Intermittent explosive disorder and other psychiatric comorbidity among court-referred and self-referred aggressive drivers. *Behavior Research & Therapy, 40,* 641–651.

Garrett, C. J. (1985). Effects of residential treatment of adjudicated delinquents. A metaanalysis. *Journal of Research in Crime and Delinquency, 22,* 287–308.

Garrido, V. (1995). R&R with Spanish Offenders and Children "At Risk." In R. R. Ross & R. D. Ross (Eds.). *Thinking straight: The reasoning & rehabilitation program for delinquency prevention and offender rehabilitation.* Ottawa: Cognitive Centre of Canada. (cogcen@canada.com)

Gaylin, W. (2001). *How psychotherapy really works.* New York: McGraw-Hill.

Gendreau, P., Little, C., & Goggin, C. (1988). A meta-analysis of the predictors of adult offender recidivism: What works. *Journal of Consulting and Clinical Psychology, 66,* 348–362.

Gendreau, P., & Ross, R. R. (1979). Effective correctional treatment: Bibliotherapy for cynics. *Crime and Delinquency, 25,* 463–489.

Gendreau, P., & Ross, R. R. (1981) Correctional potency: Treatment and deterrence on trial. In R. Roesch & R. R. Carrado. *Evaluation and criminal justice policy.* Beverly Hills: Sage.

Gendreau, P., & Ross, R. R. (1987). Revivification of rehabilitation: Evidence from the 1980s. *Justice Quarterly, 4*, 349–407.

Gibbs, J. C. (1995). Equip: A peer-group treatment program for delinquents. In R. R. Ross, D. Antonowicz & G. Dhaliwal (Eds.). *Going straight: Effective delinquency prevention and offender rehabilitation.* Ottawa: Cognitive Centre of Canada. (cogcen@canada.com)

Gibbs, J. C., & Potter, G. (1987). *Identify it/own it/replace it: Helping youth help one another.* Paper presented at the meeting of the Commision on Interpersonal Education and Practice, Columbus, Ohio.

Glad, A. (1988). *Phase two driver education: Effect on the risk of accident.* Norway: Norwegian Centre for Research.

Glassner, B. (2000). *The culture of fear: Why Americans are afraid of the wrong things.* New York: Basic Books.

Glendon, A. I., Dorn, L., Matthews, G., Gulian, E., Davies, D. R., & Debney, L. M. (1993). Reliability of the driving behavior inventory. *Ergonomics, 36*, 719–726.

Goldstein, A. (1988). *The prepare curriculum: Teaching prosocial competencies.* Champaign, IL: Research Press.

Goldstein, A., Glick, B., & Gibbs, J. (2000). *Aggression replacement training: Revised edition.* Champaign: Research Press.,

Gottfredson, M., & Hirschi, T. (1990). *A general theory of crime.* California: Stanford University Press.

Grayson, G. B. (Ed.) (1992). *Behavioral research in road safety*, Proceedings of a seminar. Crowthorne, U.K.: Transport Research Laboratory.

Graziano, W. G., & Ward, D. (1992). Probing the big five in adolescence: Personality and adjustment during a developmental transition. *Journal of Personality, 60*, 425–439.

Greening, L. (1997). Adolescent stealers' and nonstealers' social problem-solving skills. *Adolescence, 32*, 51–55.

Gregersen, N. P. (1996).Young drivers' overestimation of their own skill – An experiment on the relation between training strategy and skill. *Accident Analysis and Prevention, 28*, 243–250.

Groeger, J. A. (2000). *Understanding driving: Applying cognitive psychology to a complex everyday task.* Philadelphia: Psychology Press.

Groeger, J. A., & Brown, I. D. (1989). Assessing one's own and others' driving ability: Influence of sex, age, and experience. *Accident, Analysis & Prevention, 21*, 155–168.

Groeger, J. A., & Clegg, B. A. (1994). Why isn't driver training contributing more to road safety? In G. B. Grayson (Ed.). *Behavioral research in road safety.* Crowthorne, U. K.: Transport Research Laboratory.

Gros, J. (1989). Das Kraft-Fahr-Sicherheitsproramm. *Personalfuhrung, 3*, 246–249.

Guerra, N.G. (1989). Consequential thinking and self-reported delinquency in high-school youth. *Criminal Justice & Behavior, 16*, 440–454.

Gulian, E. (1987). *Driver stress: A literature review.* (CPERU Report). Birmingham: Aston Business School, Aston University.

Gulian, E., Debney, L. M., Glendon, A. I., Davies, D. R., & Matthews, G. (1989a). Coping with driver stress. In F. McGuigan, W. E. Sime, & J. M. Wallace (Eds.). *Stress and tension control.* New York: Plenum.

Gulian, E., Glendon, A. I., Matthews, G., Davies, D. R., & Debney, M. (1990). The stress of driving: A diary study. *Work and Stress, 4,* 7–16.

Gulian, E., Matthews, G., Glendon, A. I., & Davies, D. R. (1989b). Dimensions of driver stress. *Ergonomics, 32,* 585–602.

Guppy, A. (1993). Subjective probability of accidents and apprehension in relation to self-other bias, age, and reported behavior. *Accident Analysis and Prevention, 25,* 375–382.

Gyrl, F. E, Stith, S. M., & Bird, G. W. (1991). Close dating relationships among college students: differences by use of violence and by gender. *Journal of Social & Personal Relationships, 8,* 243–264.

Hagenzieker M. P., Bijleveld F. D., & Davidse R. J. (1997). Effects of incentive programs to stimulate safety belt use: A meta-analysis. *Accident Analysis and Prevention 29,* 759–777.

Hall, J., & West, R. (1996). Roles of formal instruction and informal practice in learning to drive. *Ergonomics, 39,* 693–706.

Halpern, D. (2001). Moral values, social trust and inequality: can values explain crime? *British Journal of Criminology, 41,* 236–251.

Hancock, P. A., & Warm, J. S. (1989). A dynamic model of stress and sustained attention. *Human Factors, 31,* 519–537.

Hansen, D. J., Pallota, G. M., Christopher, J., & Conaway, R. L. (1989). Parental problem-solving skills and child behavior problems: A comparison of physically abusive, neglectful, clinic, and community families. *Journal of Family Violence, 4,* 353–368.

Harano, R. M., & Hubert, D. (1974). *An evaluation of California's 'good driver' incentive program.* Sacramento: California Division Of Highways.

Harre, N., Field, J., & Kirkwood, B. (1996). Gender differences and areas of common concern in the driving behaviors and attitudes of adolescents. *Journal of Safety Research, 27,* 163–177.

Hartley, L. R., & El Hassani, J. (1994). Stress, violations, and accidents. *Applied Ergonomics, 25,* 221–230.

Hartos, J., Eitel, P., & Simons-Morton, B. (2002). Parenting practices and adolescent risky driving: A three-month prospective study. *Health Education & Behavior, 29,* 194–206.

Hartos, J. L., Eitel, P., Haynie, D. L., & Simons-Morton, B.G. (2000). Can I take the car? Relations among parenting practices and adolescent problem-driving practices. *Journal of Adolescent Research, 15,* 352–367.

Hattakka, M., Keskinen, E., Gregersen, N.P., Glad, A., & Hernekoski, K. (2002). From control of the vehicle to personal self-control; broadening the perspectives to driver education. *Transportation Research, 5,* 201–215.

Hauber, A. R. (1980). The social psychology of driving behavior and the traffic environment: Research on aggressive behavior in traffic. *International Review of Applied Psychology, 29,* 461–474.

Hawkins, J. D., Catalano, R. E., & Miller, Y. (1992). Risk and protective factors for alcohol and other drug problems in adolescence and early adulthood: Implications for substance abuse prevention. *Psychological Bulletin, 112,* 64–105.

Hedlund, J. H. (1994). If they didn't drink would they crash anyway? – the role of alcohol in traffic crashes. *Alcohol, Drugs and Driving, 10*, 115–125.

Heimstra, N. (1970). Effects of "stress fatigue" on performance in a simulated driving situation. *Ergonomics, 13*, 209–218.

Hennessy, D. A. (2000). The interaction of person and situation within the driving environment: Daily hassles, traffic congestion, driver stress, aggression, vengeance and past performance. *Dissertation Abstracts International.* US: University Microfilms International.

Hennessy, D. A., & Wiesenthal, D. L. (1997). The relationship between traffic congestion, driver stress, and direct versus indirect coping behaviors. *Ergonomics, 40*, 348–361.

Hennessy, D. A., & Wiesenthal, D. L.(1999). Traffic congestion, driver stress, and driver aggression. *Aggressive Behavior, 25*, 409–423.

Hertsgaard, M. (1998). *Earth Odyssey.* New York: Broadway.

Hirschi, T., & Gottfredson, M. R. (Eds.) (1994). *The Generality of Deviance.* New Brunswick, NJ: Transaction Publishers.

Hodgdon, J. D., Bragg, B. W. E., & Finn, P. (1981). *Young driver risk-taking research: The state of the art.* Washington, DC: Department of Transportation.

Hollin, C. R., & Swaffer, T. (1993). Social functioning and delinquency: A return to basics. *Journal of Adolescence, 16*, 205–210.

Horesh, N., Gothelf, D., Ofek, H., Weitzman, T., & Apter, A. (1999). Impulsivity as a correlate of suicidal behavior in adolescent psychiatric inpatients. *Crisis, 20*, 8–14.

Horneman, C. (1993). *Driver education and training: A review of the literature.* Armidale: Roads And Traffic Authority, Road Safety Bureau.

Horvath, P., & Zuckerman, M. (1993). Sensation seeking, risk appraisal and risky behavior. *Personality and Individual Differences, 14*, 41–52.

Hutchinson, J. W., Cox, C. S., & Maffet, B. R. (1969). An evaluation of the effectiveness of televised locally oriented driver re-education. *Highway Research Record, 292*, 51–63.

Hyden, M. (1995). Verbal aggression as a prehistory of woman battering. *Journal of Family Violence, 10*, 55–71.

Iversen, H., & Rundmo, T. (2002). Personality, risky driving and accident involvement among Norwegian drivers. *Personality & Individual Differences, 33*, 1251–1263.

Izzo, R., & Ross, R. R. (1990). Meta-analysis of rehabilitation programs for juvenile. *Criminal Justice and Behavior, 17*, 134–142.

Jaffee, W. B., & D'Zurilla, T. J. (2003). Adolescent problem solving, parent problem solving, and externalizing behavior in adolescents. Stony Brook University, *Behavior Therapy* (in press).

Jessor, R. (1987a). Risky driving and adolescent problem behavior: An extension of problem-behavior theory. *Alcohol, Drugs, & Driving, 3*, 1–11.

Jessor, R. (1987b). Risky driving and adolescent problem behavior: Theoretical and empirical linkage. In T. Bengamin (Ed.). *Young Drivers Impaired By Alcohol And Drugs.* Proceedings of the Royal Society of Medicine International Congress and Symposum.

Jessor, R., Turbin, M. S., & Costa, F. M. (1997). Predicting developmental change in risky driving: The transition to young adulthood. *Applied Developmental Science, 1*, 4–16.

Job, R. (1990). The application of learning theory to driving confidence: the effect of age and the impact of random breath testing. *Accident Analysis & Prevention, 22,* 97–107.

Johnson, G., & Hunter, R. M. (1995). Evaluation of the specialized drug offender program. In R. R. Ross & R. D. Ross (Eds.). *Thinking straight: The reasoning and rehabilitation program for delinquency prevention and offender rehabilitation.* Ottawa Cognitive Centre of Canada. (cogen@canada.com)

Johnson, M., & Stone, G. L. (1987). Social workers and burnout: A psychological description. *Journal of Social Science Research, 10,* 67–80.

Johnson, V., & White, H. (1989). An investigation of factors related to intoxicated driving behaviors among youth. *Journal of Studies on Alcohol, 50,* 320–330.

Jonah, B. A. (1986). Accident risk and risk-taking behavior among young drivers. *Accident Analysis & Prevention, 18,* 255–271.

Jonah, B. A. (1996). *Sensation seeking and risky driving: A review and synthesis of the literature.* Paper presented at the International Conference on Traffic and Transport Psychology, Valencia, Spain.

Jonah, B. A., Dawson, N. E., & Smith, G. A. (1982). Effects of selective traffic enforcement program on seat belt usage. *Journal of Applied Psychology, 67,* 89–96.

Jonah, B. A., Thiessen, R., & Au-Yeung, E. (2001). Sensation seeking, risky driving and behavioral adaptation. *Accident Analysis & Prevention, 33,* 679–684.

Jones, D. W. (1992). *An Analysis Of Model Driver Education Programs In The United States.* Doctoral dissertation. Texas: Texas A&M University.

Joslin, P. (1994). Traffic and crime go together. *Police, 25,* 18.

Junger, M., Terlouw, G. J., & Van Der Heidjen, P. G. M. (1995). Crime, accidents and social control. *Criminal Behavior & Mental Health, 5,* 386–410.

Junger, M., & Tremblay, R. E. (1999) Self-Control, Accidents, and Crime. *Criminal Justice & Behavior, 4,* 485–501.

Kahneman, D., Ben-Ishar, R., & Lotan, M. (1973). Relation of a test of attention to road accidents. *Journal of Applied Psychology, 58,* 113–115.

Kaplan, J., & Arbuthnot, J. (1985). Affective empathy and cognitive role-taking in delinquent and nondelinquent youth. *Adolescence, 20,* 323–333.

Keane, C., Maxim, P. S.,, & Teevan, J. J. (1993). Drinking and driving, self-control, and gender: Testing a general theory of crime. *Journal of Research in Crime & Delinquency, 30,* 30–46.

Kennedy, B. P., Isaac, N. E., Nelson, T. F., & Graham, J.D. (1997). Young male drinkers and impaired driving intervention. *Accident Analysis & Prevention, 29,* 707–713.

Keskinen, E. (1996). *Why do young drivers have more accidents?* Junge Fahrer Und Fahrerinnen. Referate der Esten Interdizipinaren Fachkonferenz, Koln, Berichte der Bundesenstalt fur Stressenwesen. Mensch und Sicherheit, Heft M 52.

Kinkade, P. T., & Leone, M. C. (1992). The effect of "tough" drunk driving laws on policing: A case study. *Crime & Delinquency, 38,* 239–257.

Klinteberg, B. A., Andersson, T., Magnusson, D., & Stattin, H. (1993). Hyperactive behavior in childhood as related to subsequent alcohol problems and violent offending: A longitudinal study of male subjects. *Personality and Individual Differences, 15,* 381–388.

Knapper, C. K., & Cropley, A. J. (1981). Social and interpersonal factors in driving. *Progress in Applied Social Psychology, 1*, 191–220.

Kochis, C. L. (1997). The alcohol expectancies and personality characteristics of driving while intoxicated. *Dissertation Abstracts International*, University Microfilms International.

Kolko, D. J., & Kazdin, A. E. (1991a). Motives of childhood firesetters: Firesetting characteristics and psychological correlates. *Journal of Child Psychology & Psychiatry, 32*, 535–550.

Kolko, D. J., & Kazdin, A. E. (1991b). Aggression and psychopathology in match-playing and firesetting children: A replication and extension. *Journal of Clinical Child Psychology, 20*, 191–201.

Kontogiannis, T., Kossiavelou, Z., & Marmaras, N. (2002). Self-reports of aberrant behavior on the roads: Errors and violations in a sample of Greek drivers. *Accident Analysis & Prevention, 34*, 381–399.

Koopman, P. R. S. (1983). *Cognitive disorders and syntactical deficiencies in the inmate populations of federal penitentiaries in Canada.* Ottawa: Solicitor-General.

Koppa, R. J., & Banning, K. R. (1981). *Young problem driver improvement project.* Washington, DC: NHTSA, Department of Transportation.

Koson, D. F., & Dvoskin, J. (1982). Arson: A diagnostic survey. *Bulletin of the American Academy of Psychiatry and the Law, 10*, 39–49.

Kownacki, RJ. (1995). The effectiveness of a brief cognitive-behavioral program in the reduction of antisocial behavior in high risk probationers in a Texas community. In R. R. Ross & R. D. Ross. *Thinking straight: The reasoning & rehabilitation program for delinquency prevention & offender rehabilitation.* Ottawa: Cognitive Center of Canada. (cogcen@canada.com)

Kroj, J., & Helleman, R. (1971). Zur progrnoseder ruchfallwahrschienlickeite. *Zeitschrift fur Verkehrssichereit, 17*, 92–104.

Laberge-Nadeau, C., Maag, U., & Bourbeau, R. (1992). The effects of age and experience on accidents with injuries: Should the licensing age be raised? *Accident Analysis & Prevention, 24*, 107–116.

Lajunen, T., & Parker, D. (2001). Are aggressive people aggressive drivers? A study of the relationship between self-reported general aggressiveness, driver anger and aggressive driving. *Accident Analysis & Prevention, 33*, 243–255.

Lancaster, R., & Ward, R. (2002). *The contribution of individual factors to driving behaviour: Implications for managing work-related road safety.* Sudbury: HSE Books.

Lane, R. C., Hull, J. W., & Foehrenbach, L. M. (1991). The addiction to negativity. *Psychoanalytic Review, 78*, 391–410.

Lastovicka, J. L., Murray, J. P., Jochimsthaler, E. A., Bhalla, G., & Scheurich, J. (1987). A lifestyle typology to model young male drinking and driving. *Journal of Consumer Research, 14*, 257–263.

Lawton, R., & Nutter, A. (2002). A comparison of reported levels and expression of anger in everyday and driving situations. *British Journal of Psychology, 93*, 407–423.

Lawton, R., Parker, D., Stradling, S. G., & Manstead, A. S. R. (1997). Predicting road traffic accidents: The role of social deviance and violations. *British Journal of Psychology, 88*, 249–263.

Lazarus, R. S. (1981). Little hassles can be hazardous to health. *Psychology Today, May,* 58–62.

LeBlanc, M. (1993) Late adolescence deceleration of criminal activity and development of self- and social control. *Studies on crime & crime prevention.* Norway: Scandinavian Univ. Press.

Legree, P. J., Heffner, T. S., Psotka, J., Martin, D. E., & Medsker, G. J. (2003). Traffic crash involvement: Experiential driving knowledge and stressful contextual antecedents. *Journal of Applied Psychology, 88,* 15–26.

Lee, M., & Prentice, N. M. (1988). Interrelations of empathy, cognition, and moral reasoning with dimensions of juvenile delinquency. *Journal of Abnormal Child Psychology, 16,* 127–139.

Lester, J. (1991). *Individual differences in accident liability: A review of the literature.* Crowthorne, U.K.: Department of Transport.

Lichtenstein, S., Slovic, P., Fischhoff, B., Layman, M., & Combs, B. (1978). Judged frequency of lethal events. *Journal of Experimental Psychology: Human Learning and Memory, 4,* 551–578.

Lipsey, M. W. (1992). Juvenile delinquency treatment: A meta-analytic inquiry into the variability of effects. In T. D. Cook, H. Cooper, D. S. Corday, H. Hartmann, L. V. Hedges, R. J. Light, T. A. Louis, & F. Mosteller (Eds.), *Meta-analysis for explanation: A casebook.* New York: Russell Sage.

Lochman, J., & Dodge, K. (1994). Social-cognitive processes of severely violent, moderately aggressive and nonaggressive boys. *Journal of Consulting & Clinical Psychology, 62,* 366–374.

Lochman, J. E., & Lenhart, L. A. (1993). Anger coping intervention for aggressive children: Conceptual models and outcome effects. *Clinical Psychology Review, 13,* 785–805.

Lofland, L. H. (1973). *The public realm. Exploring the city's quintessential social territory.* New York: Aldine de Gruyter.

Lonero, L. P., Clinton, K. M., Wilde, G. J. S., Laurie, I., & Black, D. (1995). *Novice Driver Education Model Curriculum Outline.* Washington, D.C.: AAA Foundation for Traffic Safety.

Loo, R. (1979). Role of primary personality factors in the perception of traffic signs and driver violations and accidents. *Accident Analysis & Prevention, 11,* 128–127.

Losel, F., & Koferl, P. (1989) Evaluation research on correctional treatment in West Germany: In H. Wegener, F. Losel, & J. Haisch (Eds.). *Criminal behavior in the justice system: Psychological perspectives.* New York: Springer.

Lowenstein, L. F. (1997). Research into causes and manifestations of aggression in car driving. *Police Journal, 70,* 263–270.

Ludwig, K. B., & Pittman, J. E. (1999). Adolescent prosocial values and self-efficacy in relation to delinquency, risky sexual behavior, and drug use. *Youth & Society, 30,* 461–482.

Luengo, M. A. Carrillo-de-la Pena, M. T., Otero, J. M., & Romero, E. (1994). A short-term longitudinal study of impulsivity and antisocial behavior. *Journal of Personality and Social Psychology, 66,* 542–548.

Luengo, M. A., Otero, J. M., Carillo-de-la-Pena, M. T., & Miron, L. (1994). *Psychology Crime and Law, 1,* 27–37.

Lund, A. K., & Williams, A. F. (1985). A review of the literature evaluating the defensive driving course. *Accident Analysis & Prevention, 17*, 449–460.

Lynam, D. R, Caspi, A., Moffit, T. E., Wikstroem, P., Loeber, R., & Novak, S. (2000). The interaction between impulsivity and neighborhood context on offending. *Journal of Abnormal Psychology, 109*, 563–574.

Lynn, C. (1982). *An Evaluation Of The Virginia Driver Improvement Program On Negligent Driving: Twelve-Month Report.* Virginia Department of Transportation Safety.

MacDonald, J. M. (1964). Suicide and homicide by automobile. *American Journal of Psychiatry, 121*, 366–370.

Maisto, S. A., Sobell, L. C., Zelhart, P. F., Connors, G. J., & Cooper, T. (1979). Driving records of persons convicted of driving under the influence of alcohol. *Journal of Studies on Alcohol, 40*, 240–248.

Makinen, T., & Zaidel, D. M. (2002). *Traffic enforcement in Europe: Effects, measures, needs and future.* Espoo, Finland: VTT Technical Research Centre.

Mann, R., Anglin, L., Rahman, S., Blessing, L. A., Vingilis, E. R., & Larkin, E. (1995). Does treatment for substance abuse improve traffic safety? A preliminary evaluation. In C. Kloeden & A. J. McLean (Eds.). *Alcohol, Drugs and Traffic Safety.* Adelaide, Australia: University of Adelaide.

Mann, R., Leigh, G., Vingilis, E., & De Genova, K. (1983). A critical review on the effectiveness of D.W.I. rehabilitation programmes. *Accident Analysis and Prevention, 15*, 441–463.

Mannering, F. L. (1993). Male/female driver characteristics and accident risk: Some new evidence. *Accident Analysis & Prevention, 25*, 77–84.

Manstead, A. S. R., Parker, D., Stradling, S. G., Reason, J. T., Baxter, J. S., & Keleman, D. A.(1992). Perceived consensus in estimates of the prevalence of driving errors and violations. *Journal of Applied Social Psychology, 22*, 509–530.

Marlatt, G. A., & Gordon, J. R. (Eds.). (1985). *Relapse prevention: Maintenance strategies in the treatment of addictive behaviors.* New York: Guilford Press.

Marsh, P., & Collett, P. (1987). The car as a weapon. *Et Cetera, 44*, 146–151.

Martin, A. M., & Hernandez, B. (1995). PEIRS: Efficacy of a Multifaceted Cognitive Program for Prison Inmates. In R. R. Ross & R. D. Ross (Eds.). *Thinking straight: The reasoning and rehabilitation program for delinquency prevention and offender rehabilitation.* Ottawa: Cognitive Centre of Canada. (cogcen@canada.com)

Martinson, R. (1974). What works? Questions and answers about prison reform. *The Public Interest, 35*, 2–54.

Matthews, G. (2001). A transactional model of driver stress. In P. A. Hancock & P. A. Desmond (Eds.). *Stress, workload, and fatigue. Human factors in transportation.* Mahwah, NJ: Lawrence Erlbaum Associates.

Matthews, G., Dorn, L., & Glendon, A. I. (1991). Personality correlates of driver stress. *Personality and Individual Differences, 12*, 535–549.

Matthews, M. L., & Morgan, A. R. (1986). Age differences in male drivers' perception of accident risk: The role of perceived driving ability. *Accident Analysis & Prevention, 18*, 299–313.

Matthews, G., Sparkes, T. J., & Bygrave, H. M. (1996). Attentional overload, stress, and simulated driving performance. *Human Performance, 9*, 77–101.

Mayer, R. R., & Treat, J. R. (1977). Psychological, social and cognitive characteristics of high-risk drivers: A pilot study. *Accident Analysis & Prevention, 9,* 1–8.

Mayhew, D. R., Donelson, A. C., Beirness, D. J., & Simpson, H. M. (1986). Youth, alcohol and relative risk of crash involvement. *Accident Analysis & Prevention, 18,* 273–287.

Mayhew, D. R., & Simpson, H. M. (1995). *The role of driving experience: Implications for the training and licensing of new drivers.* Ottawa: Traffic Injury Research Foundation.

Mayhew, D. R., & Simpson, H. M. (1997). *Effectiveness and the role of driver education and training in a graduated licensing system.* Ottawa: Traffic Injury Research Foundation.

McCartt, A. T., Shabanova, V. I., & Leaf, W. A. (2003). Driving experience, crashes and traffic citations of teenage beginning drivers. *Accident Analysis & Prevention, 35,* 311–320.

McCord, J. (1984). Drunken drivers in longitudinal perspective. *Journal of Studies on Alcohol, 45,* 316–320.

McCormick, I. A., Walkey, F. H., & Green, D. E. (1986). Comparative perception of driver ability: A confirmation and expansion. *Accident Analysis and Prevention, 18,* 205–208.

McFarland, R. A. (1966). The psycho-social adjustment of drivers in relation to accidents. *Police,* Jan-Feb, Special Issue.

McFarland, R. A. (1968). Psychological and behavioral aspects of automobile accidents. *Traffic Safety Research Review, 12,* 71–80.

McGuire, F. L. (1960). Suicidal impulses in the operation of motor vehicles. Journal of the Mississippi State Medical Association, 2, 331–334.

McGuire, F. L. (1973). The nature of bias in official accident and violation records. *Journal of Applied Psychology, 57,* 300–305.

McGuire, F. L. (1976). Personality factors in highway accidents. *Human Factors, 18,* 433–442.

McKenna, T. P. (1983). Accident proneness: A conceptual analysis. *Accident Analysis and Prevention, 15,* 65–71.

McKenna, T. P., Stanier, P. A., & Lewis, C. (1991). Factors underlying illusory self-assessment of driving skills in males and females. *Accident Analysis & Prevention, 23,* 45–52.

McKnight, A. J., & McKnight, A. S. (1993). The effects of cellular phone use upon driver attention. Accident Analysis & Prevention, 25, 259–266.

McKnight, A. J., & Tippetts, A. S. (1997). Accident prevention versus recidivism prevention courses for repeat traffic offenders. *Accident Analysis & Prevention, 29,* 25–31.

McMillen, D. L., Pang, M. G., Wells-Parker, E., & Anderson, B. J. (1991). Behavior and personality traits among DUI arrestees, nonarrested impaired drivers, and nonimpaired drivers. *The International Journal of Addictions, 26,* 227–235.

McMillen, D. L., Pang, M. G., Wells-Parker, E., & Anderson, B. J. (1992). Alcohol, personality traits, and high risk driving: A comparison of young, drinking driver groups. *Addictive Behaviors, 7,* 525–535.

McMurran, M. (1993) *The Psychology of Addiction.* London: Taylor & Francis.

McMurran, M., Egan, V., Richardson, C., & Ahmadi, S. (1999). Social problem solving in mentally disordered offenders: A brief report. *Criminal Behavior and Mental Health, 9,* 315–322.

Meadows, M. L. (1994). *Psychological correlates of road crash types.* Doctoral dissertation, University of Manchester.

Meadows, M., Stradling, S. G., & Lawson, S. (1998). The role of social deviance and violations in predicting road traffic accidents in a sample of young offenders. *British Journal of Psychology, 89,* 417–431.

Michon, J. A. (1989). Explanatory pitfalls and rule-based driver models. *Accident Analysis and Prevention, 21,* 341–353.

Miller, P. M., Nirenberg, T. D., & McClure, G. (1983). Prevention of alcohol abuse. In B. Tabakoff, P. B. Sutka, & C. L. Randall (Eds.). *Medical and Social Aspects of Alcohol Abuse.* New York: Plenum Press.

Miller, S. (1981). Predictability and human stress: Toward a clarification of evidence and theory. In L. Berkowitz (Ed.). *Advances in Experimental Social Psychology.* New York: Academic Press.

Mizell, L. R. (1997). *Aggressive driving.* Bethesda: Mizell & Co

Moser (1974). *Das bild des Vielfachtaters im Strassenverker Schlussbericht und Austerwertung der* vielfachterkartei kohn: Bundesanstalt fur Strassenwessen.

Murphy-Berman, V., Rosell, J., & Wright, G. (1986). Measuring children's attention span: A microcomputer assessment techniques. *Journal of Educational Research, 80,* 23–28.

Nagin, D. S., & Pogarsky, G. (2001). Integrating Celerity, Impulsivity, and Extralegal Sanction Threats into a Model of General Deterrence: Theory and Evidence. *Criminology, 39,* 404–430.

NHTSA. (1995a). *Understanding Youthful Risk Taking And Driving.* National Highway Traffic Safety Administration. Washington, DC: Department of Transportation.

NHTSA. (1995b). *Understanding youthful risk taking and driving: Database report.* National Highway Traffic Safety Administration. Washington, DC: Department of Transportation.

NHTSA. (1997). *Traffic safety facts 1996.* National Highway Traffic Safety Administration. Washington, DC: Department of Transportation.

NHTSA. (2000). *Aggressive Driving Enforcement.* National Highway Traffic Safety Commission, Washington, DC: Department of Transportation.

Noordizi, P. (1990). *Individual differences and accident reliability: A review of the German literature.* Crowthorne, U.K.: Transport & Road Research Laboratory.

Norman, J. N., El-Sadig, M., & Lloyd, O. L. (1999). *Pre-hospital emergency care: Place for police/medical coordinating units.* Paper presented at the Conference on Police and the Challenges of the 21st Century, Abu Dhabi.

Norris, F. H., Matthews, B. A., & Riad, J. K. (2000). Characterological, situational, and behavioral risk factors for motor vehicle accidents: A prospective examination. *Accident Analysis & Prevention, 32,* 505–515.

Novaco, R. W. (1991). Aggression on roadways. In R. Baenninger (Ed.). *Targets of violence and aggression.* North Holland: Elsevier Science Publisher.

Novaco, R. W., Stokols, D., & Milanesi, L. (1990). Objective and subjective dimensions of travel impedance as determinants of commuting stress. *American Journal of Community Psychology, 18,* 231–257.

Ohbuchi, K., & Kambara, T. (1985). Attacker's intent and awareness of outcome, impression management, and retaliation. *Journal of Experimental Social Psychology, 21,* 321–330.

Oldenquist, A. (1988). An explanation of retribution. *Journal of Philosophy, 85,* 464-478.

Olk, M., & Waller, P. F. (1998). *Graduated licensing for young novice drivers: Components and impacts upon state licensing schemes.* Ann Arbor, MI: The University of Michigan Transportation Research Institute.

Ostvik, E., & Elvik, R. (1990). *The effects of speed enforcement on individual road user behavior and accidents.* Proceedings of the International Road Safety Symposium, Enforcement and rewarding: Strategies and effects. Copenhagen, Denmark.

Osuna, E., & Luna, A. (1989,a). Behavior at School and Social Maladjustment. *Journal of Forensic Sciences, 34,* 1228–1234.

Osuna, E., & Luna, A. (1989,b). Impulsivity and attention-perception features in relation to juvenile delinquency. *Journal of Forensic Sciences, 34,* 1235–1245.

Owsley, C., Ball, K., Sloane, M. E., Roenker, D. L., & Bruni, J. R. (1991). Visual and cognitive correlates of vehicle accidents in older drivers. *Psychology and Aging, 6,* 403–415.

Pakaslahti, J. (2000). Children's and adolescents' aggressive behavior in context: the development and application of aggressive problem-solving strategies. *Aggression & Violent Behavior, 5,* 467–490.

Palmer, E. J., & Hollin, C. R. (1998) A comparison of patterns of moral development in young offenders and non-offenders. *Legal & Criminological Psychology, 3,* 225–235.

Palmer, E. J., & Hollin, C. R. (2000). The interrelations of socio-moral-reasoning, perceptions of own parenting and attributions of intent with self-reported delinquency. *Legal & Criminological Psychology, 5,* 201–218.

Parasuraman, R., & Nestor, P. G. (1991). Attention and driving skills in aging and Alzheimer's disease. *Human Factors, 33,* 539–557.

Parke, R., & Slaby, R. (1983). The development of aggression. In P. Mussen (Ed.). *Handbook of Child Psychology: Volume IV.* New York: Wiley & Sons.

Parker, D., Lawton, R. L., Manstead, A. S. R., & Stradling, S. G. (2000). *The attitudinal determinants of driving violations.* London: Department of the Environment, Transport & the Regions.

Parker, D., Manstead, A. S. R., Stradling, S. G., Reason, J. T., & Baxter, J. S. (1992). Intention to commit driving violations: An application of the theory of planned behavior. *Journal of Applied Psychology, 77,* 94–101.

Parker, D., Reason, J. T., Manstead, A. S. R., & Stradling, S. G. (1995). Driving errors, driving violations and accident involvement. *Ergonomics, 38,* 1036–1048.

Parker D., Stradling S. G., & Manstead, A. S. R. (1996). An intervention study based on the theory of planned action. *Journal of Applied Social Psychology, 26,* 1–19.

Parker, D., West, R., Stradling, S., & Manstead, A. S. R. (1995). Behavioral characteristics and involvement in different types of traffic accidents. *Accident Analysis and Prevention, 27,* 571–581.

Paternoster, R., & Piquero, A. (1995). Reconceptualizing deterrence: An empirical test of personal and vicarious experiences. *Journal of Research in Crime and Delinquency, 32,* 251–286.

Patton, J. H., Stanford, M. S., & Barratt, E. S. (1995). Factor structure of the Barratt Impulsiveness Scale. *Journal of Clinical Psychology, 51,* 768–774.

Pearson, D. A., & Lane, D. M. (1991). Auditory attention switching: A developmental study. *Journal of Experimental Psychology, 61,* 320–334.

Pelz, D. C., & Shuman, S. H. (1968). Are young drivers really more dangerous after controlling for exposure and experience? *Journal of Safety Research, 3,* 68–79.

Pernanen, K. (1976). Alcohol and crimes of violence. In B. Kissin & H. Begletier (Eds.). *The Biology Of Alcoholism.* New York: Plenum.

Pfefferbaum, B., Wood, P. B. (1994). Self-report study of impulsive and delinquent behavior in college students. *Journal of Adolescent Health, 15,* 295–302.

Piquero, A. R., & Paternoster, R. (1998). An application of Stafford and Warr's reconceptualization of deterrence to drinking and driving. *Journal of Research in Crime and Delinquency, 35,* 5–41.

Piquero, A. R., & Pogarsky, G. (2002). Beyond Stafford and Ware's reconceptualization of deterrence: Personal and vicarious experiences, impulsivity, and offending behavior. *Journal of Research in Crime and Delinquency, 39,* 153–186.

Piquero, A. R., & Tibbetts, S. (1996). Specifying the direct and indirect effects of low self-control and situational factors in offenders' decision making: Toward a more complete model of rational offending. *Justice Quarterly, 13,* 481–510.

Platt, J. J., Perry, G., & Metzger, D. S. (1980). The evaluation of a heroin addiction treatment program within a correctional environment. In R. R. Ross & P. Gendreau (Eds.). *Effective correctional treatment.* Toronto: Butterworths.

Pogarsky, G. (2002). Identifying 'deterrable' offenders: Implications for research on deterrence. *Justice Quarterly, 3,* 431–452.

Pogarski, G., & Piquero, A. R. (2003). Does punishment encourage offending? Investigating the "resetting" effect. *J. Research in Crime & Delinquency, 40,* 92–117.

Porporino, F. J., & Robinson, D. (1995). An evaluation of the reasoning and rehabilitation program with Canadian federal offenders. In R. R. Ross & R. D. Ross (Eds.). *Thinking straight: The reasoning and rehabilitation program for delinquency prevention and offender rehabilitation.* Ottawa: Cognitive Centre of Canada. (cogcen@canada.com)

Pratt, T. C., & Cullen F. (2000). The empirical status of Gottfredson and Hirschi's general theory of crime: A meta-analysis. *Criminology, 38,* 931–964.

Preusser, D. F., Ferguson, S. A., & Williams, A. F. (1998). The effect of teenage passengers on the fatal crash risk of teenage drivers. *Accident Analysis & Prevention,. 30,* 217–222.

Prochaska, J. O., Norcross, J. C., & DiClemente, C. C. (1982). *Changing for good.* New York: Avon Books.

Quiggle, N. L., Garber, J., Panak, W. F., & Dodge, K.A. (1993). Social information processing in aggressive and depressed children. *Annual Progress in Child Psychiatry & Child Development, 19,* 217–241.

Quigley, B., & Tedeschi, J. T. (1989). Does self defense apply to women? Effects of sex and mode of retaliation on attributed aggression. *Journal of Social Behavior and Personality, 4,* 109–118.

Quimby, A. R. (1986). *Driving errors and individual differences: An in-car observation study.* Crowthorne, U.K.: Department of Transport.

Rahman, N. (1999). Conflict and caregiving: Testing a social-psychological model. *Australian Journal on Aging, 12,* 16–19.

Rajalin, S. (1994). The connection between risky driving and involvement in fatal accidents. *Accident Analysis & Prevention, 26*, 555–562.

Rajalin, S., & Summala, H. (1997). What survived drivers learn from a fatal road accident. *Accident Analysis & Prevention, 29*, 277–283.

Ranney, T. A. (1994). Models of driving behavior: A review of their evolution. *Accident Analysis & Prevention, 26*, 733–750.

Ranney, T. A., & Pulling, N. H. (1989). *Relation of individual differences in information-processing ability to driving performance.* Proceedings of the Human Factors Society 33rd Annual Meeting. San Diego.

Raynor, P., & Vanstone, M. (1996). Reasoning and rehabilitation in Britain: the results of the straight thinking on probation (STOP) programme. International *Journal of Offender Therapy and Comparative Criminology, 40*, 272–284.

Reason, J., Manstead, A., Stradling, S., Parker, D., & Baxter, J. S. (1991). *The social and cognitive determinants of aberrant driving behavior.* Crowthorne, U.K.: Department of Transport.

Reason, J., Manstead, A., Stradling, S., Baxter, J., & Campbell, K. (1990). Errors and violations on the road: A real distinction? *Ergonomics, 33*, 1315–1332.

Recarte, M. A., & Nunes, L. M. (2000). Effects of verbal and spatial-imagery tasks on eye fixations while driving. *Journal of Experimental Psychology Applied, 6*, 1–4.

Redelmeier, D. A., Tibshirani, R. J., & Evans, L. (2003). Traffic law enforcement and risk of death from motor vehicle crashes: A case-crossover study. *Lancet, 361*, 2177–2182.

Redl, F., & Wineman, A. (1951). *Children who hate.* Glencoe: Free Press.

Redondo, S., Sanchez-Mecca, J., & Garrido, V. (1999). The influence of treatment programs on the recidivism of juvenile and adult offenders: A European meta-analytic review. *Psychology Crime & Law, 5*, 251–278.

Renner, W., & Anderle, F. G. (2000). Venturesomeness and extraversion as correlates of juvenile drivers' traffic violations. *Accident Analysis & Prevention, 32*, 673–678.

Richman, J. (1985). Social class and mental illness revisited: Sociological perspectives on the diffusion of psychoanalysis. *Journal of Operational Psychiatry, 16*, 1–8.

Robertson, S. A. (1998). *Stress related to driving: An exploratory study.* Oxford: Transport Studies Unit.

Robinson, D., & Porporino, F. J. (2000). Programming in cognitive skills: The reasoning and rehabilitation programme. In C. R. Hollin. *Handbook of offender assessment and treatment.* New York: Wiley.

Rolls, G., & Ingham, R. (1992). *'Safe' and 'unsafe': A comparative study of younger male drivers.* Basingstoke, UK: AA Foundation for Road Safety Research.

Rose, G. (2000). *The criminal histories of serious traffic offenders.* London: Research, Development and Statistics Directorate, Home Office.

Ross, H. L. (1940). Traffic accidents, a product of social-psychological conditions. *Social Forces, 18*, 569–576.

Ross, R. R. (1967). Psychology at the Ontario Training School for Girls. *Ontario Psychological Association Quarterly, 20*, 54–58.

Ross, R. R. (1980). *Socio-cognitive development in the offender.* Ottawa: Ministry of The Solicitor General, 1980.

Ross, R. R. (2004). *PROSOCIAL DRIVER: A handbook for training prosocial driving skills and values*. Ottawa: Cognitive Centre of Canada. (cogcen@canada.com)

Ross, R. R., & Abdennur, A. (1996). *Al-Maharat Al-Zuhnieh Litatweer Al- Faalieh Al-Shakhsieh Wal-Igtimaieh* (Cognitive skills for the development of personal and social competence). Beirut: Center for Cognitive Development.

Ross, R. R., Antonowicz, D. H., & Dhaliwall, G. K. (Eds.). (1995). *Going straight: Effective delinquency prevention and offender rehabilitation*. Ottawa: Air Training and Publications. (available from cogcen@canada.com)

Ross, R. R., & Fabiano, E. (1985). *Time to think: A cognitive model of delinquency prevention and offender rehabilitation*. Johnson City, Tennessee: Institute of Social Sciences and Arts, Inc. (available from cogcen@canada.com)

Ross, R. R., Fabiano, E., & Ewles, C. (1988). Reasoning and rehabilitation. *International Journal of Offender Therapy and Comparative Criminology, 32*, 29–35.

Ross, R. R., Fabiano, E. A., & Ross, R. D. (1986). *Reasoning and rehabilitation: A handbook for teaching cognitive skills*. Ottawa: Cognitive Centre of Canada. (cogcen@canada.com)

Ross, R. R., & Gendreau, P. (1980). *Effective correctional treatment*. Toronto: Butterworths.

Ross, R. R., & Hilborn, J. (2003). *Reasoning and rehabilitation 2: Short version for youth*. Ottawa: Cognitive Centre of Canada. (cogcen@canada.com)

Ross, R. R., & Hilborn, J. (2004). *Time to think again*. Ottawa: Cognitive Center of Canada. (in press). (cogcen@canada.com)

Ross, R. R., & Hilborn, J. (2003). *Reasoning & rehabilitation 2: A handbook for teaching cognitive and emotional skills*. Ottawa: Cognitive Centre of Canada. (in press). (cogcen@canada.com)

Ross, R. R., Hilborn, J., & Greene, R. (2003). *R&R2 short version for families*. Ottawa: Cognitive Centre of Canada. (cogcen@canada.com)

Ross, R. R., & Lightfoot, L. (1985). *Treatment of the alcohol abusing offender*. Springfield: Charles C Thomas.

Ross, R. R., & McKay, H. B. (1979). *Self mutilation*. Lexington, MA: D. C. Heath.

Ross, R. R., & Ross, R. D. (1988). *Cognitive skills: A training manual for living skills*. Ottawa: Correctional Service of Canada.

Ross, R. R., & Ross, R. D. (Eds.). (1995). *Thinking straight: The reasoning and rehabilitation program for delinquency prevention and offender rehabilitation*. Ottawa, Canada: AIR Training and Publications. (cogcen@canada.com)

Rossello, J., Munar, N., Justo, S., & Arias, R. (1998). Effects of alcohol on divided attention and on accuracy of attentional shift. *Psicothema, 10*, 65–73.

Ruchkin, V., Eisemann, M., & Haeggloef, B. (1999). Coping styles in delinquent adolescents and controls: the role of personality and parental rearing. *Journal of Youth & Adolescence, 28*, 705–717.

Rumar, K. (1985). The role of perceptual and cognitive filters in observed behavior. In L. Evans & R. C. Schwing (Eds.). *Human behavior and traffic safety*. New York: Plenum Press.

Rumar, K. (1988). Collective risk but individual safety. *Ergonomics, 31*, 507–518.

Russo, M. F., Stokes, G. S., Lakey, B. B., Christ, M. A. G., McBurnett, K., & Loeber, R. (1993). A sensation seeking scale in children: Further refinement and psychometric development. *Journal of Psychopathology and Behavioral Assessment, 15*, 69–86.

Sabey, B. E., & Taylor, H. (1980). *The Known Risks We Run.* (TRRL Supplementary Report no. 581). Crowthorne, U. K.: Department of Transport.

Sampson, R. J., & Laub, J. H. (1993). *Crime in the making: Pathways and turning points through life.* Cambridge, MA: Harvard University Press.

Schmideberg, M. A. (1955). The offender's attitude toward punishment. *Journal of Criminal Law, Criminology & Police Science,* 1975, 51.1–5.

Scoles, P., Fine, E. W., & Steer, R. A. (1984). Personality characteristics and drinking patterns if high-risk drivers never apprehended for driving while intoxicated. *Journal of Studies on Alcohol, 45,* 411–416.

Seltzer, M. L., & Vinokur, A. (1974). Life events, subjective stress and traffic accidents. *American Journal of Psychiatry, 131,* 903–906.

Seltzer, M. L., Vinokur, A., & Wilson, T. D. (1977) A psychological comparison of drunken drivers and alcoholics. *Journal of Studies on Alcohol, 38,* 1294–1318.

Serin, R. C. (1991). Psychopathy and violence in criminals. *Journal of Interpersonal Violence, 6,* 423–431.

Shaw, E., Ruby, K. G., & Post, J. M. (2001). The insider threat to information security systems. *Security Awareness Bulletin* No. 2–98. (full report available from Political Psychology Associates, Ltd. Bethesda, MD.)

Sheppard, D. (1982). *Experience of an accident and its influence on driving.* Crowthorne, U. K.: Department of Transport.

Shope, J. T., & Bingham, C. R. (2002). Drinking-driving as a component of problem driving and problem behavior in young adults. *Journal of Studies on Alcohol, 63,* 24–33.

Shover, N., & Henderson, B. (1995). Repressive crime control and male persistent thieves. In E. D. Barlow (Ed.). *Crime & public policy: Putting theory to work.* Boulder, CO: Westview Press.

Siegrist, S., & Ramsier, E. (1992). *Evaluation of advanced driving courses.* Bern, Switzerland: BFU.

Simon, F., & Corbett, C. (1996). Road traffic offending, stress, age, and accident history among male and female drivers. *Ergonomics, 39,* 757–780.

Simons-Morton, B. G., & Hartos, J. (2003). How well do parents manage young driver crash risks? *Journal of Safety Research, 34,* 91–97.

Simpson, H. M. (1996). Summary of key findings: Research and information needs, program and policy priorities. In H. Simpson (Ed.). *New to the road: Reducing the risks for young motorists.* Berkley, California: The Regents of the University of California.

Simpson, H. M. (2003). The evolution and effectiveness of graduated licensing. *Journal of Safety Research, 34,* 25–34.

Simpson, H. M., & Beirness, D. J. (1993). Traffic accidents and youth: Alcohol and other lifestyle factors. *Journal of the Alcoholic Beverage Medical Research Foundation, 3,* 77–84.

Sivak, M. (1983) Society's aggression level as a prediction of fatality rate. *Journal of Safety Research, 14,* 93–99.

Slaby, R. G., & Guerra, N. G. (1988). Cognitive mediators of aggression in adolescent offenders: 1. Assessment. *Developmental Psychology, 24,* 580–588.

Smith, M. (1994). *Research agenda for an improved novice driver education program: A report to Congress.* Washington, DC: Department of Transportation.

Spruance, L. M., Van Voorhis, P., Johnson, S., Ritchey, P.N., Pealer, J., & Seabrook, R. (2000). *The Georgia Cognitive Skills Experiment: Phase 1 Outcome Evaluation.* Atlanta: Georgia Board of Pardons and Parole.

Stacey, B.G. (1985). Drinking and driving: Alcohol association with traffic safety. *Journal of Alcohol and Drug Education, 30,* 1–4.

Stacy, A. L., Newcomb, M. D., & Bentler, P. M. (1991). Personality, problem drinking and personality. *Journal of Personality & Social Psychology, 60,* 795–811.

Stern, S. B., & Azar, S. T. (1998). Integrating cognitive strategies into behavioral treatment for abusive parents and families with aggressive adolescents. *Clinical Child Psychology & Psychiatry, 3,* 387–403.

Steel, Z., & Blaszczynski, A. (1996). The factorial structure of pathological gambling. *Journal of Gambling Studies, 12,* 3–20.

Stokols, D., & Novaco, R. W. (1981). Transportation and well being. In G. Altman, J. F. Wohlwill, & P. B. Everett (Eds.). *Human Behavior and Environment (Vol. 5): Transportation and Behavior.* London: Plenum Press.

Stradling, S. G. (1997). Violators as "crash magnets." In G. B.Grayson (Ed.). *Behavioral research in road safety VII.* Crowthorne: Transport Research Laboratory.

Stradling, S. G., Manstead, A. S. R., & Parker, D. (1992). Motivational correlates of violations and errors on the road. In G. B.Grayson (Ed.). *Behavioral research in road safety II.* Crowthorne: Transport and Road Research Laboratory.

Stradling, S. G., & Parker, D. (1996). *Violations on the road: Bad attitudes make bad drivers.* Presented to symposium on "Attitudes and values Concerning Road Safety," Birmingham: UK.

Strand, G. C., & Carr, M. S. (1994). Driving under the influence. In T. Hirschi & M.R. Gottfredson. (Eds.). *The generality of deviance.* New Brunswick, NJ: Transaction Publishers.

Streff, F. M., & Eby, D. W. (1994). *An analysis of the impact and effectiveness of Michigan's 1991 drunk and impaired driving laws.* Ann Arbor, MI: The University of Michigan Transportation Research Institute.

Struckman-Johnson, D. L., Lund, A. K., Williams, A. F., & Osborne, D. (1989). Comparative effects of driver improvement programs on crashes and violations. *Accident Analysis & Prevention, 21,* 203–215.

Stutt, J. (2003). University of North Carolina Highway Safety Research Center, Chapel Hill, N.C. Personal communication.

Sullman, M. J. M., Meadows, M. L., & Pajo, K. B. (2002). Aberrant driving behaviors amongst New Zealand truck drivers. Transportation Research Part F. *Traffic Psychology & Behavior, 5,* 217–232.

Sulzer-Azaroff, B., & Mayer, G. R. (1991). *Behavior Analysis For Lasting Change.* Fort Worth: Holt, Rinehart and Winston.

Sulzer-Azaroff, B., & Mayer, G. R. (1994). *Achieving Educational Excellence Using Behavioral Strategies.* San Marcos: Western Image.

Summala, H. (1985). Modeling driver behavior: A pessimistic prediction? In L. Evans & R. Schwing (Eds.). *Human behavior and traffic safety.* New York: Plenum Press.

Summala, H. (1987). Young driver accidents: risk taking or failure of skills. *Alcohol, Drugs, and Driving, 3*, 79–91.

Summala, H. (1988). Risk control is not risk adjudgement: The zero-risk theory of driver behavior. *Ergonomics, 31*, 491–506.

Summala, H., Kanninen, J., Kanninen, K., Rantanen, P., & Virtanen, A. (1986). *Passing when visibility obscured: Can we predict accident involvement from one single traffic maneuver?* Dayton, Ohio: Proceedings from the Human Factors Society 30th Annual Meeting..

Summala, H., & Pihlman, M. (1993). Activating a safety message from truck drivers' memory: An experiment in a work zone. *Safety Science, 16*, 675–687.

Svenson, O. (1981). Are we all less risky and more skillful than our fellow drivers? *Acta Psychologica, 47*, 143–148.

Svenson, O., Fischhoff, B., & MacGregor, D. (1985). Perceived driving safety and seat belt usage. *Accident Analysis & Prevention, 17*, 119–133.

Taylor, J., Deane, F., & Podd, J. (2002). Driving-related fear: A review. *Clinical Psychology Review, 22*, 631–645.

Taylor, S. (1991). *Health psychology.* (2nd ed.). New York: McGraw-Hill.

Taylor, S. P., & Chermack, S. T. (1993). Alcohol, drugs and human physical aggression. *Journal of Studies on Alcohol, (Supplement 11)*, 78–88.

Thiffault, P., & Bergeron, J. (2003). Fatigue and individual differences in monotonous simulated driving. *Personality & Individual Differences, 34*, 159–176.

Tillman, W. A., & Hobbs, G. E. (1949). The accident-prone automobile driver. *American Journal of Psychiatry, 3*, 21–31.

Traffic Injury Research Foundation (1991). *New to the road: Prevention measures for young or novice drivers.* Halifax, Nova Scotia: Proceedings of International Symposium.

Tomlinson-Keasey, C., & Little, T. D. (1990). Predicting educational attainment, occupational achievement, intellectual skills and personal adjustment among gifted men and women. *Journal of Educational Psychology, 82*, 399–403.

Trankle, U., Gelau, C., & Metker, T. (1990). Risk perception and age-specific accidents of young drivers. *Accident Analysis & Prevention, 22*, 119–125.

Tremblay, R. E., Pihl, R. O., Vitaro, F., & Dobkin, P. L. (1994). Predicting early onset of male antisocial behavior from preschool behavior. *Archives of General Psychiatry, 51*, 732–739.

Trevor-Roper, H. R. (1976). *Hitler's Secret Conversations 1941-1944.* New York: Octagon Books.

Trimpop, R., & Kirkcaldy, B. (1997). Personality predictors of driving accidents. *Personality & Individual Differences, 23*, 147–152.

Tsuang, M. T., Boor, M., & Fleming, J. A. (1985). Psychiatric aspects of traffic accidents. *American Journal of Psychiatry, 142*, 538–546.

UAE (1994). *Annual Statistical Abstract 1994.* Dubai: United Arab Emirates.

Ulmer, R. G., Preusser, C. W., & Preusser, D. F. (1994). *Evaluation of California's safety belt law change to primary enforcement.* Washington, DC: Department of Transportation.

Underwood, G., Chapman, P., Wright, S., & Crundall, D. (1999). Anger while driving. Traffic *Psychology & Behavior, 2*, 55–68.

Utzelmann, H., & Jacobshagen, W. (1997). Validation of the German system of diagnosis and rehabilitation for traffic offenders. In J. A. Rothengatter & E. Carbonell Vaya (Eds.). *Traffic and transport psychology, theory and application.* Oxford: Pergamon.

Vaaje, T. (1991). Rewarding in insurance: Return of part of premium after a claim-free period. In *Proceedings Of The AECD/EGMY Symposium On Enforcement And Rewarding: Strategies And Effects.* Copenhagen: Institute for Road Safety.

Valliant, P. M., Gauthier, T., Pottier, D., & Kosmyna, R. (2000). Moral reasoning, interpersonal skills, and cognition of rapists, child molesters, and incest offenders. *Psychological Reports, 86,* 67–75.

van der Hulst, M., Meijman, T., & Rothengatter, T. (1999). Anticipation and the adaptive control of safety margins in driving. *Ergonomics, 42,* 336–345.

Veneziano, C., & Veneziano, L. (1988). Knowledge of social skills among institutionalized juvenile delinquents: An assessment. *Criminal Justice and Behavior, 15,* 152–171.

Vingilis, E. (1983). Drinking drivers and alcoholics – are they from the same population? In R. G. Smart, F. B. Glasser, Y. Israel, H. Kalant, R. Popham, & W. Schmidt (Eds.). *Research advances in alcohol and drug problems.* New York: Plenum Press.

Wagenaar, A. C., Zobeck, T. S., Williams, D. G., & Hingson, R. (1995). Methods used in studies of drink-drive control efforts: A meta-analysis of the literature from 1960 to 1991. *Accident Analysis and Prevention, 27,* 307–316.

Walker, H. M., Shinn, M. R., O'Neill, R. E., & Ramsey, E. (1987). A longitudinal assessment of the development of antisocial behavior in boys: Rationale, methodology, and first-year results. *Remedial and Special Education, 8,* 7–16.

Waller, P.F. (1983). *Young drivers: Reckless or unprepared?* International Symposium on Young Driver Accidents: In Search of Solutions. Banff, Alberta. Chapel Hill, North Carolina: North Carolina University.

Waller, P. F. (2002). Challenges in motor vehicle safety. *Annual Review of Public Health, 23,* 93–113.

Waller, P. F., Elliott, M. R., Shope, J. T., Raghunathan, T. E., & Little, R. J. A. (2001). Changes in young adult offense and crash patterns over time. *Accident Analysis & Prevention, 33,* 117–128.

Wanberg, K. W., & Milkman, H. B. (1998). *Criminal Conduct and Substance Abuse Treatment.* Thousand Oaks, CA: Sage Publications.

Ward, T., Keena, T., & Hudson, S. M. (2000). Understanding cognitive, affective, and intimacy deficits in sexual offenders. *Aggression & Violent Behavior, 5,* 41–62.

Wark, R., Raub, R. A., & Reischl, B. E. (1998). *Psychological and organisational variables relating to the effectiveness of a remedial driver training program.* Proceedings of the 24th International Congress of Applied Psychology, San Francisco, U.S.A.

Wasielewski, P. (1984). Speed as a measure of driver risk: Observed speeds versus driver and vehicle characteristics. *Accident Analysis & Prevention, 16,* 89–103.

Watson, B. (1997). *When common sense just won't do: Misconceptions about changing the behavior of road users.* Conference on Accident Investigations, Reconstruction and the Law, Brisbane, School of Civil Engineering, Queensland University of Technology.

Weinrath, M. (1997). The ignition interlock program for drunk drivers: A multivariate test. *Crime & Delinquency, 43,* 42–59.

Wells, A., & Matthews, G. (1994). *Attention and emotion: A clinical perspective.* Hove, UK: Elbaum.

Wells-Parker, E., Anderson, B. J., Landrum, J. W., & Snow, R. W. (1988). Long-term effectiveness of probation, short-term intervention and LAI administration for reducing DUI recidivism. *British Journal of Addiction, 83,* 415–421.

Wells-Parker, E., Bangert-Drowns, R., McMillen, R., & Williams, M. (1995). Final results from a meta-analysis of remedial interventions with drink/drive offenders. *Addiction, 90,* 907–926.

Wells-Parker, E., Cosby, P. J. & Landrum, J. W. (1986). A typology for drinking-driving offences: methods for classification and policy implications. *Accident Analysis and Prevention, 18,* 443–453.

West, R., Elander, J., & French, D. (1993). Mild social deviance: Type A behavior pattern and decision-making style as predictors of self-reported driving style and traffic accident risk. *British Journal of Psychology, 84,* 207–219.

West, R., & Hall, J. (1995). *Accident liability of novice drivers.* UK: Transport Research Laboratory.

West, R., & Hall, J. (1997). The role of personality and attitudes in traffic accident risk. *Applied Psychology: An International Review, 46,* 253–264.

Westerman, S. J., & Haigney, D. (2000). Individual differences in driver stress, error and violation. *Personality & Individual Differences, 29,* 981–998.

West Midlands Police Traffic Division. (1997). *Annual Report.*

White, J. L., Moffitt, T. E., Caspi, A., & Bartusch, D. J. (1994). Measuring impulsivity and examining its relationship to delinquency. *Journal of Abnormal Psychology, 103,* 192–205.

Wiesenthal, D. L., Hennessy, D. A., & Totten, B. (2000). The Driving behaviour Questionnaire (DVQ). *Violence and Victims, 15,* 115–136.

Wiesenthal, D. L., & Jonovjak, D. P. (1992). *Deindividuation and automobile driving behavior.* North York, Ontario, Canada: The LaMarsh Research Programme Report Series, No. 46.

Wilde, G. J. S. (1994a). *Target risk.* Toronto, Ontario: PDE Publications.

Wilde, G. J. S. (1994b). Risk homeostasis theory and its promise for improved safety. In R. M. Trimpop & G. J. S. Wilde (Eds.). *Challenges to accident prevention: The issue of risk compensation behavior.* Groningen, The Netherlands: Styx Publications.

Wilde, G. J. S. (1994c). New Techniques for determining subjects' risk-taking tendency in their task performance. In R. M. Trimpop & G. J. S. Wilde (Eds.). *Challenges to accident prevention: The issue of risk compensation behavior.* Groningen, The Netherlands: Styx Publications.

Wilde, G. J. S., Robertson, L. S., & Pless, I. B. (2002). For and against: Does risk homoeostasis theory have implications for road safety? *British Medical Journal, 324,* 1149–1152.

Willett, T. C. (1964). *Criminals on the road: A study of serious motoring offenses and those who commit them.* London: Tavistock.

Williams, A. F. (1997). *Graduating licensing and other approaches to controlling young driver risk-taking.* Arlington, VA: Insurance Institute for Highway Safety.

Williams, A. F. (1996). Overview Of The Young Driver Problem In The United States. *Transportation Research Circular, 458,* 6–8.

Williams, A. F., Lund, A. K., & Preusser, D. F. (1986). Drinking and driving among high school students. *The International Journal of the Addictions, 21*, 643–655.

Williams, A. F., Wells, J. K., McCartt, A. T., Preusser, D. F. (2000). "Buckle up NOW!" An enforcement program to achieve high belt use. *Journal of Safety Research, 31*, 195–201.

Williams, E. B., & Malfetti, J. L. (1970). *Driving And Connotative Meanings.* New York: Teachers College Press.

Wilson, R. J., & Jonah, B. A. (1985). Identifying impaired drivers among the general driving population. *Journal of Studies on Alcohol, 46*, 531–537.

Wilson, R. J., & Jonah, B. A. (1988). The application of problem behavior theory to the understanding of risky driving. *Alcohol, Drugs & Driving, 4*, 173–191.

Woodward, L. J., Fergusson, D. M., & Horwood, L. J. (2000). Driving outcomes of young people with attentional difficulties in adolescence. *Journal of the American Academy of Child & Adolescent Psychiatry, 39*, 627–634.

Wright, R.T., & Decker, S. (1994). *Burglars on the Job.* Boston: Northeastern University Press.

Yagil, D. (2001). Reasoned action and irrational motives: A prediction of drivers' intention to violate traffic laws. *Journal of Applied Social Psychology, 31*, 720–740.

Yamaguchi, K., & Kandel, D. B. (1985). On the resolution of role incompatibility: A life event history analysis of family roles and marijuana use. *American Journal of Sociology, 90*, 1284–1325.

Yanovitzky, I. (2002). Effect of news coverage on the prevalence of drunk-driving behavior: Evidence from a longitudinal study. *Journal of Studies on Alcohol, 63*, 342–351.

Young, K. (1993). *Workshop to identify training requirements designed to reduce young drive risk taking and improve decision making skills.* Washington, DC: National Highway Traffic Safety Administration.

Yu, J., & Williford, W. (1993). Problem drinking and high-risk driving: An analysis of official and self-reported drinking-driving in New York State. *Addiction, 88*, 219–228.

Zamble, E., & Porporino, F. J. (1988). *Coping, behaviour and adaptation in prison inmates.* Syracuse: Springer-Verlag.

Zelhart, P. F. (1972). Types of alcoholics and their relationship to traffic violations. *Quarterly Journal of Studies on Alcohol, 33*, 811–813.

Zuckerman, M. (1994). *Behavioral expressions and biosocial bases of sensation seeking.* New York, NY: Cambridge University Press.

ABOUT THE AUTHORS

ROBERT R. ROSS

Bob Ross (Ph.D. Psychology, University of Toronto) has been Lecturer, Wilfred Laurier University; Associate Professor of Clinical Psychology, University of Waterloo; Research Associate, Human Justice Program, University of Regina; Honorary Research Associate, Faculty of Law, University of Edinburgh; and Professor of Criminology, University of Ottawa.[1] He is Director of the Cognitive Center of Canada and an International Consultant on Offender Rehabilitation.[2] Dr. Ross has had extensive experience as a Clinical Psychologist working with antisocial individuals, including twelve years as Chief Psychologist with the Ontario Government's Ministry of Correctional Services for juvenile and adult offenders. He has also been a faculty member for the Ontario Department of Education's programs for special education teachers, and a Consultant to the Department of Educational Television. Dr. Ross has been conducting research on antisocial behavior since the late 1960s. His research has been published in more than 100 articles in journals in psychology, criminology, and education and in fifteen books including *Effective correctional treatment* (1980); *Treatment of the alcohol abusing offender* (1985); *Time to think: A cognitive model of offender rehabilitation and delinquency prevention* (1985); *Reasoning and rehabilitation: A handbook for teaching cognitive skills* (1986); *Thinking straight: The reasoning and rehabilitation program* (1985); *Reasoning and rehabilitation 2: Short version for youth* (2003); *Reasoning and rehabilitation 2: Short program for families* (2003); *Time to think again: A cognitive model for the treatment of antisocial behavior* (2004). His internationally renowned "Reasoning and Rehabilitation" program has been delivered to more than forty thousand offenders in fourteen countries with significant reductions in recidivism. Dr. Ross has been awarded the Centennial Medal of Canada for his work with antisocial adolescents.

DANIEL H. ANTONOWICZ

Dan Antonowicz (Ph.D. Psychology, Carleton University) is Assistant Professor, Department of Criminology, University of Ottawa; and Adjunct Professor, Department of Psychology, Carleton University. His dissertation examined the relationship between hostility, anger, and roadway aggression. He completed a Master's of Applied Criminology at the University of Ottawa where he also served as a teaching assistant for courses on offender rehabilitation. He has worked as a research officer

---

[1] ross@uottawa.ca
[2] cogcen@canada.com

for various Canadian federal government departments such as the Correctional Service of Canada, the Solicitor General, and the Ministry of Justice. He has conducted research on offender treatment efficacy, sex offender assessment and treatment, sentencing, mentally disordered offenders, and firearms control. His clinical experience includes the assessment and treatment of adult male offenders in provincial and federal institutions. His publications include articles in international journals on the essential components of effective offender rehabilitation programs, the personality characteristics of sex offenders, and sentencing. His research on effective offender rehabilitation appears as a chapter in *Thinking straight: The reasoning and rehabilitation program for delinquency prevention and offender rehabilitation.* He has also co-edited a book with Dr. Ross entitled *Going straight: Effective delinquency prevention and offender rehabilitation.*